HOW FREUD WORKED

HOW FREUD WORKED
First-Hand Accounts of Patients

Paul Roazen, Ph.D.

JASON ARONSON INC.
Northvale, New Jersey
London

Production Editor: Judith D. Cohen

This book was set in 10 point Garamond by TechType of Upper Saddle River, New Jersey.

Library of Congress Cataloging-in-Publication Data

Roazen, Paul, 1936–
    How Freud worked : first-hand accounts of patients / by Paul
Roazen.
        p.   cm.
    Includes bibliographical references and index.
    ISBN 1-56821-556-8 (alk. paper)
    1. Freud, Sigmund, 1856–1939.   2. Psychoanalysis—Case studies.
I. Title.
BF109.F74R632   1995
150.19′52′092—dc20   95-11733

Manufactured in the United States of America. Jason Aronson Inc. offers books and cassettes. For information and catalog write to Jason Aronson Inc., 230 Livingston Street, Northvale, New Jersey 07647.

For Sylvia, Joe, Albert, and in memory of Lena

Contents

Acknowledgments   ix

Introduction: What Is Living
       in Freud's Psychology?   xi

1. The Question of Coldness: Albert Hirst   1

2. "The Right Punishment": David Brunswick   31

3. Co-Dependency: Mark Brunswick   61

4. Forbidden Sex: Dr. Edith Jackson   90

5. Officer of the Vienna Psychoanalytic:
    Dr. Robert Jokl   115

6. **Cultism: Kata Levy**   143

7. **"A Fine Thing for Normal People":**
   Dr. Irmarita Putnam   167

8. **Between Father and Mother:**
   Eva Rosenfeld   195

9. **Bloomsbury: James and Alix Strachey**   231

10. **Conclusions**   257

References   281

Index   291

Acknowledgments

I continue to be grateful to my agent, Georges Borchardt, for his patience and confidence in my work. My old friend, Michael Paul Rogin, has once again read a manuscript of mine with good consequences. Todd Dufresne, a new student, has helped me on a line-by-line basis; I hope he will reward me by continued disagreements. Johann Mohr has, I hope, found in me a worthy student.

The Hannah Foundation for the History of Medicine, and York University's Committee on Research, Grants and Scholarships, Faculty of Arts Research Grants, and Social Science and Humanities Research Council Small Grants, have all facilitated my research for this book.

Jason Aronson's copy editor, David Kaplan, has done an unusually fine and sympathetic job.

Introduction:
What Is Living in
Freud's Psychology?

A fierce controversy continues to rage about the kind of therapist Freud was. To some stalwart supporters he remains an untouchable icon whose every act reflects a consistent scientific standpoint. At the opposite extreme are those for whom Freud has been reviled as a fabricator whose successes have been largely in the realm of public relations. Both Freud's person as well as his doctrines have come under recent assault. In 1993 *Time* (November 29, pp. 46–50) had a cover story entitled, ''Is Freud Dead?'' One might have thought that anyone who could be the subject of such a discussion, over fifty years after he actually died, had already entered the pantheon of intellectual giants. But the same month of the *Time* article the *New York*

Review of Books started running a bitter discussion of how misleading Freud's claims could be (Crews 1993).

It does not help to resolve the contending uncertainties that Freud scarcely kept records about the patients he treated. Although in old age he sometimes made a list of the letters that he sent out, and usually saved correspondence that was received, Freud seems to have destroyed most of his clinical material. Despite the many cartoons about psychoanalysts with their expectant pens and pads of paper that have appeared over the years, for instance in the *New Yorker*, Freud himself declined to take notes during therapeutic sessions and specifically advised against the practice. Here he was at odds with the recommendations of some of his most enlightened contemporaries, as well as the conduct of many of today's most up-to-date clinicians.

Freud (1909) thought that the "withdrawal of the physician's attention does the patient more harm than can be made up for by any increase in the accuracy that may be achieved in the reproduction of his case history" (p. 159). On rare occasions Freud kept clinical records, usually made at the end of the working day, from which we have learned how his written accounts can vary from his published case histories (Mahony 1986). And in one striking example of the contrast between Freud's published works and, as we shall see, what I was able to learn directly from a surviving patient of his, it becomes possible to assess his case-history writing.

Freud has been sufficiently fascinating so that the literature about him continues to increase, and he has been widely acknowledged to be a central figure in twentieth century intellectual life. Because a great body of documents about Freud at the Library of Congress in Washington, D.C. has been sealed up by the principal donor, the Freud Archives of New York, until after the turn of the century, when the immense amount of documentation that has been accumulated starts to become publicly available there will be a renewed expansion of Freud studies.

Freud was a thinker who laid down some central challenges to the conventional wisdom of his own time that remain enduringly striking, and the philosophic implications of what he had to say are still disturbingly subversive to many beliefs and values that are widely accepted today. Freud's skepticism about religion, for example, and his assault on the propriety of leading Christian ethical standards, still provoke dispute. As early as 1928 a Swiss psychoanalyst, who was also a pastor, published a respectful reply to Freud's *Future of an Illusion* (see Pfister 1993).

Although the collected psychological writings of Freud make up a set of twenty-four volumes, the most interesting new information about him has been appearing in the volumes of his correspondence, which have been coming out at at steady pace. If only for commercial publishing reasons the Freud Copyrights, on behalf of Freud's heirs, do not want all the primary documents released at once but, rather, gradually. As of now there are a dozen different editions of Freud's letters, and the bulk of his correspondence still remains unpublished. People found the letters he wrote even as a young man remarkable enough to save, and what ultimately appears will have survived despite the destructive upheavals of two world wars. There are over a thousand letters alone that Freud wrote to his future wife, and they are currently being prepared to make at least one book. Knowledgeable estimates vary about just how many thousand Freud letters may be in existence, but only a small fraction of these have yet been published in their entirety.

Freud's greatness as a writer has enabled him to gain worldwide recognition not just as a representative of the cosmopolitan spirit of the old Vienna of the Hapsburgs but as someone with remarkable understanding of the complexities of the human soul. As one novelist wrote to him toward the end of

Freud's life: "Your achievement will . . . be sufficient to guarantee the immortality of Viennese cultural life in the 19th and
20th centuries" (E. Freud 1970, p. 155). No other rival psychologist Freud chanced to encounter could match him as a stylist.
Freud's intense letter-writing came naturally to him (and was
taken for granted by his family); this doubtless was a way of
testing his capacities to express his thoughts. Whatever defects
Freud may have had, and the list is considerable, he was never
charged as boring.

In the midst of the growing accumulation of material by
and about Freud, what he was like as a practicing clinician still
remains an unsettled question. People easily forget, thinking
about all that he succeeded in writing, that most of his working
days were spent not sitting at his desk but listening behind an
analytic couch. At the peak of his capacities Freud could see
eight patients a day, each of them for fifty-minute sessions, and
he regularly saw each patient six times a week. Therefore, most
of his writing was reserved for evenings, Sundays, and summer
vacations, although Freud was sometimes accompanied on vacations by patients. If judged by the standard of time devoted to
each endeavor, Freud was primarily a clinician, not a writer. On
occasion Freud could express his resentment and temperamental lack of suitability for being a physician at all. He had to
earn his living as a hard-working doctor by what he collected
from his private patients; yet relatively few of them left an
account of what he was like in his capacity as a practicing
psychoanalyst.

Freud did spend, especially in his later years, a substantial
amount of his time training people for the future. The extent of
Freud's activities in promoting the "cause" of psychoanalysis
has attracted the focus of much of the world's knowledge of
him. The fights he had with, among others, Alfred Adler and
Carl G. Jung have stuck in the public's mind, especially since
these men succeeded in founding separate schools of thought.

Freud was a political organizer of substantial proportions, and he managed to create a movement led by those whose personal therapy he oversaw one way or another. The International Psychoanalytic Association, first started in 1910, is now approaching a world membership of close to ten thousand.

Today there are numerous professional journals, in a wide variety of languages, that are subscribed to by psychoanalysts; yet the issues that come up in articles, bearing either on abstract theoretical matters or more down-to-earth examples of case histories, are characteristically related to Freud's seminal writings, while almost nothing refers to his clinical practices. The more one knows about Freud as a living historical personage, the easier it is to untangle the real meanings behind what he put on paper.

An enormous amount of attention, for instance, has been paid to the handful of papers Freud wrote on the issue of so-called technique—how a proper analyst should undertake the treatment process. He was reluctant to lay down hard-and-fast rules, but felt he had to distinguish his own approach from that of others. Mostly Freud was providing warnings for beginners about how it is possible to go wrong, although only rarely did he give concrete details about his own errors. These practical essays have been studiously pored over for purposes of training future psychoanalytic practitioners, and parts of what Freud wrote are today well known to many. Freud's influence has extended far beyond those who think of themselves as loyally following in his path; even therapists who have rejected Freud's approach can be surprisingly familiar with the steps by which he went about determining how analysts should behave. Freud has been immensely influential among social workers, marriage counselors, and child therapists, even though they may not follow his teachings.

General practitioners have picked up considerable lore from Freud, as many patients coming for the alleviation of physical problems are also seeking emotional support. The mind and the body are medically interrelated in ways that remain only partially understood. Readers have also turned to texts on child-rearing that are heavily influenced by the kind of depth psychological thinking that can be traced back in intellectual history to Freud's inspiration. Freud's influence has permeated popular culture. Woody Allen's movies appeal to an audience at ease with Freud's work.

In North America so-called biological psychiatry has gathered considerable prestige, and the high status of the somatic approach to human troubles has meant that Freud himself, at least in certain medical circles, may seem therapeutically old-hat today. Freud's standing as a pioneering innovator has been impossible to dispute, and with the collapse of European Communism his work is being revived throughout Eastern Europe and in the former Soviet Union, where Marxism once scoffed at psychoanalysis's merits. Yet even when Freud was at the height of his powers he had memorable difficulties with certain students of his, like Adler, Jung, and others, who were determined to develop their own individual ways of practiticing therapy. These breaks in the ranks of his loyal disciples, who advocated a variety of alternative approaches to clinical work, have been followed since his death in 1939 with an abundance of revisions to Freud's own approach.

Waves of fashion have succeeded one another, and the organic approach to clinical psychotherapy has received an enormous boost within the last generation. The prevalence of drugs like common tranquilizers and antidepressants demonstrates how much has been accomplished on the psychopharmacological side. There is now a wide spectrum of psychoactive pills being prescribed for a range of human ailments, and the use of this medication means that Freud's purely psychological approach has been superseded. At the same time drugs have their unwelcome side effects, and excessive reliance on them is as worrisome as any of the earlier seemingly magical solutions to human troubles.

Practitioners are once again apt now to think in terms of precise attempts at classification as in the pre-Freudian era. Diagnoses can seem not like mental constructs but like real entities. In such an uncertain field abstractions are bound to have a special appeal to those who need something concrete to grab hold of. Freud sometimes claimed to have devised a therapeutic procedure that he likened to surgery. He talked about patients presenting puzzles, as if people can be solved. He assumed that patients disguise their own secrets self-deceptively. But he also wrote about how art conflicts with science. When it comes to reflecting on the human soul, we should not expect an exact science, and in practice, as we shall see, Freud conceded as much.

Freud anticipated that future developments would come from pharmacology, and he thought his students ought to hurry in studying their psychological cases because someday soon these problems might be so easily cured through organic means that they would no longer still be available for investigation or teaching purposes. He was afraid that new drugs might be so therapeutically successful that it would no longer be possible to examine the strictly psychological dimension that so interested him. He had been convinced from early on that there was a physical basis to mental phenomena, and it might not have surprised him how immensely successful the innovations in organic medicine have been.

While there are many drugs available now that were not available in Freud's own time, he still succeeded in contributing something of lasting value to the practice of psychotherapy. For no matter what may be prescribed to a patient, a therapist has to determine the particular recommendation. And the interaction between patient and clinician, which Freud made so much of for his own kind of treatment procedure, persists in some form today. The new drugs do not become effective in a vacuum; they are prescribed to patients by primary care workers, such as general practitioners, who are apt to know their patients very well. Therapists and patients come to form unique human relationships, and Freud's concentration on this particular side of things has helped ensure his relevance today. The ties that grow between the patient and the therapist are essential constituents of therapeutic change even if medication is prescribed.

Because of all the attention Freud spent on individual patients, apart from the impact of his theoretical writings, I set out to discover, beginning in the mid-1960s, as much as I could about the founder of psychoanalysis by meeting as many people as possible who had known him. In this quest I tried to see all his surviving former patients; I succeeded in interviewing twenty-five of them, all of whom are now deceased. Some had been in analysis with him relatively briefly, while others got to know him for long periods of time. The information about their treatment came up in the context of my inquiring about the nature of early psychoanalysis, and what they could tell me about their contact with Freud first hand. Freud had been a formative experience in these people's lives. Although I was interested in learning everything about Freud's life in a distant world that I could only hope to understand indirectly, the foremost questions in my mind were, What makes for good therapy? And how did Freud measure up as a clinician?

Each of the former patients of Freud's that I saw was elderly at the time, and human memory is fallible. But the past can, in principle at least, be easier to recall than more recent events. I also attempted to cross-check what I was told. At the time I was conducting my research these patients often helped me find each other. If they gave recorded interviews for the Freud Archives, that material is still unavailable, and based on evidence I have come across it would appear that these sealed interviews had serious drawbacks because of how they were conducted. The need to idealize Freud, which accounts for extraordinary reticence about releasing documentation now, was bound to color whatever was collected by his self-appointed defenders.

Some patients I met were strikingly forthcoming about the problems they went to Freud for help on, while others remained reserved. Criticisms of Freud's tactics were freely offered, even if these people sometimes lacked adequate objectivity about how they were treated. Also, many of them were naive about psychotherapy. I was restricted in the kinds of questions I could ask; I often could not press my subjects about things they were not willing to talk about. Also, I was relatively young at the time, inexperienced at this sort of work, and the old-world culture that most of these individuals came from was unfamiliar to me.

This book is an attempt to come to terms with what I learned from these patients about how Freud conducted himself as an analyst in the course of their therapies. The contractual terms on which Freud saw them had to be unique; no one else has set off with patients the same sort of immediate reactions that Freud evoked. Partly this emotional climate affected the kinds of special expectations Freud's prospective clients brought with them to the treatment situation. He was already well known, if not a celebrity, by the time any of those I talked with first saw him; his writings were readily accessible and were bound to have a suggestive impact on the sort of material people brought to him.

Freud published five famous case histories, and they have become well known not just to clinicians but to the literary world in general. His study of "Dora" appeared in 1905 and presented his theories about hysteria; Freud had only belatedly released this case, even though it was a therapeutic stalemate, for the lack of clinical success did not seem to Freud to undermine what he had learned. Freud's examination of a "phobia" in a 5-year-old boy is known as "Little Hans" and came out in 1909; Freud did not treat the child directly but relied on supervising the investigations of the father, a member of Freud's circle and married then to one of his former patients. That same year Freud published his account of the obsessional neurosis of the "Rat Man." This patient did the best of all Freud's published cases, although his death during World War I made it impossible to follow up on how he might have fared later. Freud's discussion of a paranoia, the Schreber case, was published in 1911; it was not based on a patient Freud had actually seen but was constructed as an interpretation of a book of memoirs. Perhaps Freud's most extensive account of a patient, that of the "Wolf Man," was published in 1918; by then Freud was determined to use his clinical "findings" to combat what he regarded as the renegade positions adopted by Adler and Jung, so this case history was burdened with a heavy weight of theoretical baggage and complicated rhetoric; the Wolf Man died in a psychiatric asylum in 1979, thus living long enough to repudiate many of Freud's hypotheses about him (Roazen 1990a).

All of these patients' case histories have attracted a considerable body of secondary literature, so that experts have been able to establish their scholarly careers based on their contribution to our understanding of these clinical reports. As a pioneer Freud could be tendentious in structuring material to illustrate his theories, and some brilliant interpretations of Freud's use of language have been offered. But this literature necessarily has a scholastic air, since what we have are texts that were written about Freud's treatises but that were unable to verify findings with the people involved. The revolution Freud instigated was against a somaticist psychiatrist tradition, which looked for formalistic diagnoses, too often ignoring the human beings behind the so-called diseases. Sir William Osler had a memorable dictum that is relevant here: "The good physician treats the disease but the great physician treats the patient who has the disease." The later literature on Freud, supposedly faithful to his spirit, has in its own way joined up with the abstract classificatory psychiatry that Freud so notably opposed.

Even if one were to accept uncritically Freud's version of these five patients, there are grounds for wondering how representative these well-known published case histories were of Freud's methods. Freud's tact and discretion, as well as his conception of what properly constituted science, shaped the clinical material he chose to present to the public. And while his reports about patients have been taken by some as gospel, to others they appear to be primarily fictive. Freud worried about his own powers of persuasion; as early as the 1890s he stated "[I]t still strikes me as strange that the case histories I write should read like short stories and that, as one might say, they lack the serious stamp of science" (Freud 1895, p. 160). Disillusionment with Freud has too often meant that his whole approach has been jettisoned; and for many the pendulum has now swung far from the therapeutic procedures he had been recommending.

Unfortunately the intransigent extravagances of the early Freudians have been matched by the recklessness of a succeeding generation. Although when I first started out in my work on psychoanalysis there was apt to be no credence whatever given to criticisms of what Freud had been trying to accomplish with his explicit case histories, by now his methods have been submerged in an effort to replace them with alternative approaches. Especially when it comes to Freud's female patients the implication has been that the social changes in the roles of women have radically altered the kinds of problems that Freud's patients seemed to be suffering from. In fact Freud treated patients from a wider variety of cultural contexts than most contemporary therapists do, and it is easy to underestimate how culturally sophisticated he could be. Only the most naive could expect Freud to react as we might ideally respond today,

or to assume that necessarily there has been ethical progress
between his time and our own.

   To complicate today's conventional thinking further, there
was a wide gap between the written rules Freud proposed and
what he did in practice. Here I think that Freud and his most
loyal students did a disservice to the "cause" of psychoanalysis
that they sought to forward. For it was fairly widely known,
within the tight band of Freud's followers, that he did not
himself live up to the proclaimed ideals that he held aloft for
others. A conspiracy of silence developed, and I think that the
gap between what Freud advocated and what he did was so great
as to bind his disciples in a passionately held allegiance. The
mutual sharing of the secrets about Freud's clinical techniques
meant that the early psychoanalysts could feel themselves superior to outsiders. Insiders were not misled by the public propa-
gandizing on behalf of what psychoanalysis was all about, and
therefore they were free to go their own way in violating
various taboos that Freud had laid down for others to adhere to.

   However, once it became broadly known in what ways
Freud had been "un-Freudian," and that an effort had been
made to disguise Freud's real therapeutic practices, it was hard
for observers not to think that Freud and his students had been
guilty of substantial bad faith if not hypocrisy. Freud had, for
example, denounced certain of his former followers for behaving in a "wild" fashion, and he distanced himself from them
on the grounds that they had abandoned the specific rules that
were essential to a proper conduct of true psychoanalysis. On
examination, though, it appeared that Freud was capable of
allowing himself technical liberties at least as daring as anything
he criticized opponents for indulging in. But then Freud, as the
creator of psychoanalysis, felt free himself to chuck this or that
aspect of what he had recommended in print, confident that he
knew best what was or what was not critical to the best interests
of psychoanalysis.

None of this is, or should be, easy for impartial onlookers to follow. Freud could even chide a loyal disciple for clinical writings that were "too decent." According to what Freud (1963) wrote in a letter,

> discretion is incompatible with a satisfactory description of an analysis; to provide the latter one would have to be unscrupulous, give away, betray, behave like an artist who buys paints with his wife's house-money or uses the furniture as firewood to warm the studio for his model. Without a trace of that sort of unscrupulousness the job cannot be done. [p. 38]

Even without such a candid admission about his own commitment to artistry, there is no reason why anyone should automatically accept that anything was so simply because Freud claimed that it was. Freud was great enough as a stylist to know how to write in a way a contemporary philosopher of science might approve of. Freud, I am convinced, thought of himself as transcending traditional standards defining good and evil, which means that it can be hard to fathom what his work added up to (Roazen 1991a). I do not share the viewpoint that he can be dismissed as unethical, some kind of crook. For I have always tried to understand him in terms of the history of ideas. On the street corners of Buenos Aires and Mexico City today, for example, the first volume of his collected works in Spanish is being sold in an inexpensive package with Jean-Jacques Rousseau's *Social Contract*.

One central problem for intellectual historians has been the blind fealty with which some analysts have followed Freud. Not only do they continue to take any dispassionate criticism of the master as outrageous and a sign that such work is not to be taken seriously, but also there has been an appalling paucity of fresh

case histories written. Since Freud's death, psychoanalytic abstractions have tended to acquire a life of their own, and case
illustrations themselves have had to take a backseat.

This movement in the direction of grand theorizing had
started while Freud was still alive, and may have in fact been
accelerated by the consequences of Freud's first falling ill of
cancer of the jaw in 1923. I have long thought that it was
significant that he never wrote another case history, and that he
could no longer be as outgoing with people as he had been when
he still had his health. As Freud aged his writing grew increasingly detached from practical clinical concerns; he could on
occasion write about therapeutic matters, but his last years were
marked by his most theoretical conjecturing. Although the
earliest patient of Freud's that I interviewed was in treatment
with him in 1903, and some that I will be writing about saw him
before he got sick, by and large most of those I talked with were
analyzed during Freud's final speculative phase, which lasted
until his death.

I found that it made a difference whether these patients
were already trained psychiatrists before they came to Freud for
analysis, for in that event he was eager to add them to his
movement in order to extend the range of his following within
academic psychiatry where he himself, as a neurologist, could
not hope to have professional standing. (In some countries the
line between neurology and psychiatry still remains firmly
drawn, but in the United States the old-world distinction between those two fields was made so much more fluid that many
general readers do not realize today that Freud himself was not
a trained psychiatrist. The most seriously disturbed cases, requiring hospitalization, were not those he was best acquainted
with or most interested in healing.) Many who came to Freud
had no intention whatever of becoming clinicians, and they
remained in their previous professions or usual spheres of life.
Yet it was not exceptional for people who originally had had no
thought of becoming psychoanalysts to end up, after being

personally analyzed by Freud, as analysts themselves. And Freud could encourage such changes in professional careers.

The ten patients I have selected to write about now stand out particularly strongly in my mind. They are not necessarily the most famous individuals among those I interviewed, but my diary-like notes are the fullest about them. They were unusually candid with me and accordingly I found them especially interesting. There has to be a subjective element in my reaction to these people, and I hope the necessarily impressionistic descriptions that I provide will not seem lacking in concrete detail. For there is a false objectivity that is occasioned by too much reliance on written pieces of evidence, and I hope that the examples of Freud's patients that I am recording here will help to put in proper perspective the kinds of material that come up either in Freud's long-standing published texts or in the volumes of his correspondence that have been recently appearing in print. The written word has its own special ways of being misleading, and it would be a mistake to accept it uncritically. I am offering these accounts of Freud's patients, as they presented themselves to me, in an effort to counterbalance with human lives some of the arid-seeming concepts that have loomed so large in both the popular imagination and the professional literature.

It should become apparent how much admiration I have for all the people I interviewed. I regard them not only as historical witnesses to the early days of a humanistic form of psychotherapy, but as unusually emancipated human beings who had been willing to test out for themselves original sorts of choices. Even when they were sometimes the most hidebound in their inability to go beyond Freud's own formulations, I found these people attractive in that they were soul-searchers in the best religious sense. They were trying to reorient themselves, by changing their own outlooks, instead of expecting alterations in the external world to solve their difficulties for them. I indicate when I believe their thinking became unreliable,

but I could not have undertaken this interviewing work in the
first place, nor now report it, if I had had debunking purposes in
mind.

Although I had announced as long ago as 1969 that I had
undertaken to see all these former patients of Freud's, various
taboos seem to have inhibited organizations from inviting me to
speak about my experiences. Recently, however, I have had the
good fortune to try out various of these chapters before a variety
of receptive audiences. I have lectured about Albert Hirst at the
Department of Sociology, University of Essex, England; I discussed David and Mark Brunswick before the Cambridge Psychoanalytic Forum, Cambridge, England; I presented what I
learned from Dr. Edith Jackson to the psychotherapy unit,
Maudsley Hospital, London, England; I introduced Dr. Robert
Jokl in the course of my inaugural lecture at the University
Association for Psychoanalytic Studies, Leeds Metropolitan University, England; Kata Levy formed the substance of my discussion at the Centre for Psychoanalytic Studies, Keynes College,
Kent, England; Dr. Irmarita Putnam became the focus of an
evening I spent before the Association for Group and Individual
Psychotherapy, London, England; Eva Rosenfeld was my topic
not only at the Shelby Davis Center for Historical Studies at
Princeton University, Princeton, New Jersey, but also at an
informal gathering arranged at Eric Rayner's house in London;
and my material on the Stracheys was tried out before the
School of European Studies, University of Sussex, England.
Furthermore, I gave more general lectures about Freud's pa-
tients to the Department of Psychiatry, University of Geneva,
Switzerland; the Buenos Aires Psychoanalytic Association in
Argentina; the Psychoanalytic Seminary in Tucuman, Argentina;
the psychology department of the Buenos Aires National Uni-
versity, Argentina; the Department of Psychiatry, Toronto East
General Hospital; Division 39 of the American Psychological
Association; and the group known as AGORA in Montevideo,
Uruguay.

The Question of Coldness: Albert Hirst

A mythology seems to exist that Freud's early patients were primarily women. Since men played a prominent part among those cases I was able to interview, Albert Hirst (1887–1974) is a good person to begin with. Also, Hirst was as pure a therapeutic patient of Freud's as I ever came across; he never considered undertaking training to become an analyst. After seeing Freud, Hirst went on to play no role whatever within the movement Freud created, so that in my talking with Hirst I was never tempted to get sidetracked about any professional psychoanalytic contributions that Hirst himself might have made.

Although Hirst seemed impressed enough about my own knowledge about Freud, he took nothing for granted in spelling out why he thought Freud had succeeded in helping him. Without resorting to technical vocabulary, Hirst eloquently outlined the nature of Freud's therapeutic approach. Hirst had already, by the time I saw him, spent many hours giving taped interviews for the Freud Archives that, even though they have still not been publicly released, I saw and was able to make use of in asking Hirst further questions.

At the time I knew Hirst he was an elderly but vigorous lawyer, 79 years old, who was originally Viennese but had been successful in the United States specializing in tax matters; he lived on Fifth Avenue in New York City and was writing articles for an insurance journal. In my discussions with him we stuck closely to what Freud had been like as a clinician. And yet even with Hirst it proved impossible to restrict myself only to how Freud had behaved in treating him, and the way Hirst evaluated the results, for he felt he had to explain certain qualities of the society of old Vienna that he thought were relevant.

Although the people who had been Freud's former patients often knew one another, in the instance of Hirst I first came across his name while going through Ernest Jones's papers at the library of the British Psychoanalytic Society in London. After World War II Jones, the central figure in the organization and development of psychoanalysis in Britain, had become appointed Freud's authorized biographer, and Jones's three-volume study, which came out between 1953 and 1957, remains a fundamental scholarly source. Now that the authorities in charge of the Jones archives realize the potential significance of what they have, an elaborate system of prior restraint has been devised for future researchers; by the time the barn door was closed I had all the horses I needed.

Jones was ill by 1957 and died the next year; at the end of his life he was engaged in writing an autobiography and had not bothered to sanitize the documents about Freud that he left behind. I found in Jones's papers the names and addresses of many informants about early psychoanalysis who were still living; thanks to the help of these files, I could plan to see a number of people who had known Freud, and I was prepared in advance with the background information I had been able to pick up in London.

An indispensable aspect of Jones's work had been the help and cooperation of Freud's daughter Anna, who right up until her death in 1982 was the unofficial head of psychoanalysis. It was she who had agreed in advance that Jones write Freud's biography, although she had many reservations about both him personally and his role within British analysis; yet a good part of the responsibility for the success he achieved belongs to Anna Freud, who cooperated in giving Jones access to precious primary documents, such as Freud's letters to his fiancée, which are still not fully accessible today. While Jones wrote the biography he was living off in the country and Anna Freud resided at her father's old house in London, so they communicated mostly through letters. The informal correspondence is especially interesting to read. Jones was politically astute at psychoanalytic infighting, and whatever his differences with Freud might have been he never questioned Freud's fundamental outlook. Like others, however, Jones had to be careful in what he said about Anna Freud's father, and he submitted for prepublication review all his chapters to her; but from Anna's own point of view Jones seemed frustratingly difficult and independent-minded (Roazen 1975, 1993a). Families are rarely satisfied by the official biographers they choose.

I found Hirst's name because of a letter he had written to Anna Freud in October 1953 in connection with a chapter about Freud's involvement with cocaine in the first volume of Jones's biography, which had just been published. Hirst began by reminding her that he had last seen her in 1938 when he stopped by the Freud apartment, when the family was preparing to escape from the Nazi occupation of Vienna to exile in London;

Hirst had gone there to explain why he was taking back to the United States Freud's letters to Hirst's aunt, Emma Eckstein, who had been a patient of Freud's in the 1890s. By 1953 these letters were already deposited in the Freud Archives.

Hirst told Anna that he had been in analysis with her father from 1909 to 1910; he had then been only 23 years old, and went to Freud for daily sessions. Now Hirst wanted to correct Jones's view of Freud's attitude about cocaine. Jones had been handling a sensitive topic, because Freud not only took a good deal of cocaine but continued to do so long after he had given up recommending the drug for others. According to Jones "the cocaine episode" took place from 1884 to 1887, but we now know that well into the 1890s Freud was still relying on cocaine. The place of that drug in Freud's life still requires further investigation, notwithstanding the existence of some wild charges that Freud became addicted himself (Roazen 1990a).

When Jones described Freud's initial medical recommendation of cocaine in the 1880s for the relief of symptoms like anxiety and depression, as well as morphine dependency, Jones did not minimize the extent of Freud's unfortunate role in popularizing the positive properties of cocaine before anyone realized its addictive potential. Freud, as Jones admitted, had become "a public menace" (Jones 1956, p. 89) the way he freely prescribed the drug. This incident may have been the first occasion on which Freud's medical reputation within Vienna was damaged. In contrast to Freud, another Viennese doctor, Carl Koller, went on to win a Nobel Prize for discovering the beneficial use of cocaine in eye operations. Jones pointed out how unfairly Freud had blamed his fiancée later for his own mistake in not being thorough enough in following up on discovering cocaine's useful anesthetizing properties.

Jones's discussion of Freud's involvement with cocaine might look fair-minded, especially considering that throughout the rest of his biography Jones so accepted Freud's own view of things as to glamorize Freud's role in all the various controversies he was ever a participant in. Hirst was not writing to Anna Freud out of dissatisfaction with Jones's work as a whole, or because of any animosity toward Freud himself. But Hirst did feel strongly that he had something specific he could add in correcting Jones's account about Freud and cocaine.

As Hirst remembered it, while he was in analysis with Freud a Viennese newspaper had carried an article about Koller's discovery of cocaine's anesthetizing properties for the eye, and perhaps touched on Freud's early interest in the drug. Hirst brought it up in his analysis; he recalled that Freud then said during one of Hirst's analytic hours that Freud himself had conceived the idea that cocaine be used for eye operations, and that he had given a sample of cocaine to a friend of his, Dr. Leopold Königstein, who was an eye specialist. But something about Königstein's particular chemical solution botched the job and it did not work. Königstein then went on vacation; Koller supposedly saw a specimen of cocaine at Freud's workplace, felt the anesthetizing qualities on his fingers, and afterward went on successfully to perform the experiment that made him famous.

Hirst wanted Anna Freud to know these details, because it seemed important to Hirst that Freud had emphasized to him that when he was suggesting to Königstein the use of cocaine Freud felt he was giving his friend a "great present." Freud said he was sorry that Königstein had missed his chance, but thought Koller was quite within his scientific rights in proceeding as he had done. But according to Hirst Freud had claimed full credit for the discovery that ended up making Koller world renowned. Hirst said that Freud went into an adjoining room to get a copy of an article he wrote on cocaine, in which the concluding sentences stated that further scientific developments could be expected. It was a "very impressive" experience for Hirst. According to his account for Anna Freud, her father had intended these final words of his article to refer to the use of cocaine for eye surgery. Hirst's understanding of the cocaine episode was so different from what he found in Jones's book that Hirst felt he had to write to Anna Freud directly. Hirst knew enough where power lay in the psychoanalytic movement that he wrote to her first, not to Jones.

The correspondence in the Jones archives indicates some informal back and forth between old-guard analysts about the existence of Hirst's letter to Anna Freud. Hirst had then proceeded to write directly to Jones, in an effort to explain his discontent with Jones's version of the nature of the role of cocaine in Freud's life. While Jones made it sound like Freud had missed out on something, according to Hirst Freud had considered the cocaine story one of his triumphs. The real achievement, in Hirst's account of Freud's view of things, belonged to Freud himself, not Koller.

Jones wrote back to Hirst indicating that he thought Freud later distorted the story as compared with how it could be reconstructed from the contemporary records. Freud might have thought of applying cocaine to the eye, but that would have been for medical and not surgical purposes. Jones thought Hirst needed to remember that there was a contrast between Freud's immediate reaction of success, and months later when he came fully to realize what he had missed out on. But Hirst was sufficiently persuasive that Kurt Eissler, the head of the Freud Archives in New York, wrote to Jones about a similar-sounding version of the cocaine episode that he had heard from Freud's disciple Paul Federn. According to his tale the solution König-stein had worked with was opaque, and he had added something to make it clear that then ruined the possibility of the experiment succeeding.

When I first met Hirst, I brought up the issue of cocaine relatively early, since it gave me some written documentation to use as a basis for my interviewing. Hirst repeated to me that he had been startled to find Jones's account in print. According to

Hirst Jones had "completely misunderstood" what had happened. Jones had merely "haughtily" acknowledged Hirst's letter, but had no intention of correcting the story that he had made public. (A second edition of the first volume of Jones's biography came out in 1954.) Hirst told me that Königstein had had a druggist make up a clear solution of cocaine, which meant that it had an overdose of alcohol in it; Koller, on the other hand, had made the solution for himself, and therefore it worked.

I am bringing up Hirst's version of how Freud told him about the discovery of cocaine in order to illustrate what it might tell us about Freud's general therapeutic approach with Hirst. We know that on a number of public occasions Freud (1901) took credit for having written "a paper which introduced cocaine into medicine" (p. 325) (cf. Roazen 1975). Freud brought up the incident about Koller more than once with students, as an illustration of how Koller's kind of single-mindedness, which Freud usually shared, was an essential constituent of all genuine scientific creativity. (Koller's daughter, who loyally wrote about her father's work, was shocked, wounded, and offended by what she regarded as Jones's partisan handling of her father's discovery. She had had no idea her father had ever been treated by Freud, which Jones thought helped account for Koller's later negative attitude toward Freud. By 1927 Koller was himself saying that Freud's writings had had no influence at all on Koller's discovery.) While Freud was analyzing Hirst he still had hopes that he might one day win the Nobel Prize, but in the end he was to be deeply disappointed about being repeatedly passed over. Another contemporary of Freud's, Julius Wagner-Jauregg, in 1927 became the only psychiatrist ever to win a Nobel Prize—for the malaria treatment of paresis (Roazen 1994a).

When Hirst, over forty years after his analysis, wrote to Anna Freud and Jones in order to clarify his own understanding of the cocaine episode, it was because he felt sure about the clarity of his memory on that point. I went over with Hirst the correspondence he had had with Jones and Anna. It must have been an unusual aspect of Freud's treating Hirst when Freud expanded on the cocaine incident, but Freud did characteristically discuss with patients various significant features to the early period of his work.

I would not interpret Freud's having followed up on his role in the cocaine matter as a callous effort to make himself important. Hirst came from a substantial Viennese family, the Ecksteins, who knew both Freud and his wife. The Ecksteins were prominent within local socialist circles; Friedrich, Hirst's uncle had reviewed Freud's *The Interpretation of Dreams* in 1900, and his brother Gustav was a leader of the Social Democratic party. Therese Schlesinger, a sister, was the first woman member of the Austrian parliament, and Emma Eckstein, Freud's patient, was another sister. The Eckstein family clearly had exceptionally gifted people in it. Hirst emphasized that although Vienna might seem like a large city, it was, if one considered the upper-middle-class Jewish world his own family and that of Freud moved in, a small town. In 1900 the population of Vienna was 1.6 million, and 9 percent were Jews, (Gilman 1993); by 1910 Vienna had grown to about 2 million people. It was still the center of the ancient Austro-Hungarian Empire, and people of talent and ambition were attracted there.

Compared with the United States, Austria was then a "stabilized, frozen society." Hirst's relatives considered themselves "nobility," superior to other people. They gave their old clothes to poor people, who wore "hand-me-downs." So as a child Hirst learned that one was merely the "trustee" of one's own suits, and had to be careful with them. There were "duties" long before "pleasures"—but not "privileges" since they were "cheap." (Hirst's images reminded me of the best single book I have ever read about old Vienna, Stefan Zweig's 1943 *The World of Yesterday*.) Hirst did think that Freud must have valued his opinion, otherwise it would not have made sense for him to have told Hirst about the tale of the discovery of cocaine.

Freud did typically have a special concern with priorities, and like others in the history of science he wanted to be sure he succeeded in getting credit for having been the first to achieve certain findings (Roazen 1969, 1975). By his talking with Hirst about cocaine Freud was implicitly enhancing, even if unknowingly, his own standing as a powerful physician. Hirst's faith in Freud as a healer was bound to be increased by the series of steps Freud recounted having to do with Koller's becoming a famous scientist. Freud was also sharing with Hirst one of the problems in his own early life, which meant that in some sense he was relating to Hirst, still a young man, as a moral equal with himself. Whatever Freud was later to write about the desirability of the psychoanalyst remaining detached and aloof, as we shall see Freud himself had very little experience with any of the rules that he laid down for others. It was human of Freud to have reacted to the newspaper article Hirst brought up, and Freud's worries about priorities served to contribute to the general good influence he had on Hirst.

Hirst said he had first been sent by his family to Freud at the age of 16 or 17 (in 1903 or 1904). Hirst was with Freud for only a brief period the first time; the occasion had been what Hirst considered later as unquestionably a "very insincere" suicide attempt, if it could even be called that. He harbored a slight resentment toward Freud because of the brevity of his first analysis, but Hirst had been unaware then that his parents had not wanted the treatment to proceed. Although he had stayed with Freud only a little while, it was substantial enough that Hirst could consider his return to Freud in the fall of 1909 for an extended period of time as his "second analytic experience" with Freud. Hirst remained in analysis until the spring of 1910, when the therapy ended, at his father's say-so, not Freud's. With Hirst Freud was hardly dealing with an autonomous choice-making agent, which Freud's writings have idealized as most suited for psychoanalytic treatment.

Along the way Hirst managed to acquire through family channels a good deal of knowledge about Freud. I cannot be sure exactly when Hirst knew what about Freud, for he heard many family stories; but since Hirst left for America in 1911, and returned to Vienna only on specified occasions, it seems reasonable to suppose that much of what he understood about Freud he picked up either before he was in analysis or while he was undergoing treatment. Hirst told me he had read both Freud's *The Interpretation of Dreams* and his *Jokes and Their Relation to the Unconscious* preceding going to Freud for help; Hirst thought it would not be proper to ask Freud to treat him without having first read those central texts. From Freud's point of view it seemed "quite natural" that Hirst had read the books, even if in his technical papers he did not recommend that prospective patients could expect to benefit from psychoanalytic literature. (The epigraph for *The Interpretation of Dreams* came from Virgil: "If I cannot bend the heavens to my will, I shall move hell." Hirst said that the German socialist Ferdinand Lassalle had quoted it to mean, "If I can't move the rulers, I will appeal to the masses," and that in Freud's use it became, "If I can't get along with the conscious mind, I'll rely on the unconscious." George Brandes had used the same quotation in his biography of Lassalle, who was a hero of Freud's; the Zionist Theodor Herzl had also cited the same line from Virgil in 1898 [Pawel 1989]).

Hirst seemed to know a lot about Freud's earlier treatment in the 1890s of Emma Eckstein, who was his mother's sister. She had been a very beautiful woman, and Freud's first analysis of her was regarded as a great success. According to Hirst, Emma had suffered a relapse; Freud visited her at home in the evenings. Another physician had "faked" a diagnosis, saying she had a physical rather than a psychogenic ailment; he did so thinking it would cure her, and it did, for temporarily she "got well." Hirst reported that Freud had said then that it was hopeless, and Hirst thought he had been "perfectly right." For the rest of her life "she was ill."

Emma Eckstein and Freud stayed "friends" for as long as she lived, but the physician–patient relationship between them was over. She continued to think about Freud "as a great man," only she viewed him as "terribly stubborn" in insisting that everything had to be mental when some problems were physical. At the time I knew him, Hirst was puzzled that he had never come across anything resembling Emma's case in Freud's writings. One incident, connected with Freud's friend Dr. Wilhelm Fliess, stood out in Hirst's memory. She had had a terrible nose-bleed, following an operation by Fliess; ultimately the procedure distorted her face. Hirst brought up the subject in connection with one of Freud's fainting spells. Hirst said it was the sight of the blood that had provoked Freud's collapse. Hirst interpreted Freud's fainting as an "escape" in that he then did not have to be responsible for treating the bleeding patient. (Freud's horror of blood might have been related to his own mother's tuberculosis.) The family did not seem to blame Freud for Emma's hemorrhaging, even if it caused some "amusement" that Freud, who was supposed to control that sort of thing, faded away so at the height of the crisis.

Some more of the particulars of Emma Eckstein's case, and how Fliess had botched her treatment, later appeared in a 1984 book that was highly critical of Freud's whole approach (Masson 1984). But that version of events was only possible on the basis of certain letters from Freud to Fliess that were not publicly available when I knew Hirst. Fliess had mistakenly left gauze in Emma's nose, and its removal precipitated the medical crisis and Freud's fainting. But Freud chose to interpret some of Emma's bleeding as the expression of a psychological longing, exculpating Fliess from the consequences of his error. For what it is worth, it seems significant that despite the difficulties between

Freud and Emma, Hirst's parents had not felt deterred from sending him to Freud for analysis. And they also toyed with the idea of putting his sister in Freud's hands too; as Freud told Hirst the story, she came to him under parental instructions, but since she made it plain she did not want to be treated the matter stopped there. Freud even told Hirst that he was more intelligent than his sister, which might not seem appropriate by today's standards.

When Hirst emigrated to America at the age of 24 it seemed well known to him that Freud had a "very unfavorable impression" of the States. A somewhat lame-sounding explanation Hirst offered was that a cook in the Freud household had moved to America, and later came back to see the Freuds in Vienna presenting herself as "a perfect lady." In Vienna there was a "reactionary" government, and this sort of crossing of class barriers was supposedly a "novel experience" for Freud.

When Hirst told Freud about his own leaving for America, Freud had asked, "Why don't you go to South America?" Hirst thought that this was very characteristic of Freud, who was not then making one of his little jokes. Hirst explained that he did not know any Spanish, to which Freud replied, "Oh, hell, it takes three weeks to get there." Hirst understood Freud's meaning to be that he could easily learn the Spanish language on the ship coming over; Hirst thought that Freud felt he was not making a true choice, and that his preference for North America was because he had learned English on a trip to London.

I naturally inquired of Hirst about Freud's attitude toward the States, and he reminded me that in 1911 there was still a comparatively intense puritanical streak in the United States, especially regarding sex. Hirst also thought there was a bias in America against Freud, and that references to his work were then relatively rare. When Hirst saw them later he would clip the citations out for sending along to him. Once there was a "terrible attack" on Freud by a man returning from Vienna, and it appeared that contrary to what he claimed Freud had never met him. When I asked if Freud seemed grateful for the clippings Hirst sent him, he said that he received only postal card responses. Hirst thought Freud was probably justified in his "curtness" by his desire to wean Hirst from the emotional transference to him that had been set up in the treatment he had undergone. (Transferences are illusory emotions in patients, who mistake a present relationship with the analyst for past emotional ties. Freud proposed that analytic treatment aim to arouse transferences, and then dissolve them through rational interpretations. Patients had a unique reaction to Freud as the creator of psychoanalysis, quite unlike how they related to other analysts. And to the extent that analysts have received emotional responses appropriate only to Freud, circumstances have placed them in a false position.)

Hirst also thought that Freud was very "money-minded," and disliked not being paid for his services; to Hirst Freud had an unusual and "very honest" approach both to sex and to financial matters. Hirst related Freud's lack of interest in following up on patients with his disinclination to concern himself with patients unless he were paid for it.

Hirst knew that the absence of public toilets in the United States particularly bothered Freud. In 1909, when Freud made his only trip to the States to receive an honorary degree from Clark University in Worcester, Massachusetts, he seems to have suffered from urinary incontinence; Jung, who was along with Freud for the trip, tried treating him for a psychogenic symptom (Roazen 1975, Rosenzweig 1992). At the time we met, Hirst and I were both not quite clear about Freud's 1909 urinary difficulties in America; Hirst thought that there was "a certain ineptness" on Freud's part not to know how to find a bathroom inside a building, rather than expecting the public street facili-

ties that were common in central Europe. Hirst thought that
Freud felt that the American location of bathrooms was part of
the "suppression of sex."

Hirst had, by the time I saw him, assimilated to American
life; yet he remembered how different old-world culture was.
Before World War I, for example, there were supposedly no
public libraries in Europe; the Hapsburg Emperor had a library
that one could use if granted permission. (In reality there were
public libraries all over Austria, at least since the end of the
eighteenth century, together with the first public school system
introduced by Joseph II—who also issued the first edict of
Jewish emancipation.) Hirst still retained certain strong convictions about the civilization he had once been part of. For
example, he said he continued to "hate" the political regime in
Austria, which he thought had an "infamous" government; it
was a world in which someone like Koller could not get a
university appointment solely because he was a Jew. Hirst
mentioned that his father, like Freud, had belonged to B'nai
B'rith in Vienna, which was not at all a popular organization
there but rather an exclusive club to which "only wealthy Jews"
belonged. (Freud presented several papers to B'nai B'rith [Megh-
nagi 1993].)

Hirst said that one of the things he had most resented about
Hitler was that he had forced him to be a Jew. "What was there
to do but shout 'I am a Jew' when once it is made such a
disadvantage." An uncle of Hirst's had thought that the reason
they should not convert from Judaism was simple: one does not
run away. Personally Hirst felt closest to the Unitarians and
deists like Tom Paine and Thomas Jefferson. Freud, according to
Hirst, most likely had far more of a Jewish consciousness, and
for him to have joined B'nai B'rith had to be "a declaration"
about his position. It is important to remember how much a
Roman Catholic country Austria remained, even after the em-

pire was stripped away by the settlement of World War I. The old imperial government could not even be bothered, from Hirst's perspective, to record births and deaths; these statistics were kept by the Church for the Catholics, and the Jewish communities compiled such information about the Jews. The system was set up so that one could not even look up someone's birth date without knowing the religious affiliation beforehand. And these religious authorities also had taxing power. Hirst did not like these "congenital" allegiances, preferring to be able to choose his own citizenship. He thought that the alternative was a form of slavery, and he said that he would be "surprised" if Freud had disagreed.

Hirst thought that to insult a Viennese deeply it would only be necessary to call him a "patriot." For patriotism implied hypocrisy, subservience to a "rotten monarchy," and blindness to evil. By Hirst's standards a decent Viennese simply could not be patriotic. To some people Napoleon Bonaparte might seem an autocrat, but to Hirst Napoleon was the "son" of the French Revolution who had forced the Austrian Emperor to hand over his daughter in marriage. For Hirst every humiliation over the Austrians was to Napoleon's credit, and he was a hero to Hirst; he had had pictures of him all over his room in Vienna. For his part Freud had liked to quote variations on Napoleonic adages.

Given what Hirst had told me about the situation in old Austria, I asked about how Freud at the outset of World War I could have sided so strongly with the Austrians and the Germans. Hirst thought that the solution was "easy," in that the feeling would have been that Austria had been attacked by the "murderer" the Czar. The Austrians were freer than the Russians; by a series of diplomatic alliances England and France had become the Czar's "accomplices." While for Hirst (as well as Freud) Napoleon was a hero, Russian authoritarianism was quite another matter; Russians could be deemed "barbarians," since they went without having had a Renaissance or a Reformation, and in World War I they were threatening the cultured, limited freedoms of the Austrians.

Someone like Freud could have great affection for the Alps, the little country villages, and the Austrian landscape; such feelings could "substitute" for patriotism. So even though Freud was a Jew he did not have to feel outside the fight against the Allies in World War I. Hirst thought it was characteristic of the atmosphere of the circles he moved in that in the Vienna of his youth he had been unaware of the religion of his classmates. At the time all of them looked down equally on priests, rabbis, and ministers with the "greatest contempt." As far as he was concerned, no honest person could believe in religion, or enter a profession that exploited human ignorance. In Hirst's family there had been no religious ritual at all; he would have considered himself an atheist, but at the age of 60 he discovered that he had always believed both in God and in immortality. Growing up in Vienna he had had to deal with Catholicism as the state religion, and Hirst knew that Freud had mentioned his not wanting to offend the Church as part of his reasons for hesitating to publish his *Moses and Monotheism* in the late 1930s.

From Hirst's point of view he and Freud were very much a part of the same social world. I asked him questions about Freud's family, and in particular about Freud's wife. Hirst thought she was of the same "type" as his mother and her sister. These women were "middle class," "grey-haired," "well-dressed but not modish." On his 1938 trip to Vienna he had gone home "for a last visit." His sister still lived there then, and he went to help get her out. At the time there was "a terrible feeling" in the city itself. It was his sister who then possessed Freud's letters to Emma Eckstein, and Hirst went to Freud for permission to take the letters out of the country; Hirst's uncle had arranged for the interview.

At the time Freud was old and sick, so Hirst saw only

Freud's wife and Anna. He remembered how astonished Freud's wife was at the casual way Hirst talked about "leaving" Vienna, since the Freuds were then still awaiting the official papers allowing them to go. Hirst thought that the local Jews were then so scared that they did not dare ignore the Nazi rules on emigration. When Hirst left on a night train to Switzerland, the Nazis never even bothered to check his papers. As he talked to Freud's wife, she mentioned how much the Freuds had done for Vienna; they gave money, for example, for the restoration of St. Stephen's Cathedral.

Hirst's trips back to Vienna were relatively rare; he had also gone there right after World War I in 1919. Freud himself, when Hirst called then, was in Bavaria, but his son Martin was at home and invited Hirst to dinner at Mathilda Hollitscher's place; she was Freud's eldest daughter (Roazen 1993a). When I asked if Freud had been disappointed in his sons, Hirst recalled having had a daydream in his analysis of taking care of Freud's children when he got rich. At the time Hirst had not known that Freud's children were his own age. In America Hirst knew Freud's Bernays nieces and nephew. And in New York City he had contact with Federn, a Viennese analyst who emigrated after 1938. Hirst first met Federn before World War I, when Federn made a brief trip to the States for the sake of treating a rich young American (Roazen 1969), and then Hirst saw Federn in 1938 when he went to rescue his sister. At Hirst's home in New York he once said to Federn that Freud had not seemed to have much success with his own sons. Instead of Federn being adequately protective of Freud's boys, he gave an exceptionally "inept" answer, for he stiffened and said that it was a subject that he would prefer not to discuss, thereby giving away, as far as Hirst was concerned, the true story.

Federn had had an unusually awed attitude toward Freud as his "master." To all of them Freud was known simply as "Professor." (Even Joseph Breuer, once Freud's senior collaborator on *Studies On Hysteria*, had addressed Freud in letters, after their falling out, as "Professor.") This title was to Hirst a typically Austrian invention, in that Freud had no duties but the right to give lectures. One achieved the kind of professorship Freud had, Hirst said, through bribing the appropriate minister, and in turn he would use the money to control what the press wrote. It was a "rotten" system in which "all the titles were for sale." Freud had an intense desire for the professorship, which to be sure had a special financial value in the kinds of fees that could be charged to patients. Hirst never squared this eagerness of Freud to have the post with Hirst's own conviction that people of the Viennese "nobility" would never have been so "humiliated" as to accept a title from the Emperor, and unfortunately I failed to try to point out the apparent inconsistency. (The philosopher Ludwig Wittgenstein's father "declined the invitation to add the aristocratic 'von' to his name, feeling that such a gesture would be seen as the mark of the parvenu" [Monk 1990].)

Federn was, in Hirst's view, a "complete devotee" of Freud's. Still, Hirst thought that in Vienna it seemed "inconceivable" to go to any other analyst but Freud himself. The general attitude in Hirst's family was that it was a "pity" that the great man's disciples were so "inferior." Bismarck had a son named Herbert, who "amounted to nothing"; and Freud's spiritual sons were, according to Hirst, "all Herberts." One story had it that Federn for years analyzed a patient without knowing or finding out that the patient had a long-standing affair with Federn's own wife. That tale, whether it was accurate or not, communicates something of the Viennese feeling about the low level of Freud's students. (Patients from abroad were less likely to pick up this local Viennese conviction.) Although Hirst thought Federn was "not a very bright man," he knew his "limitations" and therefore got the maximum out of the gifts that he did have.

As for Hirst's own outlook on the inventor of psychoanalysis, Hirst thought Freud was "an absolute genius—make no
mistake about it!" Apparently Freud had written to Hirst's father
about him, without being asked. (Such letter-writing within
Vienna would not have been unusual, since Freud disliked using
the telephone. And letters have survived, for example, between
Freud and someone like Federn.) Hirst's analysis had cost forty
kronen an hour, which was about ten dollars in 1909; that meant
Freud was charging "quite a high fee." Hirst's father was "a
wealthy man," a paper manufacturer. At the time Hirst said he
was "filled with ingratitude" toward his father. Hirst's family,
though, was friendly with the Freuds.

Hirst's guess was that Freud kept few records about his
former patients. He once asked Freud how he could remember
so much with such accuracy, and Freud replied: "I make no
effort." Freud could evidently trust his free associations about
his patients. I asked if Freud had ever talked to Hirst about
aggression or hate, but Freud had never used any such notion as
"aggression." As far as technical terminology went, Freud had
brought up concepts like "identification" and "transference."
Hirst did not think, even after the distance of all those years, that
he had had much transference to Freud. Instead, Hirst saw it as
a "sensible admiration"; he had been "aware of the privilege of
being in the presence of a great man." Without his having had
his analysis with Freud, Hirst thought he would have continued
a "most unhappy existence."

It may be worthwhile trying to consider what Freud's
reactions to such feelings on Hirst's part were apt to have been.
Let us assume that Hirst's approach to Freud was a realistic one.
It would not have made sense for Freud to have rejected Hirst's
emotions, or tried to undermine them. Freud presumably accepted Hirst's tribute as what was appropriately due him. No
other therapist since Freud has had to deal with exactly the same
situation. However, Freud's surrogates, which include all later

analysts, have been the recipients of feelings aroused by the treatment setting Freud had created, including emotions that made sense in reaction to Freud but that were bound to be misplaced when directed at others.

When I asked Hirst specifically what enabled Freud to help him he talked about "the peculiar, rare form of impotency" that he had suffered from at the time. He could not ejaculate during intercourse. For some slight physical difficulties during the analysis, Freud had sent him to a urologist. But that consultation did not bear on the central symptom that bothered Hirst. Freud knew that there were other psychological aspects to Hirst that also needed straightening out, but Hirst himself was not too interested in anything else but that one symptom itself.

Hirst thought that his "final cure," his "real recovery," had come about ten years after the end of the analysis. While he was with Freud he already discovered that he could be unusually potent, and had successful intercourse several times in an hour. When Hirst attributed his sexual prowess to an inheritance from his father's family, Freud made a dry remark to the effect that for such a trait one ought to be able to forgive one's family much.

Hirst came to America representing his father's mills. Then the First World War broke out, and soon Hirst had a wife and a child. Hirst said that his "final cure" came about when he was able to connect up his difficulties in earning a living with what he had once thought about his sexual inability. Hirst remembered that he was walking down a staircase (according to Freud a sexual symbol) when he realized the connection; then Hirst went to law school and was successful ever after.

Hirst concluded that Freud had been right about him in the analysis. Hirst had brought some poems of his for Freud to read. He was surprised that Hirst had "other" gifts than those he had known of. Hirst now struck Freud as having a "strong analytical mind." Freud told him: "You aren't a weak person, you are very strong." Hirst said that to be so praised by Freud was totally unexpected. Hirst thought he had been living on half his mind, but unable to reach the rest. He said that he would attribute it "entirely" to Freud that he had been able to fulfill himself. And Freud's assurance that Hirst had a very good mind was part of how Freud had helped him.

Hirst had the idea, undoubtedly from Freud, that a hidden childhood trauma lies behind every neurosis. The Alfred Hitchcock *Spellbound* view of psychoanalysis as aiming at the recovery of a secret memory, a forgotten childhood crisis, was so familiar to Hirst that it formed a natural part of his own personal understanding of himself. (Others might see this procedure of Freud's along the lines of exorcising old-fashioned demons.) During the treatment Hirst learned from Freud that the trauma often came back to pop up in an analysis in a curious way: a daydream criticism of psychoanalysis. Hirst imagined he could recall his father holding him as a little child and saying: "I could strangle the bastard for making so much noise." Hirst thought then how stupid it was that such an incident should interfere with his life. At that point Freud maintained that a crucial core of neurosis often came back as a criticism of psychoanalysis.

When I asked Hirst what he thought had cured him, he maintained there were two features. First there was the supportive element in Freud's treatment of him, and second the subsequent possibility of Hirst's making a link between his ability to earn a living and his sexual life. Hirst said that he could not really feel that Freud had been distant with him, not when he showed so much professional interest and remembered so many things about him. Hirst had not felt that Freud kept him at bay. Because Freud's postcards to Hirst in America were impersonal and short, Hirst had felt a certain "coldness" in Freud. Hirst said his attitude toward Freud was that of an orthodox Christian toward Christ. He viewed Freud as his "savior," and thought that without him he would have been a "failure" or a suicide.

In thinking about the apparatus of psychoanalytic treatment and thinking, Hirst insisted that "any system will work if a Freud undertakes to make it!" Hirst was not struck by the importance of any individual aspect of Freud's approach. Hirst never had the impression that Freud was being confrontational about the truth; he was not educating Hirst, nor was he making propaganda. Freud behaved as one maintaining a purely professional physician–patient relationship. He was therefore not at all interested in Hirst's politics, ethics, or philosophy of life. Although I tried to contrast Freud as a scientist and as a therapist, Hirst held that Freud was both an important discoverer and a great healer.

Hirst felt that he had an advantage in life in having had more access to his unconscious than most people. Freud's attitude toward his impotency symptom had been that if Hirst began to understand his repressions and inhibitions, then the problem would cure itself. So Freud focused not on the symptom alone but on Hirst's free associations.

Initially Freud had been skeptical of Hirst's talent for writing poetry. (In retrospect Hirst thought he had been too proud of his poetic gifts, and had not had enough confidence in his inner strength and analytic powers.) One of Freud's comments in this connection stuck in Hirst's mind for life: "The sand in almost every river contains gold, the question is whether there is enough gold to make it worth exploiting." In that way Freud had tried to put Hirst's poetry in perspective. According to Hirst Freud usually had done "very little" talking during the analysis, and had not told jokes. When Hirst left him, he thought he was "cured", but he realized later that there were still multiple possibilities for how his life would turn out.

Hirst had not found Freud an intimidating presence. Both analyses had taken place with Hirst lying on Freud's couch. Hirst could not recall how much explaining Freud had to do about what psychoanalysis was like. Of course Hirst had read those books by Freud. And Hirst knew about the significance for Freud of the "original trauma" in all neuroses; it was a linear conception of Freud's implying that the unearthing of underlying causes would relieve neurotic symptoms. Hirst also knew that his grandfather had died of syphilis, and that it was Freud's predilection to relate neurosis to a syphilitic ancestry. Hirst's grandfather had died of locomotor ataxia, the last stage of syphilis. He was also injured in a fall from a bus and later paralyzed, but a relative of Hirst's, a physician, had explained the real nature of the illness. This sort of inheritance was viewed by Freud as a predisposition to neurosis and reflected a Lamarckian assumption on Freud's part. Hirst then had this family heritage in common with his Aunt Emma. Although Hirst was unsure what he learned verbally from Freud as opposed to having read in books by him, Freud's ascribing neurotic troubles to syphilis was not something that appeared prominently in print; rather, Freud tended to dismiss arguments about the heredity of such problems.

Freud's healing took place indirectly, and was not confined to his decision to use certain words or offer specific interpretations. Hirst (at odds with what he earlier reported) thought Freud was far more an educator than a healer, but Freud did not consciously lecture. He was not like a priest or a minister, telling you what to do. But he was engaging in a deeper form of education, as he sought to make one understand the workings of the psyche, providing the tools for self-analysis. For years afterward Hirst wrote down his dreams and analyzed them. To learn these insights from Freud was far more important than to acquire knowledge of medicine. Once a friend of Hirst's had said to him, "You *would* have made an excellent lawyer," which is when he came to the decision to do what he always had planned—study law.

I had suggested to Hirst that tolerance may not have been among Freud's virtues. Hirst agreed that Freud had not been

tolerant toward analysts who dared to differ with him. But Hirst
was inclined to fault Freud's disciples for the rise of factionalism
in psychoanalysis; people like Adler, whom Hirst had known,
did not make things easy for Freud. As for himself Hirst said he
had no reason to believe that Freud liked him as a person. He
may have been interested in him as a case, but it had no bearing
on the treatment itself. Freud succeeded in giving him "invaluable gifts," which Hirst considered "presents." Freud had
taught Hirst about himself, and the general significance of
self-knowledge. Hirst had never known himself until then. He
reported that he had understood that he had been in the
presence of one of mankind's great men, and this was not a
retrospective judgment for Hirst had admiringly read those
books beforehand.

Hirst knew that in principle an analysis involves both
antagonism as well as affection. I asked whether he had ever
found it frustrating that everything with Freud had to be so
exact. Hirst was reminded of how the collection of antique
figures on Freud's desk were always in the same order. Hirst
possessed one of the famous Pollock etchings of Freud peering
out over his antique-covered worktable.

Freud was "rigid" about analytic hours; you paid for his
time, from nine until ten for example; it was nine sharp and ten
sharp. Hirst said he had "often" been late. Here Hirst did not
think he was dealing with a peculiar personal habit of Freud's;
punctuality was instead a professional matter. Freud had not
seemed to mind when Hirst was late; Freud realized it was an
aspect of a neurotic problem of Hirst's. In one period Hirst was
always fifteen minutes late; Freud just mentioned it, and said he
used the time to write checks. Freud for his part never kept him
waiting. And Hirst never saw the patients whose sessions preceded or followed his; Freud's waiting room was set up so that
the entrance to his office was separated from the exit. If Hirst
met somebody coming or going on the staircase of the small

apartment building, he had no way of knowing if the person was visiting Freud.

What Hirst so admired about Freud's approach was that Freud had allowed Hirst to "run the show." When Hirst brought in the poems, for example, Freud had said, "You have finally decided that the poet in you needs to be analyzed as well"; Freud had never told him to bring them in. Freud did not decide the issues that were to be discussed. Hirst experienced an immense amount of freedom with Freud, perhaps in special contrast to Hirst's parents whom he described as "very severe" and stern "Puritans."

In my inquiring whether literature had come up in the analysis, Hirst said that novels had only been mentioned when Hirst brought them up. Freud had a great interest in the confirmation of his theories from literature. Hirst remembered one short story by Heinrich Mann in which a lover kills his mistress. It was supposed to be a double suicide, and she helped guide a dagger into her breast. "And it was strange," the author wrote, "that her most heroic action should resemble her most obscene," meaning guiding a penis into her vagina. In another story a man was married to a woman yet does not sleep with her. Then one day she says to him, "You know, we are so close and yet so distant—I sometimes wish you would beat me." And that night he slept with her for the first time; the male character understood the unconscious psychoanalytic meaning of beating fantasies. Freud was "very interested" in both these remarks when Hirst told them to him.

In reflecting on Freud, Hirst thought it striking how Freud had been hated and maligned in Vienna. Hirst mentioned that doctors always dislike medical innovators; here Hirst blamed the pettiness of practitioners who were dependent on a small number of individual fees. And then there was the anti-Semitism, which seemed to increase over time. As a result Freud was not quite considered a joke, but he was "ignored" and had no standing. Therefore his adherents felt like they were a supporting party; Freud was considered by them as a prophet under attack. At the same time, Hirst conceded, perhaps Freud did enjoy too much being criticized.

The result was that Freud was inadequately recognized, although he was not considered a "quack." The sexual element in his theory had aroused opposition. Hypocrisy about sex influenced people then, and even played a role in creating Freud's problem with Jung. Freud himself was not "completely detached" about sex. There was in him a certain "shameful-ness" about it, as something extraordinary, not like the rising and the setting of the sun, or as routine as "chewing and eating." Freud was himself a little bit puritanical, like Hirst's own family.

Yet Freud was emancipated enough to take an active part with Hirst in making out a prescription for a contraceptive to be inserted in the vagina. (The prescription later wound up at the Library of Congress.) Until then Hirst had been using a condom as protection against conception. Freud said the condom was an unsatisfactory device, and that Hirst would have more pleasure without it. Hirst thought that Freud had been trying to "wean" him from masturbation, saying, "A condom is a tissue-plate against infection, and an armor-plate against enjoyment." Freud had not implied to Hirst that he thought masturbation was debilitating; in those days it was commonly thought to "destroy the mind." Freud instead took the approach that nature expects a discharge, and it does not matter how it is brought about.

Hirst still remembered some of Freud's stories. He once told how a very dignified lady comes to a physician wanting to know what to do not to have children. The best method, he advised, is a glass of cold water. "Fine," she said, "but before or after?" "Oh, instead!" Hirst thought it was characteristic of Freud to express some wisdom in a succinct form.

Hirst knew that Freud was not apt to overdo the desirability of sexuality. Hirst recalled telling Freud that he thought after a long marriage with many children a woman would lose her attractiveness for the husband. Freud replied that when a marriage has reached that stage, the importance of the sexual relationship becomes reduced, and other emotions set in. Hirst understood Freud to mean that love can be the consequence as well as the cause of sex. That was why the marriage-broker idea had worked so well within traditional Judaism; to be sure, both of the people to be linked in such matches came from similar backgrounds.

As a detached outsider, I would rate Hirst's treatment by Freud as a therapeutic success. Nevertheless I do not believe that what Freud achieved can measure up to the high standards he publicly set for himself. Supposedly psychoanalytic treatment makes use of evoking a transference from the patient for the purpose of ultimately dissipating it. Freud's idea was that the analyst would use the patient's positive relationship to him for the sake of exploring past emotional reactions. Symptoms arose, according to Freud's thinking, because of unconscious conflicts; once these emotional problems were rationally understood, the disturbances would evaporate of themselves. (Similarly Karl Marx, who thought past history was defined by class conflict, reasoned that after the socialist revolution had eliminated the existence of classes, the state, formerly a representative of the ruling class, would logically have to wither away.)

It appears from Hirst's account that his treatment included the kind of suggestive or transference cure that Freud claimed to want to avoid, on the grounds that it would not be lasting and was reminiscent of religious help. Freud's theory stated that the purpose of arousing transference was to produce memories, and through awakening the past the patient would be freed from the shadows of neurosis. But, when Hirst was being interviewed by Eissler for the Freud Archives, Hirst had explicitly stated that the mere fact that he was talking to Freud had more of a therapeutic effect than anything that Freud had said to him. In other words the relationship, not the rationalistic substance of Freud's interpretations, had been the key curative element.

Hirst was grateful for what Freud had done for him. He felt that by speaking to me he was in part repaying a "debt" he owed to Freud. Probably for a similar reason Hirst was willing to speak with Eissler. The tapes of those interviews are not available to independent researchers until the next century. But Eissler sent copies of the transcripts to Jones in London for the sake of enhancing the biography, which was designed to bolster a picture of the orthodox version of what Freud had supposedly been like. Reading through those transcripts, which Hirst was perfectly willing for me to see again, gave me a good basis for asking Hirst telling questions of my own. (Copies also turned up in the papers of Siegfried Bernfeld, an analyst with a pioneering interest in Freud's biography.)

For example, at one point in the interchange between Eissler and Hirst one could sense the dissatisfaction Eissler, as an exponent of later orthodoxy, was bound to feel at the nature of Hirst's account. For Eissler proposed to Hirst that Freud must have called Hirst's attention "throughout the treatment" to the idea that the impotency was "not really the only thing" at issue. Hirst decisively dissented from Eissler's view of how Freud proceeded as an analyst.

Had Freud taken Eissler's attitude, Hirst finally insisted, he thought Freud would not have succeeded with him. To Hirst his symptom was "terrifically" important, for it gave him a "terrible sense of inferiority." Eissler kept trying to get Hirst to admit that Freud must have referred instead to the significance of some general character traits. Hirst stuck to his guns, however, and told Eissler that his evaluation differed from that of Freud. Hirst thought that Freud had agreed with Hirst that the impotency was the "overwhelming problem," even if there was plenty of neurosis still left after the disappearance of the main symptom at the end of the treatment.

Hirst did support the idea, in his interviews with Eissler, that Freud had wanted to give his patients the impression of his complete impersonality as a therapist. Of course Hirst must have meant this as a relative matter, since we know about the complicated social involvement Freud had had with Hirst's extended family. But Hirst maintained that Freud did not want to keep in contact with his former patients. Even as a scientific matter Hirst thought that Freud's interest in his ex-patients was "very slight." Freud was not concerned with following up on the developments in the lives of his former patients or seeing what the aftereffects of the analysis might have been (Deutsch 1965). Hirst wondered whether some mental economy in Freud meant that he did not want to burden himself with any more human problems than he had to deal with, but also it may have reflected what Hirst proposed to Eissler as "an essential coldness" in Freud. (By 1912 Freud was relying on the analogy between a surgical operation and psychoanalytic treatment: "The justification for requiring this emotional coldness in the analyst is that it creates the most advantageous conditions for both parties; for the doctor a desirable protection for his own emotional life and for the patient the largest amount of help that we can give him today" [Freud 1912, p. 115].)

When I interviewed Hirst more than a decade after he had spoken with Eissler, he told me that it would not have occurred to him to call Freud "cold." I can only surmise that this apparent contradiction resulted from Eissler's approach to the alleged insignificance of Hirst's symptom, which must have seemed inhumanly aloof to Hirst. Confronted with the abstractness of Eissler's attitude toward Hirst's earlier troubles, Hirst did then allege the existence of "an essential coldness" in Freud. But when Hirst was allowed to present his own version of what had transpired in the course of his treatment, Freud emerges as a highly activist, sometimes interventionistic, analyst, quite at odds with the stereotype of the neutral therapist that later defenders of orthodoxy, such as Eissler, preferred.

2

"The Right Punishment": David Brunswick

Eissler's outlook has had many ideological allies, not the least of them being Anna Freud herself. The line of reasoning that Eissler had taken in interviewing Hirst, that Hirst must have gotten Freud's message wrong in thinking him especially concerned with Hirst's potency problem, reflected a conviction on the part of orthodox psychoanalytic believers in the 1960s that Freud stood for a distant approach to the treatment of patients. From their point of view, therapeutic improvements were a side issue, since supposedly the removal of one symptom could easily lead simply to a substitute arising.

It would be mistaken to think that such detached thinking arose in a vacuum, with no basis in Freud's publicly expressed system of ideas, for Freud aspired to create an impartial science, and this feature of his work has continued to attract impassioned advocates. Even though genuine scientific research should ideally inspire caution and skepticism, there are still many psychoanalysts of Eissler's persuasion. Janet Malcolm, whose work has been published in the *New Yorker,* approvingly quoted the head of the New York Psychoanalytic Society's Treatment Center in 1981 stating: "There are no surprises—we haven't had a surprise since 1974" (Malcolm 1981, p. 68; cf. Roazen 1990a) and in 1992 she could unashamedly write of how analyses "today" last "an average of ten years" (Malcolm 1992, p. 51). But the absence of surprise should be, I think, a telling sign of theoretical rigidity, and ten years of analysis, instead of being taken for granted, demands a special sort of defense.

Yet orthodox psychoanalytic theory holds that the reconstruction of early childhood in the course of analytic treatment will itself eventually be curative; present-day symptoms are relatively unimportant compared with the central objective of understanding the first years of life. These analysts, drawing their inspiration from certain features in Freud's worldview, look down on therapists who have a primary interest in alleviating human suffering. Knowledge is held to be the goal of treatment, with the conviction that the truth will lead to emancipation; supposedly the relationship between the analyst and patient is a laboratory-like situation uncontaminated by emotional bias. Orthodox analysts are committed to the view that Freud succeeded in creating a well-rounded science, and that by refining therapeutic technique his aims of research purposes will be at the same time attainable.

Although I had known nothing about David Brunswick other than his having been a patient of Freud's, he was easy to find. His name was on the membership roster of the Los Angeles Psychoanalytic Society, which was publicly available then as a feature of the *Bulletin of the International Psychoanalytic Association*, included in issues of the *International Journal of*

Psycho-Analysis, which was available in research libraries. Now that the membership of the International Psychoanalytic Association is much larger, such lists are privately circulated only for the members. Once I had Brunswick's name, I obtained his address from the American Psychoanalytic Association.

David Brunswick's office was in Beverly Hills, where almost all the analysts in Los Angeles could be found. One small area of Beverly Hills had so many analysts, it was known as the analyst's "canyon." At that time psychoanalysts in California had to be M.D.'s, and Brunswick was unusual in being nonmedical; he had a Ph.D. in psychology. Like other analysts of that time who were not physicians, known as lay analysts, he had been able to qualify as a psychoanalyst under a grandfather clause; early analysts who lacked medical training were considered acceptable, but no new members could be certified without a medical education. The medical monopoly on psychoanalysis had been stronger in the United States than elsewhere, but there were a few old-time exceptions like David Brunswick (Roazen 1990b).

Now the psychoanalytic establishment in California is strikingly receptive to analysts who come from nonmedical backgrounds. Freud's own hope for the future of his movement was that psychoanalysis not become swallowed-up within medical techniques, since he was convinced that all the human sciences could contribute to keeping analysis alive as an intellectually vital enterprise. California state law has for decades now been encouraging the practice of lay analysis. And recently a lawsuit of professional psychologists against the International Psychoanalytic Association, which had allowed its American affiliates to keep nonmedical candidates from being fully trained as candidates, has been successful. So there is reason to think that in the future there are prospects for lay analysis in America.

In late 1965, however, when I saw David Brunswick, he was an exception to what was then the medical fraternity of Los

Angeles analysts. I wrote to him before my arrival in the Los Angeles area, but I have no record of his answering, so I assume that I just telephoned him when I got to town. I did not bluntly propose talking to him about his analysis with Freud; instead I asked for his help in pursuing general work on the history of psychoanalysis.

At the time there were two psychoanalytic groups in Los Angeles, and Brunswick was a member of the more "conservative" one. In fact he turned out to be a member of the establishment that Eissler so prominently represented. A split among the city's analysts had taken place in 1950, following a similar schism that had occurred shortly before in Philadelphia. In both places the more orthodox analysts were determined to maintain a puristic approach to psychoanalytic treatment. Brunswick told me, for example, that he distanced himself from those colleagues in Los Angeles who had formed a "dissident" group (the Southern California Psychoanalytic Society) believing in "short" analyses and only three sessions a week; these liberals would be the ones who concentrated on trying to improve the state of a patient's symptomatology. Although a few people managed to bridge the two groups, and taught students in training at both societies, Brunswick had remained loyally allied with the original organization. Only in recent years, long after Brunswick's death, have the followers of Heinz Kohut, the creator of the self psychology movement in psychoanalysis, succeeded in creating a third training association in Los Angeles.

Brunswick identified with the old guard, the so-called mainstream within analysis, which has always been composed of a relatively small but immensely articulate and influential band of advocates. Even Freud had sometimes argued, in contrast to Hirst's account, that the premature relief of a patient's symptoms could also remove the suffering that was an incentive to insight. Therapeutic ambitiousness, according to this line of reasoning, could be at odds with what were considered scientific goals.

Around the same time I was interviewing David Brunswick, I also met one of the "renegade" members from that second Los Angeles group of analysts, who happened to show me how he placed his analytic chair at the side of the end of his couch in such a way that the reclining patient could easily look at him by turning his head. Even such a minor variation in the standard psychoanalytic treatment setting was considered by some to be heretical, a contamination of the more traditional arrangement. Freud's own seat had been out of sight, behind the couch. Moralistic purism about proper psychoanalytic procedure has always been strongly maintained, even though in a famous 1912 paper Freud had said of the approach he was then outlining, "I must however make it clear that what I am asserting is that this technique is the only one suited to my individuality; I do not venture to deny that a physician quite differently constituted might find himself driven to adopt a different attitude to his patients and to the task before him" (p. 111).

However tolerant Freud might sound here, encouraging the reader to think that others could legitimately proceed along a different course, only a year earlier he had created a sensation in Vienna by effectively excommunicating Adler, along with his sympathizers, from Freud's group of followers (Roazen 1975). Adler's sins, from Freud's point of view, were multiple, and a "deviant" like Jung also gave up on using a couch as part of his disagreeing with the creator of psychoanalysis (Roazen 1975). Freud could be intransigent about what he regarded as any betrayal of the unique mission he felt called upon to espouse, even at the cost of expelling former allies. In everything Freud wrote one has to be wary of the metaphorical whipped cream that he, like a true Viennese, served up, and so he could modestly proclaim that the technique he was proposing was merely "the only one suited" to his own "individuality." It can be hard to detect, except when reading between the lines, what Freud's real feelings were; in his correspondence he could be at odds with his public utterances, and yet even in reading his letters now it is easy to be misled by the full complexities of Freud's manners.

David Brunswick was a straight-shooting American without the old-world charm we saw in Hirst. One has to wonder what psychoanalysis became not only without Freud's personal capacities but also in the absence of the whole culture of which he was a part. For example, Freud regularly shook hands before and after every analytic hour. A handshake can be not only a social ritual but a means of human communication and support, and some of Freud's patients remembered the special significance of the handshakes with Freud. Yet in a famous British textbook on psychoanalytic technique, one that David Brunswick thought well of, there is a lengthy paragraph on the question of whether or not to shake hands with a new patient: "[T]he decision is not perhaps momentous, but it involves considerations of certain principles" (Glover 1955, p. 24). What was perfectly natural to Freud became later, in different social settings, a procedure requiring thoughtful reflection.

Since I was new to the psychoanalytic community in California, Brunswick helpfully referred me to a local analyst who specialized in the history of Freud's movement in the area. Brunswick told me how the original society of Los Angeles analysts had been formed in 1946; before that the San Francisco Psychoanalytic Society had been the governing body for members on the West Coast. By the time I met Brunswick he had long since allied himself with those Los Angeles analysts who saw themselves as protecting the "science" of psychoanalysis lest it be lost in the clinical aims primarily concerned with being helpful to patients. Today's biological psychiatrists may seem humane in their willingness to recommend various drugs, but any system of therapy can be used for keeping patients at a distance; the *Diagnostic and Statistical Manual* is too often misused for purposes of pigeonholing, rather than helping, patients. At the time I was conducting these interviews I was aware of the existing partisan divisions among analysts, even though as an outsider, a social scientist interested in the theoretical uses of psychoanalytic thinking, I was not expected to have any doctrinal allegiances.

The other analysts I met in the Los Angeles area, with one exception, had no personal contact with Freud. But they provided me with valuable background material and helped forward my understanding of psychoanalysis. Some of these analysts were strikingly successful in terms of their having dealt with famous Hollywood producers, directors, actors, and actresses. For example, psychoanalysis became so successful in America that Marilyn Monroe's New York analyst (she also had one in Los Angeles, and both were in regular contact with Anna Freud) was chosen by Jacqueline Kennedy as well.

Although I think Hirst has to be considered a therapeutic success, his account of his treatment did not sit well with someone like Eissler, for it showed Freud behaving too much like a caring human being as opposed to how a so-called classical analyst was supposed to act in Eissler's view of things. It is possible to think of the conception of an orthodox analyst as a straw man, but Eissler's expressed discontent with Hirst's understanding of what transpired in his analysis illustrates how doctrinaire that wing of analysts could be. In contrast to Hirst, Brunswick, whom Eissler also interviewed (tape to be made available in 2013), was one of Freud's therapeutic failures—not a disaster but at best a stalemate. Yet oddly enough Brunswick, as we shall see, derived a curious lesson from his own frustrating experience. His not having thrived with Freud was attributed by him to Freud's failure to fulfill the abstract ideals of analysis that he laid down for others, and that Brunswick had then proceeded to adopt as his own.

When I initially approached Brunswick I was mostly seeking his help with understanding other patients of Freud, in particular his sister-in-law Ruth Mack Brunswick, whom I had already discovered was a special favorite of Freud's in the last decades of his life. She died in 1946, before my research began. (The idiosyncrasies of Freud's uniquely cluttered office, which offered patients a special sort of emotional rapport, contrasted with the more antiseptic surroundings of his American followers like Brunswick. Eissler's own office, the one time I interviewed him, was impressively book-lined.) In the course of my talking to David I discovered how he, his brother Mark, and Mark's wife Ruth had all been among Freud's patients. One of David's sisters had also then been in analysis in Vienna. Despite the stature that Ruth Mack Brunswick once held within the psychoanalytic movement, there was almost nothing about her in a standard reference like Jones's biography of Freud.

I was not at the outset fully aware of the familial connections among David, Mark, and Ruth. Keeping things straight became even more complicated since Ruth's father, after his first wife had died, married David and Mark's mother. Judge Julian Mack, who eventually became David's stepfather, was a well-known Zionist and a famous jurist, who played a prominent part in the era of President Franklin Roosevelt's New Deal. Even before Judge Mack married David's mother, David and Mark had been distantly related to Ruth; in fact Mark as a young man had been present at the 1917 ceremony for Ruth's first marriage to a prominent physician, Herman Blumgart, who was a cousin of his mother's. Herman's brother Leonard was a New York psychoanalyst who had been analyzed by Freud for four months shortly after the conclusion of World War I. David told me he had heard about Freud from Leonard Blumgart who, along with a whole group of New York psychiatrists, had gone to Freud for further training at a time when psychoanalysis seemed the wave of the future. David had also studied under E. B. Holt at Harvard College, who taught psychoanalysis as early as World War I and wrote an early text about it.

Of the three Brunswicks to go to Freud for analysis, Ruth had been the first, and she was the only one of them to have had formal psychiatric training. She had gone to Radcliffe College during World War I, and then graduated from Tufts Medical School. Her future husband Mark was a musician, and her brother-in-law David, although he later returned to the States and became a practicing analyst, had no such intention at the time he first saw Freud. Thus, David Brunswick was part of a larger family constellation that I wanted to understand.

In contrast to how I happened to come across Hirst's name, no written material existed then as to the significance of the Brunswicks as a group of patients in Freud's world. I knew that Freud had sent his case the Wolf Man to Ruth Brunswick for reanalysis in the 1920s, and that her published account of him formed an addendum to Freud's own famous report. But it would never have occurred to me to pursue the story of the three Brunswicks if I had not been alerted informally to the special standing Ruth had attained as an important disciple within Freud's circle. Everyone I met who was in a position to know confirmed her importance. Entirely aside from the problem of trying to establish why Ruth came to matter so much to Freud, it is at least as striking that all three of the Brunswicks were for some time in analysis with Freud simultaneously. Freud had that separate entrance and exit from his office so that patients could be allowed to maintain their anonymity, yet in the cases of David, Mark, and Ruth, Freud was treating three people who were intimately acquainted with one another, and for each of them it would be impossible not to know something of what was going on in the analysis of the others. Analytic therapy presupposes distance between the analyst and his patients; for me to put in print, as I did first in 1969, that Freud saw these three close relatives at the same time was in itself a blow to the orthodox analysts' carefully nurtured picture of Freud as an aloof and detached clinician. Almost nothing else has been written about Ruth Brunswick since two chapters on her that I published in 1975.

I met with David Brunswick, whom I was interviewing before I met Mark, in his Los Angeles office and also at a luncheon. He told me at the outset he had been in analysis with Freud from 1927 to 1930.

In contrast to a few of the other Los Angeles analysts who had become something of media celebrities, David Brunswick was correctly described to me by one reliable local source as an unusually "modest" man; in spite of his long and direct association with Freud, he had not assumed any airs. I found him honest and unpretentious, less lively and personally engaging than Hirst had been yet somehow nice and I thought also a bit peppery; while Hirst had been full of old-world manners, Brunswick was more than a trifle on the colorless side, certainly pale in contrast to how I came to remember his brother Mark. One old Viennese woman, the widow of the analyst Edward Hitschmann, strikingly once said to me of David that by her standards he was "hardly a human being," meaning that he was that dull. Similarly the wife of a Los Angeles analyst referred to David as having the personality of an "accountant." So far he has still not succeeded in making it into the history books (cf. Appignanesi and Forrester 1992). Despite how David was characterized to me, I learned some key things from him. In retrospect, though, it is understandable that in my memory he was overshadowed by his artistic brother Mark.

Although David's three-year analysis at that late stage of Freud's career, after Freud was already ill with cancer of the jaw, was by no means a short one, David informed me right away that his brother and sister-in-law were in Vienna even longer with Freud. Freud's analyses before he got sick were all characteristically shorter than afterward. The younger Freud was, the more outgoing he was apt to be with people, and the higher the turnover in his cases. He could even be so extravagant as to have told an American newspaper interviewer in 1909: "As you ask me about my own method of psychotherapy I must first mention that there are of course many sorts and ways of psychotherapy. All are good if they accomplish their objective, that is, effect a cure." At the same time Freud was holding to the belief that "there is the greatest contrast between the suggestive and the analytic technique" (Albrecht 1973, pp. 23–25). Although it seems to me that Eissler was upset to hear that Hirst's account of his treatment sounded so much like "suggestion," David Brunswick would have shared Eissler's preference for the norm of "analytic technique," and would have considered that Freud's failure to live up to it in Brunswick's analysis explained why it had run into the ground.

According to Brunswick his treatment with Freud had not been "a good analysis." By the time I interviewed him I was already well informed about Freud's possible failings as a therapist; I knew that many of Freud's former patients, at least those who had gone on to be analysts themselves, were capable of joking among themselves about some of his clinical inadequacies. None of this skepticism was inconsistent with a shared reverence for Freud, or his immense personal significance in their lives. David Brunswick may have been the first of Freud's former patients to be so blunt with me about where Freud had gone wrong with him. Yet he himself had become a practicing analyst who was strongly identified, as I have already mentioned, with that wing of analysts relatively inattentive to the immediate needs of therapeutic success. He seemed to have no suspicion that the grandiose expectations of orthodox psychoanalysis might lead a therapist to be tempted to act like a magician, and that same doctrine could be infantilizing to the patient as well.

From Brunswick's point of view it was essential to explain to me at the outset that Mark and Ruth were already with Freud before he started. But no matter how unusual the situation might have been, and it struck me then as fairly "unorthodox," Brunswick explained without defensiveness that psychoanalytically Freud had "done" them all at once. He felt Freud "should not have taken him" into analysis at the same time as his sister-in-law and brother.

Based on the written evidence one might never have expected such an arrangement to have arisen. During World War I Freud had written that "most of the failures of" psychoanalysis's "early years were due not to the doctor's fault or to an unsuitable choice of patients but to unfavorable external conditions." At this time Freud was comparing psychoanalysis to a surgical procedure, and what it would be like to proceed in "the presence of all the members of the patient's family." In dealing with Hirst Freud necessarily had to rely on the family. But with the Brunswicks he brought on himself the task of sorting out the most intimate kinds of familial troubles. Nonetheless in Freud's writings the reader is left with the proposition that "in psychoanalytic treatments the intervention of relatives is a positive danger and a danger one does not know how to meet" (Freud 1916–1917, pp. 458–459). With the Brunswicks Freud had ambitiously courted the very peril that he warned others against. (Some contemporary practitioners of family therapy thus might cite Freud as an unlikely predecessor.)

I still wonder what significance it had for David Brunswick that he knew that Freud was so blatantly violating his own recommendations. It did not seem to me that Brunswick was being theoretical about where he thought Freud had gone wrong in conducting his therapy. I do not think he was making a generalization about how analytic therapists ought not to deal with too many members of the same family at one time. True, I had never before heard of Freud's so obviously ignoring his own precepts about the analyst's striving for detachment and neutrality. Subsequently I have known of analysts who analyzed married couples—sometimes at the same time, more often not—and who reported having good success and bad results. In recent years we have learned a good deal more about how daringly unconventional Freud could be as a therapist (Brabant et al. 1993; cf. Roazen 1994b); the term *indiscretion* seems far too mild to encompass Freud's boldness.

Brunswick stressed to me that when he went to Vienna, Freud was in a different stage than in his earlier work. At one time Freud had supposedly been in favor of relatively quick analyses, which lasted only a matter of months, but this was "no longer" so, Brunswick pointed out, by the late 1920s. According to his version of things, the "interference" with his analysis came more from Freud and his "countertransference" to Brunswick than from Brunswick's own transference "resistances." Freud invoked the concept of how an analyst's irrational emotions could constitute a serious impediment to the practice of psychotherapy, but he never did more than that; in his writings he chose to emphasize the problem of the transferences on the part of patients, although since Freud's death there has been an efflorescence of literature about the existence of countertransference. According to Freud's model of treatment it was the patient, not the analyst, who produced troublesome emotions that he characterized as "resistances" to self-knowledge; it has taken a later generation of observers to think in terms of how the mutual interaction between patient and analyst shapes one another's feelings. (An analyst in 1926, who pointed out the positive possibilities of countertransference helping the analyst identify with a patient's problems, was to be a pioneering voice [Deutsch 1992].)

In Brunswick's account, Freud had been prejudiced against

him beforehand, based on what he had been told—presumably by Ruth and Mark. (Unfortunately I had failed to raise with Hirst the issue of the implications of how Freud could be indiscreet.) According to Brunswick, Freud knew the proper way for an analyst to behave, and yet he did not do it himself. Brunswick acknowledged that at an earlier point in Freud's career as a practitioner the kind of blunders Freud made with him might have been understandable. But by 1927 Freud had succeeded in understanding his own earlier foul-ups, and "should" have mastered that kind of self-indulgent temptation.

For example, at the outset of the analysis Freud indicated that he thought Brunswick should become an analyst. Although he had had some training as a psychologist, Brunswick said he entertained no intention of being an analyst. He expected that when he returned to the United States he would go into business. But Freud told him: "You must go to medical school." So he obediently started to attend medical school in Vienna, only to drop out as he had already done in America. Brunswick was willing to volunteer that his reasons for failing at medicine were no doubt "neurotic." But Freud's point had been that for Brunswick to succeed as an analyst in America, where medicine was considered mandatory for analysts, he needed to be trained as a physician. Ultimately of course he managed to become an analyst in America without a medical degree; my guess is that his having been treated by Freud personally gave him an almost automatic license as an analyst.

The issue of lay analysis, which Freud espoused, was one of the many bones of contention between himself and American analysts. (Anna Freud, who had no formal higher education, was already practicing as an analyst, and Freud was understood to be in part defending her future position.) It seemed to me natural to wonder whether Freud had not given Brunswick a hard time partly because he was an American. When Leonard Blumgart and five other analysts had come over to Vienna right after the end of World War I, Freud said he had only thirty hours available, and therefore one of them would have to go to another analyst instead. Those were the days of the six-day analytic week. When none of the six prospective American patients would give up the chance to be analyzed by Freud, he accepted them all on the condition that they each agree to only five sessions a week. But Freud did not cut down similarly on the number of times that he was then seeing his British patients, and at least one of the Americans in treatment with him felt resentful at his obvious preference for the British (Kardiner 1957).

It would have been understandable if Freud, who so frequently expressed his disdain for American culture as a whole, conducted himself somewhat harshly toward his American patients. They had the most to offer in the way of financial resources, and Freud, who hated being dependent, must have minded his need for American money. He objected to how they in particular mumbled from the couch. "This race," he predicted, "is sentenced to disappear from the face of the earth. They can no longer open their mouths to speak; soon they will also not be able to do so to eat, and they will die of starvation." This wish of Freud's, that the Americans vanish, can also be tied to his own particular problems, for at the time he was expressing this animosity about the Americans, he was himself suffering from difficulties in speaking, and due to his cancerous jaw he was ultimately endangered by starvation.

Even if Freud tended to project onto the Americans his own special difficulties, it was not easy for Brunswick to accept the idea that Freud was apt to give American patients a hard time. He did not think Freud had any prejudices against America, an observation that helped convince me how psychologically obtuse Brunswick could be. Yet from his perspective Freud had been exceptionally interested in his sister-in-law Ruth and his brother Mark. If, among all his other mistakes with Brunswick, Freud had "not" succumbed to anti-Americanism, Brunswick thought that Freud instead had been guilty of being overly involved with Ruth and Mark.

It seemed natural to me to be interested in inquiring whether Freud had conducted the analysis in English. Brunswick said that at the time he could read German but was unable to understand spoken German, so they started the analysis in English. Freud, however, preferred that Brunswick proceed in German, so he complied. (It can be easy to miss how damaging to Freud's style as a writer it could be to have to listen to patients who spoke German badly; Freud wrote about this in letters [Brabant et al. 1993], and one can usually infer some meaning from the language Freud chose to correspond in.) Later they switched back to using English again. The idea of Brunswick's speaking German, like the suggestion that he go to medical school, was to him an aspect of Freud's punishing attitude. "If Freud said I must go to medical school, I went!" But he protested to me that he "did not need to be punished." In his view he had been punished enough as a child.

Brunswick's analysis with Freud went on for three years, and one has to at least wonder why, if it went so badly, he stayed on in treatment. (There does not seem to have been any special historical reconstructions of early childhood, since they "never got that far" in the analysis; this was in contrast to what Hirst reported, although both he and Brunswick shared the conviction in the childhood origins of neurotic symptoms.) Perhaps it would have been expecting a lot of Brunswick to have walked out on Freud, terminating the analysis. But other patients were able to find the strength to break off an unsatisfactory relationship with Freud. Perhaps some rivalry with his brother Mark, who was more satisfied with Freud, may have helped hold Brunswick in the analysis. His expectations about analysis also helped keep him in treatment, and he swallowed the whole scientistic line of propaganda about what an analysis is supposed to be like.

Afterward Brunswick went to a whole bevy of other analysts, which did not disabuse him of the ideal of analysis as an aloof instrument. In California he was analyzed by Ernst Simmel, Otto Fenichel, and Frances Deri. He was treated by Anna Freud finally in London. He remembered her having said to him once, "But now I am asking questions, and that is always a mistake," at which point he said that he "almost cried," since her willingness to admit a mistake was so opposed to the experience he had with Freud. (Freud had written in 1895: "It is of course of great importance for the progress of the analysis that one should always turn out to be in the right *vis-à-vis* the patient, otherwise one would always be dependent on what he chose to tell one" [p. 281].)

Brunswick readily admitted that he had been "a stubborn patient" with Freud, but did not think this excused Freud's attitude toward him. He remained unsure whether, in the end, Freud admitted his mistaken approach to him. As an effect of Freud's criticism of him, for the first three or four weeks of the analysis he told Freud the story of his life, but this was done without the help of free associating, since he was unable to relax with Freud. From Freud's point of view that meant that a patient was not compliant enough to obey the "fundamental rule" of analysis, which entailed allowing everything that came into the patient's head to be verbalized. In defense of himself Brunswick told Freud that it was Freud's "fault," not his, that his free associations were blocked; the problem lay, he felt, in the way Freud had started the analysis. Freud at one point said in his own behalf, "Suppose I were to admit a mistake, what would you think?" Brunswick replied: "that you might make more of them!" Freud took that response as confirmation of why he ought not to admit an error. But Brunswick thought Freud should never have gotten into that sort of struggle of wills with him in the first place.

In Brunswick's view, Freud had a "fear reaction" toward him, and this anxiety on Freud's part explained how the treatment had misfired. He felt Freud did not want to get into any "trouble" in an analysis. Freud had been told that Brunswick was very intelligent, but that he would use intelligence as a "resistance." Therefore Freud decided Brunswick should speak in German and go to medical school. Brunswick felt that Freud should not have been afraid to see for himself what Brunswick was like. In Brunswick's view Freud was "a wonderful scientist," but he faulted Freud's conduct with him as a therapist, and was touchingly eager to hear from me about any other instances of Freud's having had failures with patients.

Once the analysis got off on the wrong foot, evidently it could not be corrected. I was never sure whether this was true only with Freud, or with psychoanalysis generally. But I had heard that Freud had a similar-sounding experience with another American patient, Clarence P. Oberndorf; an early dream interpretation Freud offered had been deeply wounding to the patient's sensitivities as a southerner, and it was never possible to right the situation afterward. Following the first month of Brunswick's analysis, Freud said that he guessed he had "intimidated" Brunswick at the outset. In retrospect Brunswick thought this was the "best" thing Freud had ever said to him.

I inquired what Brunswick might have known about the Wolf Man, whom Ruth had treated. Brunswick said that he had once met him at Ruth's office. At that point the Wolf Man was suffering from a paranoid delusion, and Brunswick told me he thought that Freud's financial help to the Wolf Man had been responsible for precipitating the paranoia, a psychoanalytic interpretation that seemed to me almost unbelievably crude. But the reasoning was that Freud's being good to the Wolf Man had mobilized a paranoid defense against homosexual love. (Ruth

Brunswick herself wrote that it was Freud's illness, and the possibility that he might die, that had undermined the Wolf Man's earlier stability.) Yet in David Brunswick's understanding of the case Freud had a therapeutic success with the Wolf Man; his earlier symptoms were no longer present, and he had become an actuary for an insurance company.

Freud had suggested, during Brunswick's analysis, that he read the theoretical papers, although not the clinical ones, that Freud had written. A later school of orthodox psychoanalytic thought considered it a mistake for analytic patients to do much reading in the professional literature. But Brunswick did not think there was anything surprising about Freud's recommendation; it was in keeping with the way in which candidates in psychoanalytic training were later admitted to theoretical seminars in the first year of their program. It was presumed that this sort of contact would be less likely to be an interference with a student's therapeutic progress than immediate involvement with the clinical aspects of psychoanalytic material. (I think Brunswick was building false continuities in the history of psychoanalytic training, and would have been better advised to have acknowledged another inconsistency with orthodoxy in Freud's approach here.)

In the course of analyzing Brunswick, Freud had by no means won the admiration that he got from Hirst; yet Brunswick was the one to have gone on to be a practicing analyst. There was already a small study group of Los Angeles analysts by the time Brunswick came to California. It was at the urgings of one of the local analysts that he decided to become an analyst himself. Freud sent him a letter then in Gothic script, which Brunswick could not read; he went to someone to have it translated for him. He said Freud knew that he could not read that form of German; Freud could write in English for American relatives, and wrote mostly in English to his British disciple Jones. Freud's letter to Brunswick on this occasion amounted to

Freud's formal acceptance of him: "That you have become an analyst is the right punishment for you." But Brunswick did not seem to enjoy any of the irony in Freud's communication. When he was in analysis with Freud, Brunswick had not wanted at all to be an analyst, and "had resisted so much." He was unhappy enough about the experience he had with Freud as to be unable to see any humor in Freud's joking about what course his career finally took. (Although I tried my best to persuade Brunswick to publish the letters he had from Freud, he brushed the idea aside on the grounds that they were just "personal"; he was not in any way implying that this correspondence was private but that it was basically trivial.)

Brunswick had also heard informally from Ruth Brunswick about Freud's reaction to his becoming an analyst. She told Brunswick Freud's response:"If it hits the target." My understanding, and I think Brunswick's too, was that Freud was being tentative about how Brunswick would do as an analyst. Freud was not expressing disapproval, but rather was saying something like the proof of the pudding would be in the eating.

Yet Brunswick felt fully confident, when I saw him, that he understood what psychoanalysis was supposed to be like: it was largely a reversal of how he thought that Freud had conducted himself. Brunswick was highly moralistic about psychoanalytic treatment; according to him, "Freud knew what was right and yet he did not do it." Brunswick was not just generalizing from his own experience, but he also had in mind how Freud had treated Ruth and Mark. Brunswick thought that Freud's countertransference reactions had played a role in interfering with Ruth and Mark's analyses, as well as with his own. Brunswick had attended the wedding ceremony for Ruth and Mark, which was held in the Vienna City Hall, at which Freud had been an official witness. He remarked on how well Freud had looked on that occasion. But Brunswick repeatedly described himself as having struggled to steer clear of personal contact with Freud, in an effort to succeed in getting a "proper" analysis.

Brunswick seemed to admire Freud more as a scientist, for what he had discovered, than as a healer, a distinction Hirst had repudiated. I was inclined to think that Brunswick was imposing on Freud some of his own special concerns, as his work had originally been in physiological psychology. When I saw him he still spoke of his "dream" of uniting that sort of thinking with psychoanalysis, although he conceded his efforts were going "slowly." When I remarked on the fact that he was following a similar route to that taken by Freud himself, he agreed, but he said that in those days he had not known anything about the very early period in Freud's work when he was concerned with physiological psychology.

I specifically asked whether, as with Hirst, Freud had mentioned any material from the early history of psychoanalysis, such as the story about the discovery of cocaine by Koller. In striking contrast to how Freud had behaved with most of his patients, he had not filled Brunswick in on any of his earlier struggles. As far as Brunswick was concerned, such legend-building would have amounted to further contamination; he thought it fine that Freud had not tried explicitly to propagandize with him, and that after the "opening mistake" in his analysis, consisting of telling him to go to medical school and to speak in German, Freud had been "a good analyst."

Brunswick had subsequently played a part in the organization of psychoanalysis on the West Coast; he wrote to Simmel to invite him to come from Berlin to Los Angeles. The intention was that Simmel would function as a senior figure in training analysts in California, and Brunswick said that both Franz Alexander and Hanns Sachs, who had once been in Berlin themselves and were both prominent training analysts in America, approved the choice of Simmel. Brunswick had himself first met Simmel when Brunswick, along with two or three other patients of Freud's, had followed Freud to Simmel's sanatorium (Tegelsee) for treatment and rest. (It was customary in those days for all analysts, not just for Freud, that patients, especially foreigners who did not have time to spare, would be expected to accompany the analyst on vacation.)

Simmel therefore became the founding European in Los Angeles psychoanalysis. (The Nazis were to have a broad impact on the flight of intellectuals to America.) Simmel first invited Mrs. Deri to come to Los Angeles from Prague (originally she had been in Berlin), and "Mrs. Deri" invited Otto Fenichel, who had been in Norway and had succeeded her in Prague. Later on Alexander would be a great figure in Los Angeles psychoanalysis. He was an organizer, and Brunswick labeled him a *macher*. Alexander had been an inspiring leader in Chicago analysis from the early 1930s until he decided to go west in 1956; he died in 1964. He remains one of those figures in the history of analysis about whom we know far too little. One Los Angeles analyst I interviewed then, who had been closely associated with Alexander, mentioned having seen on his desk a stack of about fifty letters from Freud. Alexander was one of the great lights in Freud's movement in the 1920s and 1930s, and after Freud's death Alexander was an original thinker, full of new ideas. Oliver Freud, Freud's middle son, went to Alexander for a personal analysis in the early 1920s, which was a sign of Alexander's standing then in Freud's own eyes (Roazen 1993a). The particular significance of the Freud–Alexander letters is that they likely discussed clinical issues, unlike some of Freud's more belles-lettristic exchanges of views. In Chicago Alexander left a legacy of fear associated with his name, because analysts there have been piously afraid of being stigmatized for Alexander's so-called deviancy.

No matter how difficult it might be for Brunswick to consider the history of analysis with scholarly detachment, he was fully aware of the special place that his sister-in-law Ruth had played in Freud's last phase. She had left Vienna for the United States after the Nazis occupied Austria in 1938, but twice visited Freud in London; she was then an analyst in New York City, and her death in 1946 seemed to David Brunswick "a great loss." According to him her psychological illness was based on too close a dependency on Freud. Yet Brunswick emphasized that Freud was not "in love" with her. He agreed that she had been very devoted to Freud, and he to her; in Freud's last years the two women pupils who were closest to Freud were Ruth and the Princess Marie Bonaparte. Brunswick conceded that others "might well" have been jealous of Ruth's intimacy with Freud. Dorothy Burlingham, who like Ruth and Marie was in analysis with Freud for years, was "closer" to Freud's daughter Anna than to Freud himself. It is striking that even now, when full biographies have appeared about both Marie Bonaparte and Dorothy Burlingham (Roazen 1990a, 1991c), so little attention has been given to pursuing Ruth's tale.

In Vienna David Brunswick had gone to only one meeting of the psychoanalytic society; the occasion was when Wilhelm Reich returned from his trip to the Soviet Union. Reich was "very enthusiastic" about Communism, which was at odds with Freud's own attitude. It was shortly after that in 1930 Freud wrote his *Civilization and its Discontents*, which Reich later correctly claimed had been directed at combatting the attempt Reich had made to unite Marxism and psychoanalytic theory (Higgins and Raphael 1967).

In those days, according to Brunswick, Freud did not want to have anything to do with the official Viennese group of analysts. Freud was physically well enough to attend meetings, according to Brunswick, and he was well enough to attend his weekly game of cards, so Brunswick refused to attribute Freud's failure to continue going to professional psychoanalytic meetings to his cancer. However, chronologically Brunswick was wrong, in that it was the cancer that made a difference in Freud's behavior; before 1923 it was unthinkable for Freud to have missed a public session of his followers in Vienna. But I think Brunswick was also right in his judgment, and that in all probability Freud had inwardly not wanted to go for some time. Afterward Freud saw his special students on a monthly basis at small gatherings that he held in his apartment; Brunswick was not invited to such select meetings, which were reserved for about a dozen regular Viennese analytic participants, and occasional visitors.

Based on Brunswick's clinical encounter with Freud, as well as his later experience as an analyst, he thought that a patient's knowledge of the standard technique of analysis might, if it were acquired too early, interfere with the treatment. According to this sort of reasoning, a patient's "resistances" to self-understanding might be directed to issues of technique, and such intellectualized resistances can supposedly be harder to handle than others. I specifically asked whether Freud had talked about theoretical issues in the analysis. But the answer I got was "no," with the understanding that any such discussion would have been a technical error, in getting away from the patient's emotional problems.

Brunswick kept reiterating that there was an "uncorrectable mistake" on Freud's part at the beginning of the analysis. It almost sounded like a trauma for Brunswick. According to his version, Freud later in the analysis became "a good analyst." But even so, Freud had behaved in a "wrong" way toward him at the outset. Freud should not, in Brunswick's view, have accepted him as a patient in the first place. And second, Freud ought not to have let what he knew about Brunswick affect him. In Brunswick's view Freud was "afraid" of him, which is why Freud had told him "on the second day" of the analysis that he should go to medical school and speak in German.

Yet from Freud's point of view I think that his accepting

Brunswick for analysis was a special sign of his favoring Ruth. In retrospect Brunswick might reproach Freud for having taken him for treatment; curiously enough, he made no mention of the possibility that Freud might have referred him to someone else once it was apparent that the analysis was not going well. It was clear to him, however, that Ruth had been the central channel by which he had reached Freud. While Ruth was in America for the summer of 1926 she and David spoke about his going to Freud. David wrote to Freud finally in the spring of 1927. Unlike in his earlier years, Freud was no longer undertaking those "short analyses," which David puristically looked down upon.

It should be clear that Brunswick was not personally hostile to Freud. He had found him to be "very nice," a "pleasant" man. Photographs of Freud are misleading in making him look stern, since his failure to smile was part of the photographic conventions of his era. David pointed out that it is an American custom to say "cheese" in front of a camera. Brunswick remembered having visited Freud on vacation in the summer of 1929 at Berchtesgaden, and he remarked how friendly Freud was, but Brunswick did not feel that he had gained a human or personal foothold with Freud. He would not have expected or wanted that sort of contact, and seemed to consider it appropriate that even Freud's published autobiography (1924), written after he had fallen ill, was "really a history of the movement" rather than a personal testament. By that time Freud had completely identified his own life with the cause of psychoanalysis itself.

I asked Brunswick about his knowledge of Ruth, and in particular about Freud's possible disappointment in her. Such disillusionment was news to him. But he did volunteer, as a possible explanation, that she had remained "still sick" despite Freud's treatment. She was, he said, "a drug addict." This was the first time I had heard her described that way. Brunswick said Ruth not only took sleeping pills but "there was always medicine" she was taking. He agreed with me that Jones did not pay adequate attention to her in his biography of Freud. (Brunswick, who reported he had trouble reading, had not finished all of Jones, and was unaware of much of the invaluable information there.)

I asked Brunswick what Freud had admired in Ruth. Brunswick responded by pointing out her natural psychological ability, her intelligence, as well as her interest in psychotics. He said her life was a "great tragedy" in that she was not well. He specified that her death was not a suicide—but that it may have "unconsciously" been a suicide. Freud had died, and Mark had left her; she still had her daughter Mathilda, who was named for Freud's eldest daughter. Ruth had already had a tendency toward abusing drugs when she was in analysis with Freud; by the end of her life there was a "great dependence" on them. Of course as a doctor she could prescribe medicines for herself. Over the long run this drug-taking undermined her health; her death was caused by a fall in the bathroom, in which she hit her head and fractured her skull.

Ruth worked very effectively until the last part of her life. Freud's death had not been a disturbance to her; he was so old and sick by then that his dying was a deliverance for him. She was five years older than Mark, from whom she was divorced in 1945. Mark was formally uneducated—the sum of his schooling was a year at Exeter Academy—yet more cultured than David. It was through a sister of David's, who had gone for a while to Radcliffe, that Mark and David had met Ruth.

David Brunswick agreed with the idea I proposed that Freud would have found a drug addiction a particularly difficult problem to deal with. Freud did not generally approve of self-dependencies, and would have wanted to have nothing to do with alcoholism, for example. He would recognize an addiction as a sickness, to be understood and treated, but still Freud would have found it distasteful. Ruth could not have invented an illness like that to express her ambivalence to Freud, since it was there all along and it must have come up in her analysis.

Despite Freud's own use of cocaine he had not himself become an addict, but he was more or less enslaved to cigar smoking, and this nicotine addiction no doubt was a contributing factor in the jaw cancer he developed. But Freud, who in principle ruled out addicts from psychoanalytic treatment, was capable of behaving at odds with his own principles when it came to someone he especially admired. And before World War I he treated Loe Kann, who had been living with Ernest Jones, although she was addicted to morphine (Roazen 1993b). Oddly enough, Freud attended Loe Kann's 1914 wedding, like that of Ruth and Mark later, although he did not go to his own children's marriage ceremonies. David Brunswick remembered how retiring he felt at the Brunswick wedding in 1928. He had tried to stay away from too much personal contact with Freud, because he was "trying" to get analyzed.

In Brunswick's view, Freud's countertransference had interfered with Ruth's analysis as well as with his own. But in Ruth's case Freud had liked working with her "too much." She was enjoying being dependent on him. When that sort of relationship happens to develop Brunswick thought it should be treated as a problem rather than just savored as a pleasure. The dependency should have been pointed out and analyzed. He went so far as to maintain that Freud liked Ruth too much to be analyzing her at all. He thought that Freud had as much reason to be disappointed in his treatment of Ruth as in her herself.

Freud's analysis of Ruth was in stark contrast to the essays he wrote in which he recommended an appropriate technique for analysts to adopt. Brunswick summed up Freud's attitude with the injunction that others should "do as I say, not as I do." Freud was capable of "allowing" himself a special liberty with Ruth, just as he had made an exception in taking on David, Mark, and Ruth simultaneously.

When I asked about Freud's own possible neurotic symptomatology, Brunswick refused to accept any generalizations I
proposed about Freud's possible emotional conflicts. He did not
think that Freud was an "obsessive-compulsive" type, in that he
was not discontented with partial knowledge. But Brunswick
agreed that one could find in Freud certain compulsive signs. He
thought Freud (whom he referred to as "Professor") might not
have had a fluid-enough personality to adjust psychoanalytic
technique in order to treat psychotics. Freud had a very well
organized personality. He was distinctly on the "normal" side,
rather more so than most people. Freud had his personal
difficulties, but Brunswick thought he had worked them out
through his self-analysis. When I asked if any parts of psychoanalytic theory were off base because of Freud's own neurotic
tendencies, Brunswick could not say one way or the other; it
seemed to me then a striking aspect of what I considered to be
Brunswick's infantile relationship to Freud that he could not
think of any way in which Freud's subjective characteristics
interfered with or colored the theories he proposed. Nor could
he say which sorts of patients Freud would be better with.
Brunswick bought the party line about what psychoanalysis
should be like, even though it meant isolating his own immediate personal experiences with the founder of the discipline.

To Brunswick Freud deserved to be remembered as the
"discoverer" of the id and the unconscious; he also knew about
the resistances and the ego, yet Brunswick was convinced that
Freud had not taken the so-called higher layers of personality
enough into account. Brunswick thought it was "left" to Anna
Freud to develop that part of the psychoanalytic system. (For
some reason Brunswick had the idea that Edward Hitschmann
had analyzed Anna Freud; I did not then know that Freud had
himself analyzed his youngest child. I had heard some stories to
that effect, but was not satisfied that the rumor could be
confirmed.)

Although Freud is often publicly associated with proposing the significance of the Oedipus complex, Ruth was herself intimately identified with the notion of there being "pre-oedipal" layers, an aspect of human psychology that Freud accepted only relatively late in his career. The implications of her theorizing would be the legitimacy of examining the young child's mother-bonding, prior to any sorts of triangular rivalries that might arise. Of the three Brunswicks, it was Ruth who matters most to the history of psychoanalysis, and David thought it was she, rather than Mark, who could be blamed for having made Freud afraid of the possible difficulties he would encounter in treating David. The prospect of "intellectualized resistances" from David evoked, he thought, Freud's decision to make things difficult for David at the outset of the analysis.

Ruth was emotional and free in her free associations, and David thought I should write to Mark about the existence of her surviving papers. I asked whether the kind of long analysis that Freud conducted with Ruth was not designed to induce just exactly the sort of dependency that David thought was wrong in the relationship of Ruth to Freud. He said he was "not sure." But Freud and Ruth were, he thought, surely "too close." Despite how much Brunswick had tried to stay away from the circle of analysts in Vienna, he saw a lot of his brother and Ruth. In my effort to learn more about Ruth, it seemed natural to try and see Mark. Although David did not want to go so far as to say that Ruth had been like an "adopted daughter" to Freud, he agreed that it was true she was intimate with the Freud family. He thought it was a sign of Freud's being a "normal" man that he got along with his female pupils (like Ruth) better than with his male ones.

As far as Brunswick knew, Ruth's marriage to Herman Blumgart was already on the rocks before she went to Vienna. She had already completed her psychiatric residency, and went to Freud to work on her personal difficulties as well as to learn how to become an analyst. Ruth was in training in Vienna; after her marriage to Mark, Ruth certainly continued to see Freud for personal help as well as for the supervision of her own cases. While in later years the practice was that one did not go to one's own analyst for the supervision of clinical cases, but consulted with others instead, in Vienna Freud saw Ruth for both purposes.

Right from the early years of Freud's presenting his ideas and developing the therapeutic approach he recommended for neurotic patients, there were skeptics who doubted the validity of Freud's claims. Amid the storm Freud evoked he went on undeterred. If one examines the reviews of his works that came out while he was alive, for example, those that appeared in the first decade of the twentieth century, one finds that some of the most basic questions about his ideas were being raised with sympathy and respect (Roazen 1990c). Freud himself did not appreciate how he was being received, and scarcely paused to answer any of these original critics.

I believe Freud already sensed what a special sort of power he had created in the psychoanalytic treatment itself. Despite all the dissatisfaction Brunswick felt at his own therapeutic experience with Freud, he nonetheless became a loyal follower. Although Freud did not seem to have understood the role that old-fashioned suggestion was capable of playing, or the place of rational insight, he knew that his method of working was attracting converts and disciples. By the end of the first decade of the twentieth century it was apparent to Freud as well as to outsiders that he had succeeded in inaugurating a new school of thought.

3

Co-Dependency: Mark Brunswick

Within a month of seeing David Brunswick in California, I was interviewing his younger brother Mark at his Greenwich Village apartment. I found Mark as uninhibited as his brother was innerly restricted. Mark's mind darted around in surprising directions, and subtle points he made continued to resonate in my mind for years afterward. Mark was so spontaneous and intuitive that I often magically wished, long after his death in 1971, that he had been still alive to talk to. Although hindsight has given me many fresh ideas I wish I had thought to discuss with all Freud's patients, I do not think I ever met anyone who gave a more vivid and individual picture of Freud than Mark provided. He appeared in sharp contrast to David, who had telling individual points to make but seemed altogether the more limited personality. Mark's conception of Freud was rich, complicated, and realistic; Mark remains one of the great highlights of all my interviewing.

At the outset Mark stressed that he had little knowledge of scientific matters in connection with psychoanalysis, but that he could only offer "personal information." He was relaxed and friendly, and early on indicated that he was willing to be contacted by me again, although he also mentioned that I might try asking him some questions by mail. I not only wrote to him subsequently, but interviewed him later at his current wife's home in Princeton, New Jersey, where she taught mathematics. Unlike David, whom Freud had sent off to medical school, with Mark Freud never expected him to become a doctor; according to David, the explanation for Freud's behavior was that Mark was already set with his career as a composer and musicologist. Mark told me that he knew nothing at all about medicine, and that Freud had once remarked on what an accomplishment that must have been considering that he was married to Ruth.

Before going to Vienna in 1924 Mark had read Freud's *Totem and Taboo*, a bold and imaginative account of the origins of human civilization written in powerful and incisive prose. Mark had liked the book very much, since to him it was "anthropology" rather than medicine. (Modern anthropologists have never been happy with that book.) During the analysis itself Freud "made" Mark read the case histories of the Wolf Man and Little Hans. (When Freud asked Mark to read the Wolf Man case, it was "pure agony" for him, sheer "resistance," but Mark complied.) Otherwise Mark had never been able to read Freud, who evidently thought that if Mark had contact with this clinical material it might "bring things out" in Mark's own analysis. Part of the contrast to what Freud had expected David to read may have stemmed from the fact that Mark maintained that he would never have dreamt of becoming an analyst himself.

It would be wrong to assume that after Freud's earlier period, as exemplified by his analysis of Hirst, Freud changed his ways of clinically proceeding; there was a continuity in his work in spite of the appearance of the technical papers that he published just before World War I. In 1912 Freud had written that the analyst "should be opaque to his patients and, like a mirror, should show them nothing but what is shown to him" (p. 118). Since Freud himself so rarely, in his treatments of David and Mark for example, fulfilled this standard of what supposedly "true psychoanalysis" consisted of, it is hard to fathom what status his ideals were supposed to have. (A revisionist school of psychoanalytic thinking has challenged the image of the analyst as a mirror, on the grounds that it is a mistaken objective. One bold idea would be to substitute "window" as an alternative.) Freud's recommendations were largely negative, indicating where a practitioner might go wrong, but they have seriously misled many subsequent generations about Freud's own procedures.

Mark's analysis started out in English, and then after a month Freud wanted to switch to German. Mark knew that language from his one year at high school, and he was taking lessons in Vienna. Freud gave him a week to make the change; Mark came in to his next analytic hour, and Freud said let's start now, for Mark would not know it any better in a week. Mark asked if the use of German would not interfere with his free associations, but Freud said that on the contrary it would help. Shortly thereafter Mark made a meaningful slip that he would not have committed in English.

I did not understand the nature of Mark's career intentions at the time. I asked him whether his family had been related to the bowling people. He answered that he wished it were, for then he "would be rich." I had raised this line of questioning because it only gradually dawned on me that I could not understand how Mark had supported himself during his many years in Vienna. (David told me that he had paid Freud twenty-five dollars an hour for his analysis, and that the money had come from David's father.) I had wondered about Mark, and what he had existed on in Vienna, although the same question did not come to my mind in connection with David; partly this was because Mark was in Vienna so much longer and without any professional prospects that were clear to me.

It crossed my mind that Mark had been living off Ruth, but I did not dare to ask anything along those lines. It turned out, as I learned some ten years later, that Mark had been fairly wealthy. The extent of Mark's assets were itemized in an affidavit Mark and Ruth had filled out to help get a Viennese bookseller [1] to the United States in 1938. According to Mark's obituary in *The New York Times* (May 28, 1971) he had assisted many others as well: "from 1937 to 1941 he was chairman of the National Committee for Refugee Musicians, and placed hundreds of European colleagues in positions here." (The FBI therefore kept files on both Mark and Ruth.) In Mark's later years, at the time I knew him, his fortune may have dissipated, but he came from a background that was as noticeably well off as Ruth's own family.

In Vienna the Brunswicks had a house and a car, and were considered millionaires. (Mark failed to mention that they also had a chauffeur.) Although Mark thought their financial standing was exaggerated among the analysts, the extent of Ruth's close friendship with Marie Bonaparte may have colored how Ruth was perceived (Meisel and Kendrick 1985). Freud had originally

---

1. He told me a story typifying old Viennese political cynicism. After the Nazis had marched into Vienna his concierge hung a swastika outside the small building he lived in. When questioned about the surprising nature of his political allegiances, the concierge took him upstairs to show a closet full of all the flags of the multiple Viennese political parties—from the Communists through the monarchists.

sent some Dutch patients to Ruth. One "followed" the other, and "most" of her cases were from Holland; they were rich enough to pay the analytic fees easily. Mark, Ruth, William C. Bullitt (Roazen 1989), Marie Bonaparte, and an American named Blumenthal, had "cornered" the market on Freud's time. Originally Mark had in the 1920s been paying Freud twenty dollars an hour, but then in the 1930s Mark and the others voluntarily decided to raise their payments to twenty-five dollars. Analysts in New York City were getting as much; Ruth was herself receiving twenty dollars an hour in Vienna. (Mark somehow thought that "nobody knew" about Freud in America until after World War II; that was probably the high point of American medicine's enthusiasm for psychoanalysis.)

At one point in 1931 Ruth and Marie Bonaparte had "chipped in" to pay for a new prosthesis to be made for Freud's mouth; when I met Ruth's daughter, some twenty years after Mark's death, she said that the bulk of that money, which came to some five thousand dollars, must have been from Marie. (The physician in question reported having been paid by Ruth.) It was Ruth who thought that Freud's Viennese doctor was not the best, and she arranged for an expert from Harvard University, where her father was on the Board of Overseers, to make a fresh device. It was, however, not a success, and Mark thought that Freud "somehow resented" Ruth's intervention. Throughout Freud's career he was touchy about being beholden to anybody financially. And if he could have "afforded" the Harvard doctor, he would not have "chosen" to spend the money that way. Still, in 1927 Freud had written to his son Ernst that Ruth "almost belongs to the family. . . .," (Molnar 1992, p. 58), and she was to play a special role in looking after Freud's health.

Mark first went to Freud about six months after Freud's initial bout with cancer of the jaw. Freud was 68 years old then. Mark was "a shy and timid" 22; he was "a prodigy in one way, and yet totally undeveloped." He remembered Freud's remarking: "Is it possible for anyone to be so young?" I asked, thinking of the full circumstances around David's analysis, whether Mark's treatment had been arranged through Leonard Blumgart. According to Mark, Leonard had been the channel through which Ruth herself got to Freud; Leonard was, to repeat, Ruth's husband Herman's brother, therefore Ruth's brother-in-law. She went to Freud first in 1922. (Ruth had been born in 1897, and was five years older than Mark.) Herman Blumgart, Mark said, had traveled at one point to see Freud for a short visit in Vienna; Mark's view of things was that Freud "preferred" Mark to Herman as Ruth's husband. Mark's own analysis with Freud was arranged by Ruth herself. Her marriage was already in serious trouble, for Mark and Ruth were lovers at the time; she wanted Mark as a spouse. Her relation to Blumgart had been "very neurotic," so Freud was not disrupting a good marriage. (Mark repudiated the suggestion that Eissler had made to me that by the 1930s Ruth had been "dilapidated" because of drugs; Mark thought Eissler probably never knew Ruth, just as Eissler had never set eyes on Freud.)

Mark went only once or twice to meetings of the psycho-analytic society in Vienna; he was "terribly shocked" at the words they used in public with both sexes present. One has to remember, he thought, that it was in the early 1920s when standards were different from nowadays. Freud himself had "quite a Victorian side to him." And he turned off his work when he was with the family, which is where Mark saw a lot of him.

To Mark, Freud seemed "often quite naive." For example, one night Ruth and Mark stopped off at the Freud apartment on the way to the theatre or the opera. Jofi, Freud's chow dog, was clearly having a dream, and Ruth pointed it out. Freud then simply commented: "I've told them they are giving her too much to eat!" Instead of Freud being fascinated by an animal's dreaming, he used the occasion to indicate his relative helplessness as an authority in the home. Freud seemed to live "in two separate worlds." He was "very nice" and "self-protective" within his family. Mark would not have "dared" to point it out to him, or rather it "never occurred" to him enough to say that he would not have dared. Once Freud "teased" the husband of his older daughter, Mathilda, about being so "flirtatious" with Ruth, and Ruth was Freud's patient at the time.

In Mark's view Freud simply shut off being an analyst at home. Once Federn, a man whom Mark considered "nice but rather fatuous" and someone who made "the most obvious" slips of the tongue, was commenting at Freud's place about a slip that Federn had committed at a memorial meeting for a dead analyst, Karl Abraham. Federn, as vice president of the Vienna society, had become in Freud's absence its presiding officer; Federn had publicly referred to the person sitting next to him, Theodor Reik, then a favorite of Freud's, instead of the dead man who was being honored. According to folklore Freud was so angry about the ambivalences he had created among his students that the incident led him to stay away from any further meetings. Mark said that Federn went through an elaborate explanation of his slip one night at the Freuds. At that time Freud's wife commented, "It is so interesting, we never hear such things." She was being "ironic," a trait that Mark thought was seldom mentioned about her, and yet he thought it was true that Freud did isolate his work from his family life.

Mark was impressed with how "strange" the Freuds could be about what gets published. It was considered all right for Freud's eldest son Martin to write a book about his father (M. Freud 1957). But Mark was indignant that Eissler would not allow the movie that Mark had made of Freud to be shown or provide historians access to other material that was in the sealed Freud Archives. Mark had taken a film of Freud in which he was relaxed and at ease, in his customary manner instead of posing in an artificial way for a camera; Mark sold the movie to the

Archives, after they were set up following World War II, in an effort to recoup some of the expense of his own analyses. But the Archives then adopted the policy of disallowing others to see the film, although portions of it are now publicly on display at the Freud Museum in London, with Anna Freud as the narrator. Many donors shared Mark's resentment about the way documents given to the Archives were being restricted.

In describing how Ruth had gotten to Freud, Mark thought that Leonard Blumgart must have gone to Vienna for an analysis himself with Freud in 1919 along with people like Philip Lehrman, Horace W. Frink, and Abram Kardiner. (Mark's dates turned out to be a bit off, but he had the right general period.) Analysts were all "pretty raw" then, and rather "unstable." Seeing Frink through Ruth's eyes, Mark would say that Frink was really brilliant, but that the other Americans at the time were less so.

Freud had a "complete countertransference" for Frink, and by that Mark meant excessive confidence in Frink, which Mark thought had "contributed" to Frink's "downfall." Mark thought that Freud had been too incautious with Frink; expressed overt affection from an analyst, who also "happens to be Freud," can be a special problem to bear. Freud encouraged Frink to replace A. A. Brill, who had been Frink's first analyst, as the leader of the American psychoanalytic movement; it would be "only human" for this mission to be disturbing to Frink. (Freud had sanctioned Frink's divorcing his first wife in order to marry a rich patient he had fallen in love with. Frink suffered a mental collapse, and his second marriage soon ended in divorce.) Mark thought that the combination of being both a patient and a pupil had, with Frink, meant his "inadvertent debauching" (cf. Edmunds 1988, Roazen 1975, Warner 1994).

Ruth was such an important link between Freud and his American following that she knew a lot about what happened to Frink. According to Mark she played a role in mediating between

Frink and Brill. She understood the task Freud had entrusted to Frink; she was a good friend of Brill's, although she knew his "defects." In the back of Mark's mind, I think, there must have been an analogy with Frink to what subsequently happened to Ruth. But Mark wanted to soft-pedal the seductiveness of Freud's countertransference feelings for Ruth, highlighting instead the mutual fondness and intellectuality of their relationship. Yet the kind of emotions Freud encouraged—he called these unique bonds examples of "transference love"—meant that a sort of spiritual incest was an inevitable component of Freud's work.

Ruth's "best friend" was Marianne Kris, who was the daughter of a close friend of Freud's; she herself had a "short," didactic analysis with Freud, but he took her "for granted" and therefore she was not really an important figure in her own right. Marianne had mentioned to Mark a while before I saw him that she still had Ruth's papers, or some of them anyway. (When I alluded to Mark's name in interviewing Marianne Kris, her face clouded over as if in wary disapproval of my having seen him.) Mark thought that Marianne Kris was not just "close to Anna" Freud, but that she saw her as "God." (Marianne died while visiting Anna in London.) It is worth noting that in contrast to his brother David, Mark was not an analyst and therefore Anna had no special hold over him. Mark was convinced that there was a second article that Ruth had completed on still another continuation of her analysis with the Wolf Man, who was at the time doing well, but Mark had never been able to find it among the papers of hers that he had gone through. (As far as I could tell it was already sealed up in Eissler's Freud Archives.)

I could not help, given Mark's profession, asking about Freud's attitude toward music. It was, Mark said, "a very strange one." Freud said that he disliked it, and that music meant nothing to him. He was "obviously irritated" by it. Mark disapproved of Jones's discussion of the subject. Mark had read through all of Jones on Freud, and considered Volume III of the biography "the worst"; the art and music sections at the back were "very inadequate." Freud "adored" opera, and his taste was "very good"; he "despised" Richard Wagner but loved *Die Meistersinger von Nürnberg*. Freud pointed out many things in *Meistersinger* that Mark said he would not have noticed on his own. (Mark had never read Freud's *The Interpretation of Dreams*, so he said he would not know that music comes up there [Diaz de Chumaceiro 1990].)

Mark was insistent that it is impossible to love opera and not like music; to someone who was as unmusical as Jones described Freud "a good play would be spoiled by the music." Of all the arts Mark thought music was closest to "the id," which was how Freud conceptualized unconscious instinctuality. Music per se, without any words, left Freud with no guide from the upper part of his mind; it therefore induced in Freud "a subconscious malaise." Mark's own kind of abstract music contained too much "id" for Freud. (Mathilda Hollitscher, Freud's eldest daughter, recalled to me how shocking Mark's music had seemed to her and her husband.) In general, Freud's taste in art was "normal" for a person born in 1856; Freud had "bourgeois" inclinations here, and not much else was needed to explain his preferences. "Even Ernst Kris," Marianne's analyst husband who had started out as an art historian, "could not understand this." Freud was not just magically a genius; "he hauled himself up by his bootstraps, but they were those of 1856."

Accordingly Mark thought that he, by his own standards, had detected in Freud a certain "prudishness"; Freud described in print how repellant at first his own "discoveries" were. Mark thought that Freud was "very moralistic." Mark once purchased for $14 a beautiful book on Rome, and showed it to Freud. Freud, who loved Rome and saw how marvelous the book was, said, "See that you deserve it!"

Mark picked for Freud's seventieth birthday present in 1926 four volumes of the Cambridge series on ancient history. (For that same birthday Otto Rank sent Freud a wonderfully bound edition of the works of Nietzsche, which Freud did not really like, since Mark thought Freud interpreted it as a "bribe." The falling out between Freud and Rank partly centered on the issue of money [Roazen 1975]. I think Freud also resented being reminded by a former pupil of one of Freud's own predecessors.) Mark and Freud would discuss archeology, since both loved ancient history. Freud really appreciated the present of those books, and as each succeeding volume came out Mark presented him with a copy. The last one appeared in 1938, by which time Freud was "disappointed" in Mark and Ruth. Freud had already ordered the book for himself, and wondered who was to pay for it. Mark thought that had Freud been "more himself" he would not have expressed himself so.

Mark described himself to me as "partly a son-in-law to Freud." Had Anna Freud ever married, especially if she chose someone from within the psychoanalytic movement, Freud would have then faced a formidable human presence, for any such man would have been able to speak with the kind of authority that would have exceeded someone like Rank, who proved troublesome enough. But Mark, as Ruth's husband, could pose no such threat, since he was determined to stick with his music. In contrast to David, Mark often saw Freud outside of a clinical context, and Mark remained astonished at how "completely unpsychological" he was with his family. According to Mark, Freud was "not always peering into everything." Yet one wonders how any sort of family life could have survived had Freud behaved differently. Some of Freud's disciples, for example, who tried to be more royal than the king and were psychologically intrusive with their families, developed terrible relations with their children.

While Freud was tolerant at home, to Mark Freud had one

strikingly "fixed," inflexible idea: "his great emphasis on the physical basis" of neurosis in dammed-up libido. In analysis Freud used *libido* as a term, without referring either to ego or id. Mark himself suffered from a symptom of "compulsive masturbation," which seems to have persisted throughout the total of seven years he spent in analysis with Freud. (Ruth reportedly took pride in her own masturbatory techniques [Bertin 1982].) Freud had told Mark, right from the start, in the first month or two of the treatment, that he would never get "anywhere" in the analysis unless he stopped masturbating. Mark thought that this stand of Freud's "vitiated the analysis" from the outset, and that his sexual practices had no biological connection to *sublimation*, Freud's term for the best of which we are capable. Although I did not think of it at the time, Mark's own complaint was a variant on those of his brother David's. Mark thought that Freud had been behaving "just like my parents," which was "psychologically fatal," when to "cure" him he would have had to be just the opposite. When Mark came down in the morning, his parents would ask him if he had been a good boy—referring to masturbation. "Somehow they always seemed to know"; he said that he must have looked very guilty when he did it.

Mark felt in Freud "real moralism." Masturbation was commonly enough considered injurious physically; Freud saw it as wasted energy that needed to be preserved for higher activities. From Mark's point of view it would have been better for Freud to accept even "a dribble" of material from Mark rather than to act as a parent. At the same time Freud could be helpfully pragmatic about masturbatory fantasies in intercourse; Freud thought that anything that contributed to heterosexuality was all right, and Mark found it "very liberating" for Freud to say so. I asked about homosexuality, which Mark said (as Hirst had too) was not one of his problems; Mark thought that if people were decent homosexuals, with good characters, Freud would have been accepting of them.

After being analyzed by Freud in Vienna, Mark had later gone to Robert Bak for an analysis in New York City, and he was "strictly Freudian" about masturbation. And the analysis with Bak went "two hundred percent better" than that with Freud. In retrospect Mark thought that because Freud was dying, Mark could not let out his full aggressions during the treatment process. Mark had accepted everything Freud proposed and then "acted like a mule." So despite the many differences between Mark and David, there were underlying similarities in their analyses with Freud.

Mark did not seem to know very much about David's analysis, not even its length or the dates; at one point Mark said that David's analysis with Anna Freud was "a really good one." I think that in his obvious preference for Mark Freud had made the right human choice between the brothers. In Mark's view Freud was "very unstrictly Freudian," and this was confirmed to me by Freud's other patients. Freud was strikingly "not a mixer," and all the personal contact Mark had with him proved an "enormous interference." At one point Mark said that it had "ruined" him; although he also thought Freud's social presence had done him "a lot of good," it had confirmed some of his "pathological traits." Mark reported that Freud could be "irritatingly silent" for quite a lengthy period, not saying a word while sitting there "jingling" his keys. (A Freudian might not be surprised that given Mark's symptomatology he was the only patient of Freud's I met who recalled what Freud had been doing with his hands.) Although Freud probably talked "too much" to Mark, at the same time he could seem "the most silent" of men; yet compared with Bak later, Freud was "garrulous." Mark felt that as the years passed Freud did not speak any less because of the pain in his mouth; Freud had supposedly not "let the illness" affect him that way. But when Freud did talk his moralistic attitudes would come out.

The clinical implications of Freud's libido theory, the idea that libidinal energy that remains undischarged gets converted into anxiety, seemed to Mark "not as stupid as it sounds." But Mark thought that one can explain the "pathogenic character of masturbation" and the guilt that it involves without invoking the concept of libido. Mark remained struck with Freud's "literal belief in the libido theory," even though in his writings Freud seemed to have changed his mind about the origins of anxiety. (While once Freud held that anxiety was a response to undischarged sexuality, by 1926 he proposed that anxiety was a signal to the ego of approaching danger.) Yet Mark felt that Freud's approach implied the necessity for holding back sexuality. In Mark's view Freud "had these sexual inhibitions," and as a result he had a theory justifying repression. (Wilhelm Reich had come to the identical conclusion as Mark.) Freud told Mark that masturbatory gratification means that one does not dream the way one should for the sake of analysis.

Because of what David had already told me I wondered whether Freud's outlook had intimidated him, and Mark exclaimed how it had "intimidated the life out of me." In Mark's view Freud's clinical "indiscretions" were "bad" for him. For example, Freud said to him one day, after David had been in analysis with him for a while: "What have you and Ruth done to me! Your brother is the most boring person!" Somehow instead of Mark being flattered by this comparison with David, Mark thought Freud had made a mistake because this remark "just fed" his "long-standing jealousy of David." Yet David was "a goody-goody," and Freud "hated" them. Freud was not moralistic "to the point of nausea." Mark referred to how David in the end was "tremendously helped" by his analysis with Anna Freud.

But for Freud to have analyzed Anna himself was, in Mark's view, "criminal." Freud's motives may have been the best, yet there were other good analysts around, and the cards were thereby "stacked" against Anna. By now I seem to have heard from others too about Freud's analysis of Anna. In contrast to Marianne Kris, who did not want me to mention the subject publicly for fear it would get "misused," Mark thought Freud had actually damaged Anna by analyzing her himself. No other action of Freud's more closely resembled the "wild" analyses he could condemn in others, although other analysts, like Ernst Kris, also analyzed their own children. Somehow Mark did not think that Freud's treating Anna himself contradicted what he had said earlier about how "unpsychological" Freud could be at home. (Freud's analysis of Anna can be understood perhaps as Freud's effort to protect Anna from what any other analyst might do to her, and this curious treatment of her may also be seen as an aspect of Freud's own continuing self-analysis.)

Mark had initially consulted Freud because of "severe character disorders." He felt that if Freud had not taken him into analysis, because Ruth was already in analysis with him and Mark was involved with Ruth, it would have been "traumatic" for Mark but better in the long run. So both brothers independently agreed that Freud should not have treated each of them.

Three and a half years after Mark had first gone to Freud, he stopped the analysis because Freud had "pronounced" that he was "cured." It was not really so, but Ruth wanted to marry him; Freud was not that "stupid" to consider him cured enough to be a capable husband for Ruth. In 1928 Mark and Ruth got married; Marianne Kris's father and Freud were the witnesses. Mark did not know how "historic" it was for Freud to attend a wedding ceremony until he read about it in Jones. (Freud's not attending his own children's weddings may have been a way of his not wanting to acknowledge their independence.) Ruth and Mark went back to the United States for the birth of their daughter; they stayed for a year and then returned to Europe in 1929.

In 1934, or at the end of 1933, Mark told Freud during the course of a shared taxi ride that he still had all his symptoms, but that in some sense he was now worse off because he was trying to be "a grown-up." The only change in Mark was that he now had better feelings toward his father; by then Mark "adored" Freud, and therefore afterward his negative feelings could also apply to Freud. Mark persisted in his belief that Freud had much preferred him to Blumgart, even though Blumgart went on to a most distinguished career in Boston medicine. Mark saw himself as someone who had originally come to Freud in love with a married woman, and that Freud had set out "to patch up" Mark so that he and Ruth could get married. That objective remained the same as Mark undertook his second analysis with Freud.

Freud had been disturbed, "very upset," to hear that Mark had not been cured of "a single symptom," and was "very good about it"; Freud took Mark "right back" into analysis. During the first analysis, from 1924 until 1928, Freud and Ruth had talked over Mark's case "in complete detail." (We know today that Freud, while Jones was in analysis with Sandor Ferenczi, received regular reports about Jones from Ferenczi. And Jones was in close touch with Freud about Freud's own analysis of Loe Kann. Freud analyzed Ferenczi and also his future stepdaughter Elma Palos, who both before she went to Freud as well as after was analyzed by Ferenczi.) Mark was the only one I met who had been as intimately caught up in Freud's capacity for clinical indiscretion. He maintained that Freud talked to Ruth as if she were his "mother."

For Mark's second time with Freud he said that Ruth must not know about Mark's analysis in the same way; Freud acknowledged it had been "a serious mistake" on his part. Mark would not have known enough, he thought, to tell Freud he had made a mistake; it seemed fitting for Ruth and Freud, as Mark's parental substitutes, so to communicate. Freud was "natural and open" about the error he had made. (This was in contrast to how David felt Freud had behaved with him.) Mark then fell rapidly in love with "a girl," and it was "very important" to him. He asked Freud if it were proper to violate a marriage bond, and Freud said "yes." Mark made "considerable progress" until 1938. (He had one bad barbiturate reaction, which Freud "mistook" for a psychotic episode.) Toward the end of the 1930s none of Mark's musical friends remained in Vienna. Mark left in October 1937, returned in December, and finally departed for good and alone at the end of January 1938.

Freud's (1938) posthumously published essay, "Splitting of the Ego in the Process of Defence," which he never finished, contains an account of Mark's case. Freud started writing it around the time Mark finally left Vienna. Jones said that the case is not Mark's, but Ruth and Mark thought Jones was wrong. The toe "fetish," his inability to bear having his little toes touched, as well as other details of the case history, convinced Mark and Ruth that Freud had been writing about Mark. If ever one had doubts about Freud's capacity to tailor his cases for his own special concerns, this example should be telling; it would be hard to imagine a greater contrast between the man I met and the problems that bothered him, with what Freud chose to write about. Of course Freud was preserving Mark's anonymity, but other clinical examples Freud used show how he could disguise key aspects of material. (In the writings of Freud that appeared after his death, concealment was undertaken by those who edited Freud's papers. Dr. Ernst Falzeder brought to my attention certain suppressed lines from the manuscript of Freud's (1921) "Psychoanalysis and Telepathy" (cf. Grubrich-Simitis 1993).

I wondered whether by the time of this second analysis of Mark Freud was disappointed in Ruth. Mark thought that Freud's disillusionment with her was only "near the very end," toward 1937 or so. As Freud's illness grew worse, the disappointment "came out." Mark was not quite sure on this point, and he thought that on reflection the date for the change in Freud's attitude should be placed earlier than 1937, when Ruth was "becoming very demanding." Ruth and Mark were divorced in 1937, and then came together again in six months; Freud was displeased, and in hindsight Mark thought Freud had been right to be angry at their remarrying.

The "cooling" on Freud's part toward Ruth may not have been noticeable until 1935 or 1936. (As early as 1933 Freud had been writing in a letter that Ruth was "a very irregular patient and difficult to grasp owing to organic complications"[Molnar 1992, p. 140]. She was "eternally ill" [p. 152] with coughing and fevers.[2]) Freud would analyze her again, then stop, and start up again. Mark thought that Freud "should have sent her to someone else; she would have gone." Back in America she later went to the analyst Herman Nunberg "for a bit." (Ruth's daughter later agreed that Nunberg, who was misanthropic [Menaker 1989] even if impeccably orthodox, had been "a terrible choice."[3]) Ruth may even have been seeing Nunberg at the time of her death; he was the only one to publish an obituary of her in an analytic journal (Nunberg 1942; cf. also the obituary notice in *Shakespeare Fellowship Quarterly* 7 (4):54).

Ruth's use of drugs, including barbiturates, was paralleled by Mark's increased reliance on drinking (when he first came to Vienna he had never drunk at all). Yet for an American he thought he did not drink much. Until the last two years Ruth was very much against Mark's drinking, and he had to do so fur-

---

2. In thinking about Ruth it is hard not to be reminded of what Freud wrote about Loe Kann: "The uncertainty about the real nature of her pains was a great obstacle to a consequent treatment. After studying her latest reactions I strongly incline to the solution that the far bigger part of it is hysterical indeed" (Paskauskas 1993, p. 290).

3. Nunberg was notoriously sour. He had once declared, instead of saying that the patient had been unsuccessfully treated, "The patient has been successfully mistreated."

tively. Freud's case history never touched on what we now would think of as the co-dependency between Ruth and Mark. For she so intimidated him over his use of alcohol that he never challenged her use of drugs. Intimate areas of their lives will remain unknown, although from a historical perspective it is possible to learn a lot.

Freud himself had an exceptionally naive approach to alcohol. He reported to Mark that when he was once traveling in England he had had some whiskey, and found it was good. Freud "hated" to be dizzy; taking an aspirin meant to him that he was "lost" in the medication, and he so disliked giving up his activity that he could not relax. Perhaps part of Freud's intolerance could be connected with a special outlook on what was properly masculine. But then Freud could be "deep," in telling Mark, for instance, as a compliment, that he was so feminine that he could not let his creativity out.

Ruth had gone from New York to England in the summer of 1938, and Freud had analyzed her again. She was "ecstatic" about the analysis and what she had gotten out of it. Then Freud's disappointment with her started to manifest itself. By January 1939 he was suffering very much, "horribly ill," and therefore "not himself" but instead "very strange." His wife said he was "not the same"; he had a "pathological" relationship to certain things of the past. For example, he failed to remember Ruth's daughter, whom he had once "adored"; Mark quoted Freud as having remarked, "I think I've heard of her." According to Mark, areas of Freud's personality were restricted by the pain of his illness and the consciousness of the approach of death. At the very end he was "completely" disenchanted with Ruth, but his irritability was exaggerated by the state of his health.

I asked why Ruth had not been among those in Freud's retinue invited to go with him to London. Ruth had been unable to leave for England when Freud did in 1938. Her father was very sick; his eyesight and memory were affected. Ruth had not wanted to leave Freud in Vienna. Mark kept telephoning her across the Atlantic. His mother was there in Vienna with Ruth and his daughter. Mark told her that she simply had "got" to come home. The Nazis were about to take over in Austria, and her father needed his only child. After all, Freud "had Marie" Bonaparte to protect him. According to Mark, Ruth had returned to America "very reluctantly."

By then Freud was already beginning to become "disillusioned" with Ruth. She could be domineering and in fact "aggressive"; Ruth was "jealous" of Anna Freud's special role in taking care of her father. Ruth had not only analyzed Max Schur, Freud's doctor, as well as Schur's wife, but for years Ruth had helped function as Freud's personal physician. Although Schur's posthumous book about Freud has received a lot of attention, he successfully disguised Ruth's stature and her role in his becoming Freud's physician (Roazen 1990a). (Schur was, incidentally, also David Brunswick's internist in Vienna.) Mark remembered one conversation between Ruth and Freud in which she had been "laying down the law" to him in their front porch. Mark only saw what happened, without being able to hear what was said, but Mark thought Freud's face "froze" in anger. Mark felt that Freud was probably depressed much of the time because of the pain in his mouth, which he moved a good deal.

Everything between Ruth and Freud remained all right on the surface, but inside their relationship things had changed. The final "estrangement" between Freud and Ruth was "only there very close to his death." Not only were Ruth and Anna jealous of each other, but Helene Deutsch was another more distant rival. Mark thought that Helene was "very queer and hysterical," a temperamental prima donna. Helene Deutsch was not especially intimate with Freud in the years Mark knew about. Ruth was "the closest to him of all the females." Among his other pupils Freud was fond of Heinz Hartmann and Ernst

Kris, and also Marianne, but Mark wanted me to understand that Marianne was "very young" in those days.

Ruth's "work block" came out toward the end, and she never succeeded in publishing as much as Freud and she thought she should. (That lack of productivity in itself helps account for why Ruth is not better known now.) Once Freud had made Ruth a "present" of an idea; for the development of the aesthetic sense, he thought that the relation of the infant to the mother's breast was of exceptional importance. (I am not sure Freud was aware of it, but Melanie Klein would have been interested in such an insight.) But instead of overcoming her work inhibition, Ruth grew demanding of Freud out of jealousy. Mark thought that maybe Freud had treated her in too close a way, and then tried to make the relationship between them more distant than he should have been realistically able to expect. I asked whether Freud's daughter Mathilda, a close friend of Ruth's, would have agreed; Mark thought that such an insight would have been "too subtle" for her.

In his books Jones "suppressed" Mark and Ruth's daughter "Tilly." Out of all the children in those last years, Mark said she was the principal child for a long time, one of Freud's "favorites." Anna was a little "jealous" on this score; she was envious of Ruth because Anna, who remained unmarried, could not give a child like that to Freud, and Anna was also jealous of "Tilly." Mark thought that this jealousy on Anna's part went "very deep," and was unconscious. The last time Mark had seen Anna, after some fifteen years, she had even failed to ask about "Til." But "Frau Professor," Freud's wife, had, like Freud himself, been especially fond of Ruth's child.

Unfortunately Ruth had begun to deteriorate by the end of her stay in Vienna. Her psychological problems converted into physical symptoms, and she had a tendency to hypochondria. She had a gallbladder operation, but even afterward the doctors were not sure that the gallbladder had been bad, and there was a "cloud" over it. She had "played around" with drugs in the 1920s; she would have terrible pain from what appeared to be gallbladder attacks, and she used morphine to combat the pain. According to Mark the addiction was a very gradual process, which really "blossomed out" when she left Vienna. (But her daughter thought she had spent time in Vienna at the Cottage Sanatorium in order to break an addiction.) When she had great pain in her eye, she prescribed medication for herself; she went blind in that eye. Aside from her relationship with Freud, her own family was disintegrating; first her mother died, then her father, and she and Mark finally broke up.

In Vienna Ruth was found to have arsenic in her; at least one "reputable" doctor said she had too much in her blood. "Was it the cook who was responsible, as they once thought?" Mark still felt he could not say whether or not she had been "poisoned." He saw her the night before her death in 1946. Six hours later she was dead; it was "a great shock." Ruth had been very ill with a "near pneumonia," and was getting better, but could not go to a party for Marie Bonaparte who was visiting from Paris. (Marie had stayed with them in Vienna, and they visited her in Paris; they regularly took houses together for the summer holidays.) That last night Ruth had been very friendly with Mark.

Thinking about the circumstances of her death, he recalled how she would get horrible diarrhea and then take morphine for it, often falling asleep on the bathroom floor. Mark would find her there and carry her to bed. Once her right to medicate herself was taken away in New York by the federal narcotics agency, she drank paregoric the way one might drink whiskey. That last night she must have taken too much of something, possibly just too many barbiturates. Mark said she died from a fall that fractured her skull, but that it was not a suicide. Tragically, she did not produce as much as she should have, and her physical illness made her prone to drugs. She had been clinging to what she was attached to. All the losses in her life, including that of Freud, confirmed her addiction; everything she was attached to was crumbling, and so she fell apart, too. Ruth's death was given out as a heart attack (obituary, *New York Times*, January 26, 1946), but that was "made up." She died of too many barbiturates and the fall. An autopsy, Mark was told, would show a great proportion of opiates in her blood (in contrast, cf. Young-Bruehl 1988).

Ruth's stature in Freud's world was striking partly because she was such an exception to his general hatred of America. His attitude was that "some of his best friends" were Americans. Mark was himself "ambivalent" toward America. Two things about the United States struck Freud as really horrible: the food, since he seemed to have eaten at railroad station restaurants when he came for his 1909 honorary degree from Clark, and the absence of public toilets in New York, which Hirst had mentioned too. But Mark had come to Freud at a period when his special antipathy for President Woodrow Wilson was known; it was "axiomatic" that Freud hated him. Mark predicted that the book about Wilson that Freud collaborated on with Bullitt, which was in those days still unpublished (and is now out of print), would be "terrible." It was always "a sword of Damocles" hanging over their heads (Roazen 1968).

Mark thought that Bullitt and Freud had "fallen in love at first sight" on the basis of their mutually hating Wilson. Mark had no special allegiances to Wilson, and thought that Bullitt was "a pathological liar," charming and unstable, who would help produce a "crazy" study of Wilson. (Ruth was specially favored by Freud having sent her a few pages of the Wilson manuscript.) Wilson might be one of Freud's "pet" hates, but he was Bullitt's "great" one. Austrians like Freud had a special reason for disliking Wilson, since his policies broke up the old Empire; it was not just patriotism on Freud's part (which Hirst had denied could really exist), but that World War I ruined everything economically in Vienna. Freud thought that the conflict should have ended in a "stalemate," and the Germans should not have won the war either. Freud "hated" the Germans. Mark had once bemoaned the lack of barbarians to bring freshness into a declining civilization, and Freud commented: "We have ours, the Prussians."

Throughout his analyses with Freud, Mark associated with other regular analysands of Freud's, such as Bullitt. Once someone mentioned the concept of the "phallic woman" and Bullitt got very upset; "Freud must have had a time with him on the next day!" Although the literature mentions almost all the others in Freud's circle, nothing yet is known about the American named Blumenthal, who was so rich that he had "three" floors in a big hotel in Vienna. Two floors were supposedly empty, both above and below him; he had a phobia about disease, due to his brother having had measles, as Freud had explained the case to Mark. (Once again this sounds like the same kind of trauma theory that Hirst picked up.) The number of towels that Blumenthal consumed was "astronomical."

Mark was a special source of information about Freud's final days because Ruth had gone, like a selected few others, to visit him a month before he died. He passed away after having had to disband his practice, and he endured terrible suffering. Schur was the physician who administered the drugs that Freud asked for to put himself out of any further torment. At the end, Anna and Schur let the illness drag on too long. Freud's Viennese specialist had "rough ways," and at the slightest sign of trouble he would operate. Once Freud got to London he was treated as such a personage that his physicians were afraid of him. (Perhaps Freud's medical condition helps explain why he waited so long to leave Vienna.) In London they permitted his cheek to be pierced from the outside and a terrible odor developed; even Freud's favorite dog would not come near him. A mosquito netting was needed to keep off the bugs from his wound. But

Schur and Anna waited until Freud specifically asked for the end.

Mark saw Ruth's analysis of Schur and his wife as a continuation of how Freud had analyzed her and Mark. (She also treated Muriel Gardiner, Karl Menninger, Robert Fliess, Walter Federn, and the actress Myrna Loy.) Within orthodox limits she was a somewhat activist analyst. Mark thought it was amazing that Ruth was not even more activist, having had Freud as her own analyst. She had, Mark thought, "a marvelous intuitive sense"; she was an enthusiastic woman, and there was no overt decline in her ability to analyze almost to the end. Ruth was "sensitive," "responsive" to literature and poetry.

It must have been painful for her to have Freud reproach her in the last months of his life. He charged her with an "eternal feminine" need of wanting to see her father die. Too much concern was a cover, Freud thought, for the opposite; his "bitterness" was exacerbated by his illness. The world was receding from Freud as he clung to Anna and Schur. Ruth must have felt left out, for her Freud had been the greatest person imaginable—scientific mentor as well as father substitute. She had "a very ambivalent relation" to Judge Mack, and for years had neglected him for Freud; Freud was for Ruth "the great solution." And until the end Ruth and Freud's relation was "very fine."

One early source of tension between both Mark and Ruth was the darkening political scene. The Brunswicks were both keenly disappointed in Freud when the socialists were violently put down in the 1934 Vienna civil war; the Brunswicks helped to smuggle things out of Austria. (Ruth comes up in Muriel Gardiner's *Code Name "Mary"*: *Memoirs of An American Woman in the Austrian Underground* [1983].) According to Mark, Freud had "turned completely," and supported Engelbert Dollfuss, the Austrian chancellor, whom Mark and Ruth considered a fascist. Freud's son Martin went so far as to hang

Dollfuss's picture on the wall of the psychoanalytic press office, even though the office was financed by money coming from Freud's American supporters. In Mark's view one had to understand that Freud was a dying man who wanted to stay in Vienna. Ruth and Mark used to tell him regularly that he had to leave, and he did not like it; they became the bearers of bad news, telling him things that he did not want to hear. And it was "hell" for everyone when the Nazis finally did come; many of the members of the analytic community could not leave until Freud did himself, for it would seem they were deserting "a sinking ship."

In February 1934 Freud and Mark had agreed to part for awhile, interrupting Mark's second analysis, because he was so "bitter" about Freud's support of Dollfuss. It was "an anti-intellectual government," representing "everything" that had "kept Freud down" over the years. "And the socialists were his friends!" Freud could not "handle" this political issue in Mark's analysis, and Mark hypothesized that Freud's technical incapacity was due to his guilty conscience.

Mark, if only because of Ruth, was kept aware of the various power struggles within the psychoanalytic movement itself. So he knew, for example, about the "great explosions" over Sandor Rado and Franz Alexander, both of which were concerned with their moving from Europe to the United States. Mark also heard a little about Freud's troubles with Otto Rank and Sandor Ferenczi. Around 1937 Mark explained Ferenczi's having "gone bad" with the analogy of the early use of x-rays, when people were overexposed because the dangers were not yet known. Mark, with disbelief, said that Freud thought that Mark had offered a "brilliant" explanation. Freud used the x-ray analogy himself in his 1937 paper, "Analysis Terminable and Interminable."

However ambivalent Mark described himself as being to-ward Freud, I trusted some of his observations since they appeared so lifelike and unstereotyped. It sounded right to me, for example, that Freud's jokes were always both Jewish and wonderful. Mark appreciated Freud's warmth and humanity, and thought his "sins" were those of "outgoingness." In many ways Anna was like him, but Mark found her too self-centered and completely absorbed in her work. Freud himself worked "ten times harder" than most, but Mark said that one never felt it. Freud was "interested in everything," perhaps too much so; yet Mark never experienced a lack of human concern on Freud's part. Each time the subject of the worst difficulties between Ruth and Freud came up in our discussion, it was obviously painful for Mark to recall it.

The only quality Mark maintained he did not like in Freud was the way he admired success. (His theory, however, I understand to treat failure, or neurosis, seriously; Freud focused his work on the problems of such outsiders as neurotics.) With Mark personally Freud had done "his best"; but Mark felt Freud was too keen on thinking worldly success was wonderful. Kris already in Mark's time had an academic appointment, which Freud approved of, since Freud himself "never" got over not becoming a regular faculty member at the University of Vienna. Despite outside pressures, Freud did manage to maintain his integrity. But Freud still had a little bit of the "snob" in him. Mark thought that helped explain Freud's interest in Bullitt, who was so well connected in the United States, as well as Freud's attraction to Marie Bonaparte. Mark thought she was an impressive personality, "whose mistakes were as amusing as her virtues"; her family money might be tainted, since a grandfather was involved with creating Monte Carlo, but she was well known within Parisian society. She had married into the most respectable royal family in Europe, and "one never knew" which "king or duke" might turn up at her home.

Marie's life as a princess was absorbed into that of being a psychoanalyst. But Ruth was only just starting out with Freud, and therefore Mark considered that she had been "nothing" before psychoanalysis. Ruth had been a "tabula rasa" within Freud's world. (This was true for someone like Otto Rank as well.)

Mark thought that the conditions of Freud's analyzing were unique; he was not a vain man, but proud and harshly protective of his doctrines. Freud was like Bismarck; once he was gone, his whole way of running things had to be changed. (Heinz Hartmann made the identical analogy.) Freud had had a highly specialized way of conducting analyses. Mark said he never found anything "remotely" petty in Freud, even if he had not been cautious enough in handling his own creation; everything he did stemmed from good will, and also from the need to protect himself. When Mark told Freud a dream, Freud had commented, "Now you are going to get well." Freud had raised Mark's hopes enormously; because psychoanalysis was his discovery he had a "special handicap" in using it. Mark still was impressed with what he considered to be the complete identity between what Freud said and what he believed, and Freud had taken seriously what others had ignored. It was when one was in Freud's presence, looking at his deeply piercing brown eyes, which were "almost melodramatic," that one could detect the founder of psychoanalysis.

Freud could still be curiously credulous, which Jones had related in a "complicated" way to Freud's capacities as a genius. Freud believed, for example, in all the stories that had circulated about Hitler's supposed sexual perversities—that he got satisfaction from a prostitute's urinating in his mouth. But Mark was also able to appreciate how Freud had created, despite his personal fallibilities, a unique treatment situation in which the patient is ideally provided with an opportunity to make himself known. I think it has to be impressive that despite how Ruth had tragically gone under, Mark still was able to value Freud's contribution.

4

Forbidden Sex:
Dr. Edith Jackson

By the time I met Edith Jackson in the summer of 1966 I was so far along in my interviewing that I came equipped with a long list of questions that I could fall back on if her account began to slacken. Unlike with Mark Brunswick, however, in seeing Edith Jackson I felt I had to be careful. She had once been a practicing analyst, and when I first met her she wondered aloud if Anna Freud would approve of what I was doing. Fortunately I had already seen "Miss Freud," as she was called in those days, and my having visited her in London was a reassurance to Edith Jackson that my work was considered acceptable (Roazen 1993a). It did seem to me that Dr. Jackson, who was known to her old friends as "Edie," had quasi-religious feelings about Anna, or at least felt a special political allegiance to her.

After Edith Jackson's death in 1977 she left a small bequest of money directly to Anna, to be used presumably for furthering Anna's clinic for children, and Anna herself wrote a memorial tribute about Edith Jackson (A. Freud 1978).

Although Edith Jackson was in America and therefore would not be able to talk immediately with Anna about my work, I had to be on my guard in how I spoke with her. It may have helped that I was seeing Dr. Jackson at her sister-in-law's house on Cape Cod, so our surroundings were relaxed. I brought a tape recorder, but she did not allow me to use it. In 1954, however, she was interviewed by Eissler on tape, and I have recently seen a transcript that Professor Sara Lee Silberman helped me obtain. Eissler was duplicitous enough to claim that he needed "the machine" only because of his supposed inadequate memory, but that would imply he was using her material for his own research, as opposed to locking it up for later inspection. But as we shall see, with Dr. Jackson Eissler missed the forest for the trees.

Edith Jackson explicitly asked whether I would be submitting what I wrote to Anna before publishing it. Edith did not want to see it herself, but felt she should defer to Anna's authority. When I indicated as gently as I could that I would be pursuing my own path, with all due respect for Anna's position, Dr. Jackson did volunteer that she had found it curious that Anna had taken such objection to the movie about Freud starring Montgomery Clift, when she herself did not think it so bad.

As a neutral starting point I asked about the timing of her own analysis with Freud, how it had been arranged, and the other people she had known there at the time. She had been in analysis with Freud from 1930 until 1936, which is a relatively long spell. She was 35 years old when she began the analysis. She had graduated from Vassar College in 1916 and from Johns Hopkins Medical School in 1921, and then completed her internship. She had also embarked on her first job; after thinking she was going to be a pediatrician, and having worked on a rickets-prevention project at Yale, she was just starting to get into psychiatry. She had an appointment for a year at St. Elizabeth's Hospital in Washington, D.C. Her friend Dr. Smiley Blanton, whom she had known in her medical school days, said to her that he was going to Vienna to be analyzed by Freud, and suggested that she do the same. (Blanton's diary of his contact with Freud was subsequently published in 1971.)

When Blanton went to Europe, he spoke to "Professor" on Dr. Jackson's behalf, and she got the next available "niche." Both Blanton and his wife, who went into analysis with Ruth Brunswick, were "very effervescent and ebullient" people. (Dr. Jackson accounted for Jones's neglect of Ruth on the grounds that "probably he was jealous of her.") Although Blanton's wife had never had any formal education, she was "widely informed and amusing"; Blanton himself looked terribly "sober" but Dr. Jackson found him "full of wit." She acknowledged, when I raised the point based on my own contact with him, that Blanton was not much of a scientist, and she volunteered that he really did not think in psychoanalytic categories. Still, having met him myself, I found it hard to believe how seriously she continued to take him. She had received a letter saying when she should come to Europe, and she guessed that she had heard from both Blanton and Freud himself. She arrived in Vienna at Christmastime 1929. She first stayed at a pension with the Blantons.

Dr. Jackson did not start going to meetings of the Vienna Psychoanalytic Society "right away," since it was not "allowed." She was conscientious enough to call to my attention that her memory was "poor," and that she had "kept no records." But she reasoned that because foreigners might not be able to stay in Europe too long, they were permitted to go to psychoanalytic meetings rather sooner than others might. She could read German, but she had trouble when it was spoken rapidly, so it would not have done her any good to have gone to gatherings at the outset. It was, she supposed, eight or nine months before she went, which would have placed it after the summer vacation of 1930. By then she was properly "settled into" her analysis.

Dr. Jackson started reading Freud's works in German in the fall of 1930, as soon as it was clear she was going to be enrolled at the Training Institute of the Vienna Psychoanalytic Society. That Institute had first been set up in 1924, with Helene Deutsch as its head; by the time Dr. Jackson enrolled as a candidate, which had to have been with Freud's approval since he was analyzing her, the Institute possessed a full roster of courses. Freud had thought it was a good idea that she proceed to study his writings; she was not quite sure whether it was before she started going to formal meetings or coincident with her attending those discussions. But she had come to Vienna wanting to learn German "better" as well as to study the analytic literature, so reading Freud served both purposes.

She reported that Freud could listen with equal ease whether the analysand spoke in English, French, or German. At one point he thought she was using English as a "resistance," so they shifted over to working in German. But he "could not stand" her German, so they went back to English. He had no trouble with that, for she spoke slowly.

She remembered how once in the analysis she had given him a best-selling novel, *Ramona* (1884) by Helen Hunt Jackson, who was her father's first wife, then deceased. Freud read it "that night" and the next day was able to discuss anything about it. Dr. Jackson was the child of her father's second wife, who was a niece of the first one. (Dr. Jackson never mentioned to me, or Eissler, the suicide of her mother when she was almost 5 years old [Silberman 1994].) Although Helen Hunt Jackson had passed away, Dr. Jackson's family lived in the same house she had, but none of the children had known her. *Ramona* was about a

Spanish girl who had married an Indian, and it was written to illustrate the bad treatment of the Indians. Helen Hunt Jackson had earlier written a book called *The Century of Dishonor* (1881), but it had not gotten anywhere in influencing Congress, so she then wrote *Ramona*. Dr. Jackson thought Freud was interested in the novel. He liked to collect antiquities, and over the holidays she picked up something for him from the American Southwest. But she thought whatever she had chosen was not antique enough for him.

Dr. Jackson came from a socially prominent American family, and she was known among Freud's pupils for having money. (I presume that Dorothy Burlingham's being a Tiffany put her in a special category, but in the end not much was left for her heirs.) She had grown up in the same Colorado town as the Harvard sociological theorist Talcott Parsons, and he had in fact mentioned her name to me; she seemed a bit hurt that he had just given her out as a possible source, without mentioning the old personal tie. Edith's brother, Gardner Jackson, was a prominent lawyer and had been a leader in the defense of Sacco and Vanzetti in the 1920s; he became notable throughout the New Deal period. I therefore asked whether Freud had ever discussed American politics with her, in connection with the Leopold and Loeb case, the Scopes trial, or Prohibition, but she said that such issues "never" came up. She thought that Freud had "probably" talked about such matters with Bullitt, who in the days she was in Vienna had an hour with Freud. She was "never sure" whether his time with Freud was for a personal analysis or for the book he was working on with "Professor," but Bullitt's presence in Freud's circle was memorable.

With Dr. Jackson I had a special interviewing agenda, in that I had heard that she and Freud's eldest son Martin had been romantically involved. (Eissler spent his time with Dr. Jackson going over the details of the handful of letters from Freud to her, while Eissler ignored this most sensitive subject.) I knew from

Jones's biography of Freud that during the summer of 1932 she
had sent some two thousand dollars to help support the psychoanalytic publishing house, with which Martin was then closely
associated. (Dr. Jackson had never finished reading Jones's
biography but she thought it had been "well done.") Edith
Jackson struck me as both straitlaced and old-maidish; Mark
Brunswick had not been shocked by the idea that she might have
had a love affair with Martin Freud, whom Mark knew as "a real
Don Juan." (One family member characterized Martin to me as
"a case of arrested development.") Knowing how puritancial
Dr. Jackson seemed, Mark thought that Freud might well have
been tempted to recommend that she get herself someone in her
life who was sexually experienced, but that sounds to me more
like Mark himself speaking rather than how I would have
expected Freud himself to react. I would not have discussed the
possibility of Martin and Edith having had a relationship, in the
course of my talks with Mark, until after I had met Dr. Jackson
herself. In fact, she made a personal impression on me of being
so strikingly spinsterish (she never married) as to make a liaison
with Martin Freud, who was married and had a number of affairs
(Roazen 1993a), all the more unlikely.

The only way I could steer the conversation toward Martin
Freud was by raising the more general issue of Dr. Jackson's
knowledge of Freud's family. I asked about Freud's mother, who
lived on until the fall of 1930 but about whom the scholarly
literature remains thin; Dr. Jackson, however, said that she had
never met her. She remembered Freud's once apologizing for
missing an analytic hour due to the death of a relative, but she
did not think it was his mother. (Freud had chosen not to attend
the funeral in Vienna, but did write some letters; I do not know
whether he saw his regular analytic cases that day but it is
conceivable.)

Dr. Jackson told me how she had met "only" Freud's

immediate family. She had found Freud's sister-in-law Minna to be a "very outgoing, warm, generous, and outspoken" person. Minna, along with her sister Martha, Freud's wife, were interested in being sure that the visiting American ladies like Edith were well situated in Vienna. Edith eventually stayed at the home of a neurologist's widow who was a good friend of both "Tante" Minna and Martha Freud.

Until coming to Vienna Dr. Jackson had not known Ruth Brunswick, but Ruth looked out for the Americans in town, too. Ruth was "very important" at the time, and Edith recalled how jealous she was of Ruth since she had such an "in" with Freud, which was unlike that of any of Freud's other patients. In the summers Ruth would walk with him in the garden. They all felt that Ruth was a "specially favored" pupil, who could talk over not just her cases with him but what she was writing too. Freud regarded Ruth as connecting him to the whole American group of analysts. Dr. Jackson was modest about her own intellectual attainments although she was a Phi Beta Kappa; on several occasions she indicated that Freud must have raised more abstract and theoretical issues with others than with herself. So that when she was commenting on how "bright" Ruth had been, it was partly in order for me to be able to appreciate what her own more limited talents amounted to.

Dr. Jackson thought that perhaps what had singled Ruth out was the special time when she had come to Freud. If Dr. Jackson had to guess why Ruth mattered to Freud so much, it would be that Freud could feel that through Ruth his work would be interpreted correctly to the American circle of his following. He had felt rather "wounded" by his own personal visit to the United States in 1909. She knew about his having had "gastrointestinal" problems then, and that he had found everything so different in America from what he had been accustomed to. He had discussed his experiences in coming to America during Edith's analysis. She imagined that he would feel at loose ends in such a different environment, where he could not easily "run out" to get writing paper or cigars.

She felt that Freud had "tremendously" admired the Harvard medical professor James Jackson Putnam, and it was at his camp in the Berkshire Mountains in western Massachusetts that Freud had not been feeling well; life there was "hardy" and "simple," whereas Freud was used to being always "looked after" in Vienna. (Alan Gregg saw Freud at the Putnam camp, and it made a big difference because Gregg had such a "wide vision." Gregg later was able to steer Rockefeller Foundation money in behalf of supporting analysts who were emigrating from Europe to America [Brown 1987].) If Putnam had lived longer—he died in 1918—Freud thought that the history of psychoanalysis in America would have been different. Freud "revered" Putnam both for his dignity and his position, and there was "mutual admiration" between Freud and Putnam. (Dr. Jackson may or may not have known about the Frink episode, but it did not come up in our time together.)

Matters connected with the history of psychoanalysis in America would only have been raised during her analysis with Freud, since she practically had no contact with him outside of her analytic sessions. It was the custom for local Viennese analysts to invite analysands like herself who had come from other countries to occasional Saturday evening get-togethers. But nobody but the Brunswicks were seen by Freud in a social way. In Edith's time Freud was "relatively strict" about any extra-analytic contacts with his patients.

However aloof Freud might appear to have been with Dr. Jackson, still she was "quite sure" that he had mentioned the "divergences" of Adler, Jung, and Rank. (But Freud had not done that with David Brunswick.) In her view Freud was "not averse" to saying certain things, even if he himself did not bring the subject up, and then proceed to discuss it at length. Sometimes if he took some such controversial matter up it was because he was "bored," or he wanted to "precipitate" something in the analysis.

Dr. Jackson knew that Anna had access to a car in Vienna, and thought (rightly) that perhaps it belonged to Anna's friend Dorothy Burlingham. But the only time Edith saw Freud outside of an analytic hour was when he got in and out of that car. Anna and Dorothy shared a small farm in the country to which they could sometimes retreat.

Dr. Jackson remembered Freud's having mentioned his friend Dr. Oskar Rie during the analysis; she thought he was one of Freud's physicians. (Mark Brunswick considered Rie a "sweet" man; he had been the doctor for Mark's daughter Til.) "Professor" thought of Rie's daughter Marianne Kris as "a saint." She was one of those women Freud admired very much. To Dr. Jackson the essence of analysis consisted in getting over the envies and jealousies that might arise in connection with Freud's fondness for such people. Marianne Kris had two children who were "very young"; both Marianne and her husband Ernst were exceptionally "kind" to the American visitors. Also, other couples in Freud's circle—the Waelders, the Deutsches, the Hitschmanns, the Bibrings, and the Sterbas—invited foreign analytic students to their homes.

Dr. Jackson had paid Freud twenty-five dollars an hour, which she acknowledged was "a lot of money" in those days. She had to learn to get over her "secret feelings" about money; she turned out to be a banker's daughter. (According to Dr. Jackson, and in contrast to what Mark Brunswick had thought Ruth was able to earn in Vienna, someone as outstanding as Helene Deutsch would only have been able to expect about ten dollars an hour.) Dr. Jackson agreed that Martin Freud was in those days "in charge" of Freud's publishing house; when I asked about any money of hers going to help subsidize the press, she said that it was "quite possible." In 1932, besides the two thousand dollars, earlier that winter Freud recorded Edith as having donated an additional one thousand dollars. (During a lunch break, Dr. Jackson's sister-in-law spontaneously mentioned the example of money as the sort of issue that a callous interviewer could be brazen enough to raise, and Dr. Jackson and I just exchanged glances. An historian has estimated that Edith's financial investment for analytic sessions came to $33,000 [Silberman 1994].)

Dr. Jackson was continuously in analysis with Freud for over five years, with periods off for summer breaks, which lasted for a month or more. She came back to the United States for two summers. And on occasion in Vienna she would give up an hour when someone was in town temporarily and in need of Freud's time. She also recalled interruptions like short Christmas or Easter vacations. She herself later did some psychoanalysis back in New Haven, Connecticut, although she stopped conducting analyses in 1947. She found that she could not manage both clinical work and being a psychoanalyst. Her specialty was pediatric psychiatry, and her appointment was in a department of pediatrics (Wessel 1978). She felt "a little ashamed" about not going further as an analyst. But neither she nor Freud seemed to have expected her to do analysis when she returned to America. "Professor" did not "hold it against me" the way she was planning her career, and she saw him after she began working again at Yale—he thought it was "all right." She did assure me, though, that she "always" continued to maintain her membership in a local psychoanalytic group.

Unlike others who returned to the United States from having been with Freud in Vienna, Dr. Jackson had not come home with any special jobs to do on Freud's behalf. She repeatedly minimized her own role compared with that of others. As far as she knew, Ruth Brunswick was not herself in analysis with Freud "very much" after Dr. Jackson arrived in Vienna, but Ruth was on such intimate terms with Freud that she could always talk about her problems with him. As for Marianne Kris, Freud would take her into analysis for "a few weeks at a time," as he would Marie Bonaparte when she happened to be in Vienna. In those days Anna Freud's power extended over not only Freud's health but some parts of his clinical practice as well; she was an important factor in his deciding to accept certain cases.

Dr. Irmarita Putnam was in analysis with Freud, independently of Anna's influence, at approximately the same time as Dr. Jackson; Dr. Putnam and Dr. Jackson had been classmates together at Johns Hopkins Medical School. Freud knew that they were "talking our analyses out with each other"; in Edith's view Freud "could handle it." But Dr. Putnam was, from Edith's point of view, far more of an "intellectual type" than she was, and therefore Freud would be apt to bring up real theoretical matters with Dr. Putnam. In Dr. Jackson's opinion Freud was "equal to almost anything." And she followed this comment up by adding: "If he could analyze his own daughter. . . ." She thought Freud's analysis of Anna was out of the ordinary, yet she was not startled or scandalized by the matter, nor, like Mark Brunswick, critical of Freud because of it. While Marianne Kris wanted the subject kept under wraps, Dr. Jackson was faithful to a fault; she simply accepted Anna's analysis as part of Freud's extraordinary capacities. She found out about the analysis of Anna by her father "fairly soon" after arriving in Vienna, and "maybe" she heard about it directly from Freud himself.

Relatively early in her analysis with Freud Dr. Jackson had been asked by him to translate an article of his, "The Acquisition and Control of Fire" for the new American journal *Psychoanalytic Quarterly*. She enjoyed doing it "very much," and it appeared in print in 1932. She knew that Jones had been angry about the work Freud commissioned from her, since Joan Riviere in London had also been asked to translate the same article into English. Jones not only minded that Freud had set two people to the same translating chore when only one English version could survive, but Jones was horrified that by Freud's permitting a paper of his own to appear in *Psychoanalytic Quarterly* Freud was sanctioning a fresh publication, which had to cast doubt on how authoritative Freud felt Jones's own *International Journal of Psycho-Analysis* was. (Riviere's translation also appeared in 1932, and James Strachey later revised it for his own *Standard Edition* version.)

As we talked about publication matters, it made it easier for me to ease into trying to discuss the touchy matter of Martin Freud. According to Dr. Jackson, Martin was "not like" his father. She had the feeling that Freud himself was a "devoted father." When I raised the possibility that Freud had been disappointed in his sons, she indicated that Freud would never have "let on" about any such feelings with her. It was "such a close-knit family." In her view Martin had his own special place at the psychoanalytic publishing house. She said that she did not know how "well" he fulfilled his responsibilities there, but that the family consulted with Martin, who was a lawyer, about a variety of legal matters.

Although Dr. Jackson had virtually no contact with Freud outside her analytic sessions, she picked up a good deal of informal knowledge about Freud. (Living abroad, cut off from her familiar sources of emotional support, it was inevitable that she be thrown back on whatever straws she could pick up. Otherwise her life would have been inhumanly isolated.) If she went to the opera, Mozart's *Don Giovanni* for example, Freud indicated how much he loved it, and although he was "not musical" he would begin to hum some of the opening bars. She also knew how fond Freud was of Marie Bonaparte, and he also approvingly commented on the singer Yvette Guilbert. Freud's mentioning these things would not take "any length of time," but he would feel free to respond to something that he liked. "Freud knew his own rules," and free-associating on the patient's part was "an absolute rule." Also, the listening ear of the analyst was crucial for him. Yet Freud was not afraid to be "a little of himself." She did not know Freud's "personal life"; and yet he was not afraid to let you feel he was "a person."

She confirmed that Freud did shake hands at the beginning and end of each analytic hour. He had a hard, firm handshake, almost a "brusque" one. It made "an impression" on her, and she said she still did a lot of handshaking. Once she left something on the couch, and he held on to her hand looking back at what she had forgotten. But she reported, unlike a similar story that Helene Deutsch told me, that she was not "sophisticated enough" to have felt Freud was in any way being "seductive" toward her. He did once comment on a dress she wore; he so respected the analytic distance that anything beyond that was bound to be striking. She had once worn a black satin dress, and Freud remarked that he liked it. He was "an absolutely disciplined person"; but she felt he was a "warm" man, that you could feel it as he passed his children in the corridor. (It is not easy to convey what Dr. Jackson was like as a person, and I fear she may come across as too cold and one-dimensional; it would take a novelist like Hawthorne, who I think specialized in people like Edith, to make her come fully alive.)

She knew a bit about Freud's other cases in those years. In addition to Marianne Kris, Irmarita Putnam, and "the Princess" (Marie Bonaparte), Freud also was treating Dorothy Burlingham; while Putnam was, like Edith herself, in Vienna for a set period of time, people like Marianne Kris, Marie Bonaparte, and Dorothy Burlingham would "come in" for analyses for "short periods." Suzanne Cassirer (who later married Bernfeld) was also with Freud for an extended period; Dr. Jackson remembered having been "jealous" of her. Sometimes Dr. Jackson got to know about these other patients being analyzed by Freud because when he was on holiday over the summer, she would be seeing him then too for her analytic hour; Freud "liked to keep up his income," and therefore allowed himself a relatively short vacation. In her view of Freud's clinical practice, he took only five regular analytic patients and then "scattered in" the rest.

While she was in analytic training in Vienna, Dr. Jackson did some supervised analyses. Since analysts were not then supposed to supervise their own analysands, she had to find two others (besides Freud) to help her. The rule was that each candidate was to have two adult patients in supervised analysis, and two children if one was going on as a child analyst. She never had any doubts as to Freud's positive feelings about the profession of child analysis, which had already become Anna Freud's special area; Freud had not said much to Dr. Jackson about Anna's main rival in the field, Melanie Klein. For Edith the leader in child analysis was Anna; she was "outstanding," and that was "it."

Dr. Jackson had, under supervision, a Communist patient in analysis. She could not see how any such partisan could really be analyzed, since to her a person's ideological allegiances were at odds with their truly free-associating. She had been undertaking to conduct supervised analyses under the official auspices of the Vienna Psychoanalytic Society's Training Institute. Even though she was personally in analysis with Freud, at this late stage in Freud's career Dr. Jackson was bound by the regulations of the Institute. Even a few years earlier David Brunswick could skip that whole procedure; he had not yet decided—despite Freud's expectations—to be an analyst, and presumably never had any formal psychoanalytic training apart from his many personal analyses.

Although Dr. Jackson was formally a student in training, at a time when new bureaucratic procedures were in place, she spent so much time with Freud that she also picked up informal knowledge about his preferences. As far as she knew, Freud admired the special interest that someone like Ruth Brunswick had in working on the application of psychoanalysis to the psychoses, and she also thought that Freud liked the work of Federn, who had his own approach to psychotics. (Whereas someone medically sophisticated like Dr. Jackson took for granted Freud's own lack of psychiatric training, as a lay person Mark Brunswick had been unaware of it.) Dr. Jackson thought that other people might know Freud's preferences better, as she was not aware of them. Freud could certainly talk "against" people; Freud would not have been averse to expressing his antipathies. He was frank about saying that he just did not like America, for example; he always retained the memory of the discomforts associated with his trip to the United States.

Dr. Jackson emphasized that she did not really know Freud personally, and that she failed to grasp a lot of psychoanalytic theory. (Freud felt far more alienated by Federn's ego psychology than she seemed to understand.) I asked if she had looked at Freud for any signs of his personal neurosis, and her answer was "no." She had had an immediate and positive "father transference" to Freud that began even before she left America from just looking at a picture of him, which may have been when she saw him in the movie that Mark Brunswick had made. Her father had also had a beard and gray hair; her transference to Freud consisted of the feelings of a little girl toward an old father. She had read hardly anything about psychoanalysis before she started her treatment; her only preparation for coming to Vienna was leaving her job. Her introduction to psychoanalysis was so completely novel to her that she would not have thought of looking for any neurosis in Freud. In fact she had not had much exposure to neurosis since in her training she had encountered only psychotic men at St. Elizabeth's Hospital. All one was supposed to do in those days in American psychiatry was routine note taking; analysis itself was therefore quite new to her. I allowed her to pull the wool over my eyes, since it turns out she was analyzed by Lucille Dooley in Washington, DC (Silberman 1994).

In Dr. Jackson's description of Freud's therapeutic technique, he wanted to orient a patient and make them at ease. His "blank screen" (the mirror image) approach fitted in with her own transference attitude toward an older parent figure. Freud's attention and attentiveness were never to be questioned, and she always felt it. Although she herself never saw Freud really angry, she would not doubt that he could get hostile. Someone like Irmarita Putnam, because of her previous analytic experience, would have supposedly had a freer give and take with Freud.

I asked whether Freud was capable of rapping his hand on the couch. "Oh, yes," she replied. (He had not done so with David Brunswick.) Freud sat in a kind of a corner, almost as if he rested his arm on the back of the couch. (The hearing in one of Freud's ears was damaged by an early operation on his jaw.) If he did not hear what she said, or to indicate some insight he suddenly saw, he would tap to make his point, but it was a "gentle" rapping.

I also inquired about Freud's no longer going to the regular Wednesday evening meetings of the psychoanalytic society. Dr. Jackson understood that that day of the week would always retain special emotional significance for the older analysts around Freud. She thought that Freud's absence was due to his age and frailty; also, he wanted to encourage others to carry on without him. He did, however, continue to see old friends for cards on Saturday evenings. He was 74 years old when Dr. Jackson first was his patient, and he was ready to retire from his local leadership, leaving the active teaching at the Institute to others.

There was much psychoanalytic instruction going on in Vienna. For individual work Dr. Jackson liked Robert Waelder, who loved teaching and was the most systematic presenter; he would tell you clearly and slowly where he was going, explain himself, and then summarize what he had accomplished. (In the 1960s I found Waelder awfully smug and sure of himself, not at all an impressive model of psychological understanding.) She mentioned Richard Sterba, Eissler's analyst, as another notable teacher. Sterba's wife was more effervescent, and both Sterbas would express opinions about the United States although they understood nothing about the country; Edith found this off-putting. (I thought Sterba was insightful and artistic.) Dr. Jackson found Nunberg not easy to understand because he did not talk clearly, and she had "a hard time" following Helene Deutsch. (Both Nunberg and Deutsch were Poles.) Deutsch's seminars were scintillating, for she did seem able to bring out the best in people, but some of the proceedings went too fast for Edith, and therefore she found it difficult to keep up. Dr. Jackson felt sure she was not a very good student.

As a student in training there were other evening classes outside of the formal monthly meetings on Wednesdays. Dr. Jackson found both Edward and Grete Bibring harder to understand than Robert and Jenny Waelder. She paid for extra consultations with August Aichhorn. She reported seeing relatively little of Felix Deutsch, who seemed "jolly and pleasant." Grete Bibring was memorable for trying to smooth feelings over when Edward Hitschmann was making the others "impatient"; Edith thought there was a noticeable group irritation about Hitschmann, one of Freud's earliest Viennese followers, while Grete felt that someone that old should be "treasured and respected." Edith herself always found Hitschmann's "slow remarks" annoying. She was never invited to any of the private meetings at Freud's house, since she "still was in psychoanalysis." (Nonetheless Marie Bonaparte, when in town, or Ruth Brunswick would be invited, even though they both were also Freud's patients.)

Freud once gave Dr. Jackson a photograph of himself, without, she thought, her having asked for it. When she requested that he sign it on the back, he made a joke that now it would be "worth a thousand dollars." This is what he thought of Americans, that they were after money; if he wanted to "tease" he would allude to their being money-minded. (Freud was himself by then almost wholly reliant on Americans in his practice.) Dr. Jackson did not have the famous photograph of Freud holding a cigar, taken by his son-in-law in Berlin, which somehow she did not like; rather she had a full-face photo, which had been taken before she first saw him, showing Freud's head and shoulders.

I asked if Freud had ever fallen asleep in her sessions, and she replied that "as far as" she "knew" he had not. Although the conversation might be absolutely boring to him, she never felt that he was not carefully listening. She thought that his cigar smoking might have helped in keeping him alert. She hardly ever turned around to look at him; she herself was of a "trusting" and "obedient" nature. She said she herself might have fallen asleep, at least she thought that the balance might have been in favor of her having been the one to drop off. There were periods of his "silence." He would have had every right to fall asleep, as far as she was concerned; she found she had a hard time keeping awake when she conducted analyses herself.

In rethinking what she had just told me, she thought she might have gotten that photo at the psychoanalytic publishing house and then taken it to Freud for an autograph. The important point she wanted to make was that Freud did not mind "giving." He was "not threatened by me at all." He gave "each" of his female patients then a ring or a stone; he gave Edith an antique stone and she had the setting made. (Earlier in Freud's career such ring-giving had been reserved for key disciples within the psychoanalytic movement, but later on it became watered down in its significance. Whatever the mythology might sound like, Freud always retained the real power within the psychoanalytic movement. Freud also gave such presents of rings, Dr. Jackson specified, to Suzanne Bernfeld, Dorothy Burlingham, the Princess Marie, and Ruth Brunswick. Irmarita Putnam had already left Vienna, so she did not get one. (Although Dr. Jackson did not mention it, other women also got rings from Freud: Katherine Jones, Anna Freud, Lou Andreas-Salomé, Gisela Ferenczi, Jeanne Lampl-de Groot, Henny Freud, and Eva Rosenfeld were among those receiving this present.)

Dr. Jackson said she had never found Freud "indiscreet"; he certainly did not encourage indiscretion. She maintained she was not especially curious about others, and never doubted Freud's discretion for a moment. However, it turned out that Freud knew something intimate about her family, which he only had the "right" to find out from her. (This may have been the circumstances of her mother's death.) He said something to the effect that "you know we find out things." Edith was "horrified" at his knowledge; she thought it might have been Smiley Blanton who had been Freud's source.

I asked to what extent she thought Freud had helped her, and she replied it was "impossible to say." When she first went into analysis, she did not know what she wanted to do or what she could do. And in hindsight she supposed she was "depressed" about it. She had gone into psychiatry because she was not ready to practice pediatrics. But at the end of the analysis she could take Dr. Marian ("Molly") Putnam's offer of a job back in the States. (Molly was James Jackson Putnam's daughter and a fellow classmate of Edith's at Johns Hopkins Medical School; she had been analyzed in Vienna by Helene Deutsch.) So, "sure," the analysis helped her; it gave her the assurance to know about psychoanalysis, and she did not feel depressed about her inability. From Freud's point of view, work and the enjoyment associated with it was the most important thing. (I wonder now whether implicitly she might have been critical of how the analysis had left her unable to marry.) Freud thought that the analysis had been of assistance. Dr. Jackson felt that she was not quite as "reticent" as before; there was "quite a difference." Above all the fact that she had been in Vienna and analyzed by Freud proved to be an asset, even though she had not gone into it seeking that special status. As the years went by she found that having been analyzed by Freud was considered something special.

In the summer of 1937, after the end of her first year's work in America, she went back to Vienna. She had returned to the United States finally in the spring of 1936. It was then, after her spell working in America, that Freud gave her the feeling that it was perfectly satisfactory and he did not object that she was not doing analysis all the time. She had received only a handful of letters from him, which were really "friendly communications"; in her view he had "just answered his correspondence." (Nonetheless Eissler, as I have said, spent all his interviewing time on this one area. If I myself had been properly bold, I would have wanted to know what sort of model of heterosexuality or family life Freud had held out for people, and whether she had been disappointed in what analysis had done for her.)

Since it was a subject that interested me, I asked Dr. Jackson about Freud's Jewishness; she thought that it was "noticeable" but "not at all disturbing" to her. She reiterated that he was gray-haired and bearded, which was enough to mean to Edith her father. Her own background was about as aristocratically WASP-ish as any American could be. In her view Freud wanted to make sure that she had no anti-Semitic prejudices; maybe he just accepted that she was not bigoted, but he did not overdo the matter.

Dr. Jackson knew that Dr. Roy Grinker, whom she considered a "strong, bumptuous" person, was also in analysis with Freud, as were Blanton and Bullitt. But she thought that these men were the exceptions, and that Freud's patients then seemed to be primarily women. She did not personally remember Dr. Joseph Wortis having been with Freud; she supposed, from Wortis's (1963) book, that he witnessed Freud becoming angry. Dr. Jackson said she thought Freud could be "intolerant," but she did not find him so in her own contact with him. She admitted that with "humor" Freud would admit being hard on Americans. He was intolerant, though, in his idea of America— his whole outlook on America was "wrapped in" intolerance. But then she thought that anyone traveling to a country for the first time would have some such response. She said Putnam's untimely death had doomed for Freud the progress of analysis in the "right way" in the United States.

Although I mainly stuck to Dr. Jackson's general memories, I did try my best at last to zero in on her reported relationship with Martin Freud. I knew that Martin collected women the way his father collected antiquities. Martin's romance with Edith was obviously a hard subject for me to bring up, since I did not want to wreck the interview as a whole. I suspected that she gained some idea of what I was after, for she stopped at one point and asked me bluntly what I was hinting at. It was necessary for me to grow evasive, for I did not want any backlash with Anna Freud by revealing my sources, which might damage any other interviews I might want to conduct.

Dr. Jackson resolved the dilemma of how much to reveal to me by reporting that Freud had not allowed his female patients to have sexual relations while in analysis. That was his "rule." He had said, "You will think this unfair," and she still thought it was unjust. Maybe she was one of his few unmarried women patients. Freud had some theoretical reason for having taken this position; it bore a relation to the material that he thought should be necessary to come out in the course of an analysis. In any event her abstinence was to be his rule for the beginning of an analysis, and was to last "for a certain period."

I had never heard of Freud, with any other patient, making any similar precondition for analysis. If the man Dr. Jackson had in mind was Freud's eldest son, and it does seem certain that they were emotionally involved with each other, it would make a certain kind of clinical sense for Freud to do his best to put a stop to it. About this whole subject of the restraint Freud expected of her, Dr. Jackson told me somewhat stiffly that she could have "skipped" my asking the questions.

Earlier she had told me how sometimes an analyst could forbid someone to take a vacation with a friend, but "Professor" had never done so with her. She smiled at this point, but she was distinctly unamused when I tried to ferret out more about her and Martin. She had mentioned having gone on skiing trips outside Vienna, and how various members of the analytic community could be helpful to her in getting outfitted. Martin was known for being the sportsman in the family, and his wife dimly associated Edith Jackson, and skiing, with Martin.

The kind of sexual restraint on a patient's part that Dr. Jackson reported Freud required would fit in with how Freud had felt about Mark Brunswick's masturbation. Edith knew that Freud believed that there was something important in sexual self-control for the bringing out of analytic material. She related this general theme of restraint to the sacrifice involved in making the monetary payment for an analysis; Freud held that without such an monetary incentive there would be no reason for a patient ever to try to get better. (As we shall see, Freud was capable of breaking this rule with other patients whom he saw for free.) It would be in keeping with Freud's general outlook that he expected people to give up certain pleasures in order to free certain fantasies. She repeated that Freud may have applied the rule requiring abstinence only to people who were not married, but she was clear that Freud expected this "restraint" from her.

I had been told on good authority that Martin Freud had

had an affair with Edith Jackson; Helene Deutsch had had this report from Dr. Helen Ross, one of Edith's close friends. So, despite what little Edith allowed herself to tell me, I put the following paragraph in print in 1969:

> Although puritanical by temperament, on some occasions Freud could close his eyes to misdoing. One of Freud's sons became an accomplished Don Juan, and picked a patient of his father's to have an affair with while she was in analysis; the conditions of analytic treatment would insure that Freud knew of the affair and very likely of the details as well. As a father Freud had been on the whole tender, but remote and perhaps neglectful of his sons. He was early on discontented with the three of them, since none had the talent to carry on his genius; perhaps this also explains why Freud needed to make surrogate sons of his pupils. For a real son to keep an aged father so informed of his sexual exploits may well have constituted a kind of revenge. [p. 41]

Ten years later D. M. Thomas, in his best-selling novel *The White Hotel*, built his narrative around the relationship of a Freud son and a patient. But the book in which my own paragraph appeared was subjected to the closest sort of scrutiny by Anna Freud. I had deliberately been publishing while she was still alive and able to contradict any points where I might have gone wrong (Roazen 1993a). I had not in 1969 mentioned Edith Jackson's name, since after all she was still alive. But although Anna wrote down the most detailed objections to a whole number of points that she dissented from in my book as a whole, she passed by this paragraph without any comment whatsoever. In that same text I had, for the first time in print, mentioned

Anna's having been analyzed by her father. Once again she skipped any chance to contest that fact.

It will have to be left for others in the future to decide how much weight should be assigned to Anna Freud's silences. I am confident that I went as far as I could, interviewing Edith Jackson herself, in alluding to this issue. Subsequently more evidence has been examined about the possibility of a liaison between Martin and Edith; Martin did not frequently have unconsummated affairs, and there is no doubt that he and Edith spent a good deal of time together. And I also think there is little question about her own romantic involvement with him. This tie to Martin may have been enough to explain Freud's having taken the extraordinary precaution of his forbidding her to have sexual relations, at least at the outset of the analysis.

I think Dr. Jackson was not being falsely modest when she saw herself as having played a very restricted role in Freud's esteem. When I mentioned Hilda Doolittle, the poetess known as H. D., to Edith, for example, she knew that H. D. had been in analysis with Freud "for a short time," and that Freud had liked that special sort of "giftedness." Edith never saw herself as being in the front rank of Freud's pupils, and on several occasions mentioned others of Freud's students with whom he would have been more likely to discuss intellectual issues.

She said she would expect Freud to have been "possessive" about his ideas. But with Dr. Jackson, Freud would not have been likely ever to talk about anybody else's concepts being "unintelligible" to him, although with others I found that Freud could so stigmatize work that he found "foreign" to him. Edith thought that she just did not know enough to qualify for any such remarks from Freud. She reported again that she was like "a little girl" in her analysis. (Still, she had been in her mid-thirties; she was remaining girlishly unchallenging in not batting an eyelash over Freud's having analyzed Anna, and in accepting Freud's requirement of sexual abstinence.) Edith had not been especially oriented toward a career in Freud's profession. She knew that analysis could be used therapeutically, and for a time she did go on to do so. Freud knew that she expected to continue medical work in the United States.

Dr. Jackson was so modest that she never brought up the fact—which I was then unaware of—that she had in Vienna provided the money for starting an experimental nursery for children between 1 and 2 years old. This nursery was to become a source of information about the psychology of early childhood, and Anna Freud considered it a forerunner of the later Hampstead War Nurseries that she and Dorothy Burlingham set up in London during World War II. Dr. Jackson herself may be most notable, aside from having been one of Freud's patients, for having pioneered in advocating lying-in facilities for young babies to be with their mothers at the earliest possible opportunity (Silberman 1990). She also served for many years on the editorial board of the annual publication *Psychoanalytic Study of the Child*, which functioned as a forum for professional orthodoxy; its four managing editors were then Ruth Eissler, Anna Freud, Heinz Hartmann, and Marianne Kris. Only recently have we learned of Freud's own pediatric training and how it bears on the origins of psychoanalysis (Bonomi 1994); this whole subject, unknown until now, would have been intriguing to have talked about with Dr. Jackson.

5

Officer of the Vienna Psychoanalytic Society: Dr. Robert Jokl

Edith Jackson gave me an outsider's impression of what the Vienna Psychoanalytic Society had been like. But Robert Jokl was an insider. When I saw him he was a practicing analyst in Los Angeles, a member of the same "conservative" group as David Brunswick. Unlike Brunswick, Jokl had maintained the European tradition of having his office attached to his home. When I first contacted Jokl, I knew virtually nothing about him except that he had been a member of the Vienna Psychoanalytic Society in the years between the wars. It turned out that in the spring of 1919 he had been analyzed by Freud for two and a half months. Freud kept him for only "a short time"; Freud had told him in advance that he would "give him" to someone else once he had a chance to decide who would be best. When Freud referred him elsewhere, Freud reminded him that he had told him from the beginning that he had foreigners then pressing for his time, and that he could only keep local Viennese for a brief period. Since Freud had indicated that once he got to know him he would then be in a position to refer him to another analyst, Jokl was not offended about being sent away. Subsequently Jokl was analyzed by Edward Hitschmann, and later by Siegfried Bernfeld.

By the fall of 1919 Jokl had become a guest member of the Vienna Psychoanalytic Society, and in 1922 he was a full member. He stayed with Freud and the analytic group until the Nazis entered Vienna in 1938; after the Anschluss he went first to the Menninger Clinic in Topeka, Kansas, and then settled in Los Angeles. It was his Viennese years that interested me most. From 1924 until 1930 he was secretary of the Vienna Psychoanalytic Society, and from 1930 until 1931 he served as vice president; he was the only officer I interviewed. Jokl provided me with the details of his formal position at the outset of our contact, which established the basic parameters of his standing within the history of psychoanalysis.

I began by inquiring about Freud as a Jew, on the grounds that I felt that Jones's study of Freud had neglected this important aspect of Freud's background and character. This proved a poor opening move on my part with Jokl, for he was disinclined to discuss the Jewish side of Freud's life. He told me he thought that the issue of Freud as a Jew had little to do with "the science" of psychoanalysis, but he conceded that Freud's Jewishness had contributed to his independence. Freud had said as much in print himself, but there is a long history of sensitivity about Freud's Jewishness that still exists today (Gay 1987, Roazen 1990a). To discuss the cultural sources of Freud's work seems to some to compromise the objectivity of what he accomplished.

An alternative tack I took was to inquire who was Freud's

personal favorite when Jokl came to the Viennese society; Jokl hesitated, and then answered, "Bernfeld." (From others too I got confirmation of what special status Bernfeld had once possessed; as one old analyst put it, Bernfeld had been a "genius" who then somehow stopped.) But the real question, Jokl volunteered, was not who ranked highest in Freud's esteem, but rather who he did *not* like. And here Jokl elaborated on the position of Herbert Silberer, whom Jokl regarded as a "good friend" of his. Freud supposedly "never liked him," although "nobody knew why." Silberer committed suicide in 1923. Jokl expounded on how Silberer had felt very offended and rejected by Freud; Silberer was depressed about Freud's behavior to him. Freud was never friendly toward him or accepting, "and so on." To Jokl "it was very difficult."

Silberer was "devoted" to Freud and among other works did a study of hypnagogic phenomena, the images one sees when especially tired and falling asleep, which was very important at the time. He was not a psychiatrist but had a Ph.D., perhaps in psychology; he had come to the Vienna group long before Jokl himself. Yet Freud did not like him. Either Freud appreciated somebody or he did not, but "the motivations were not always clear." Sometimes Freud could be fond of those who did not work hard, and he could feel no respect for some who labored steadily to further Freud's work (Roazen 1975).

I already knew the story of Freud's difficulties with Victor Tausk, and what Jokl told me about Silberer reminded me of what seemed to others as "the Tausk problem" (Roazen 1969, 1990a). At the time I was seeing Jokl I had not yet published anything about Tausk, but Jokl already seemed familiar with the particular issues Tausk had with Freud. Jokl thought that the conflict with Silberer was "not the same" as with Tausk, in that Freud had supposedly "liked" Tausk. Tausk was entitled to feel "offended but not rejected." In Jokl's view Freud had "preferred" Tausk very much, and Freud had spoken highly of

Tausk's article on the influencing machine" (Tausk 1991). Although it was true that Freud refused to take Tausk into a personal analysis, Jokl knew that Freud had sent Tausk to someone else for an analysis. When I suggested that that was worse, in that by Freud's sending Tausk to Helene Deutsch, at a time when she was in treatment with Freud himself, Freud exacerbated the problem with Tausk, Jokl fully agreed.

According to Jokl, Tausk had had a "paranoic" streak and was very touchy. (As Reich once wrote to Federn in 1926, "My activity—which, like all positive things, also has its negative aspects—has earned me the reputation of being aggressive. I share this fate with Tausk" [Higgins and Raphael 1967, p. 150].) Otto Fenichel had once said that Tausk could not have written his famous article on the influencing machine except on the basis of self-observation, and Jokl thought that was so. Jokl had had a patient of his own with clinical material just like that described in Tausk's influencing machine paper, and Freud had agreed that Tausk's concept was "true."

Jokl said that he himself had never had any difficulties in dealing with Freud, and he cited how in 1927 he had given a paper on resistances to analysis, and attacked analysts for sometimes being overbearing and contributing to the buildup of resistances; Freud had agreed then with Jokl's approach. From others I learned, however, that in Vienna Jokl had at one time expected analysts to give him a percentage of the fees of patients referred by him. After a tortured discussion of the moral difficulties Jokl's position had raised it was made clear that Freud disapproved of any such practice. This may have been the occasion when Freud, after an analyst's breach of ethics was traced to psychological origins, ended the matter by saying: "This may all very well be so, but malpractice is none the better morally for having psychological bases." Later, while working at the Menninger Clinic, Jokl led a strike of émigré training analysts requesting more money (Friedman 1990).

Every patient that Freud sent on to him Jokl later discussed with Freud. Jokl became an analyst before the period when Edith Jackson was in Vienna, and no Training Institute had yet been set up; so in those days Freud himself was completely in charge of the education and supervising of future local analysts. Freud preferred the most informal approach. According to a reliable-sounding account that Bernfeld (1962) later gave:

> In 1922 I discussed with Freud my intention of establishing myself in Vienna as a practicing analyst. I had been told that our Berlin group encouraged psychoanalysts, especially beginners, to have a didactic analysis before starting their practice, and I asked Freud whether he thought this preparation desirable for me. His answer was, "Nonsense. Go right ahead. You certainly will have difficulties. When you get into trouble, we will see what we can do about it." Only a week later he send me my first didactic case. . . . [p. 463]

Bernfeld was not a physician, but had first joined the Vienna Psychoanalytic Society in 1913. The proposal that all future analysts be themselves analyzed was first advanced before World War I by Jung, and was probably in part intended as a criticism of Freud himself as suffering from unanalyzed unconscious conflicts. When Nunberg in 1918 publicly proposed implementing Jung's idea—without acknowledging Jung—Nunberg's motion was rejected "because Rank and Tausk energetically opposed it" (Roazen 1969, p. 66). Only after Freud's illness with cancer did the rule become formalized that all new analysts be themselves analyzed. (In France today a handful of the most distinguished analysts, because of the possibilities of indoctrination through a requirement of a didactic analysis, have been forthrightly trying to challenge the continuation of the practice.

In England during World War II Edward Glover was already concerned about the way in which the Kleinians were gaining power in Britain by supposedly misusing training analyses for political purposes [Roazen 1992a].)

According to what I could find out from questioning Jokl about Freud's own clinical skills, Freud was able to treat obsessive-compulsive cases, the classical neuroses, and borderline problems. In an effort to cut through possible idealizations about Freud on Jokl's part, I raised the issue of what had gone wrong between Freud and Otto Rank, since their falling out took place during Jokl's years in the society. In Jokl's view Rank had made more and more theoretical statements contradicting those of Freud, as Rank tried to substitute his own formulations instead. Freud publicly discussed his problems in dealing with Rank at small meetings of the society. Rank grew angry, and Freud asked him to "take it back," but Rank refused. Rank and his wife formerly had come very often to Freud's house for dinner, and then they stopped. Jokl quoted Freud as having said to Rank, "You make the whole question more complicated and more superficial," and supposedly Rank then angrily resigned.

Although Jokl's account of Freud's difficulties with Rank will not stand up as accurate history, in that the falling out between them took place over a period of several years and was fraught with painful ambivalences on both Freud's and Rank's part, Jokl had accurately put his finger on some of the key emotional issues involved in trying to exist in Freud's school. Rank had been such a personal favorite of Freud's that it was tempting for the jealousy of others to widen the breach once it had started (Roazen 1975).

While I think that Rank's situation with Freud should be considered a unique one, for Jokl Rank had had "the same problem" as Wilhelm Stekel and Alfred Adler had earlier encountered, which was how "to make his own theories and not be dependent on Freud." Tausk's situation was not "identical," in that he was "always accepted" by Freud. Tausk's suicide was to Jokl "very surprising," although his influencing machine article might have led them to expect it. Tausk had "a schizoid personality," with perhaps something more pathological "underneath." Silberer's suicide, though, was "no surprise." Silberer was "a very normal personality" who was extremely depressed about the dilemma he faced with Freud. Yet Silberer never admitted how Freud felt about him. (Jokl was not blaming Freud for Silberer's fate.)

Although Jokl had brought up the difficulties between Freud and Silberer, I tried to steer my questions in the direction of what could be learned directly from Jokl about Freud's clinical practices. I asked Jokl whether Freud had engaged in any historical reconstructions about his early childhood. Jokl was both curious and a bit puzzled by my interest in this subject. In those post–World War I days the phrase "primal scene" was not known, but that was the kind of traumatic material of the child as witness to parental sexual activity that Jokl understood me to be inquiring about. Very early in the analysis Freud had in fact mentioned some such "early states" in Jokl's childhood.

Jokl was eager to place himself alongside his contemporaries in analysis. Reich and Fenichel were part of the same group that Jokl had belonged to; so was Helene Deutsch, although she was seven years older than Jokl. Freud had not much respect for Isidor Sadger, an early follower of his, whom Jokl considered merely a "sexologist." Federn was one of the disciples whom Freud had thought well of. When I pointed out that Freud had never given Federn a ring, Jokl dodged my point by saying that there were "other reasons" for that.

I asked why someone like Hanns Sachs, also a local Viennese, had got a ring from Freud and not Federn. Jokl thought that Freud respected Sachs "very much," and missed him when he left Vienna to be a training analyst in Berlin. Sachs was an "apostle" of Freud's, yet in spite of that public role Sachs was "a

likable'' person. In his behavior Sachs was very much like
Theodor Reik; Sachs (like Reik) took great pleasure in speaking
and writing, but Jokl considered Sachs "the more serious" of the
two. For Jokl, Federn on the other hand was "no apostle."
"Having a beard is not enough to qualify!" Freud did not always
approve of what Federn was doing with his patients. In reality I
think there were substantial differences between the clinical
approaches of Freud and Federn (Roazen 1969). Jokl also knew
that difficulties existed between Federn and his wife, which
might have led to a divorce; Freud proved to be "very helpful"
in avoiding this marital breakup.

Jokl then spoke of his own attitude toward Freud. Jokl
thought that Freud was "never able to understand women
completely," and on the issue of femininity considered Freud
"almost blind." (My interview with Jokl was several years
before people like Germaine Greer and Kate Millett had popu-
larized their critiques of Freud; within psychoanalysis Karen
Horney had been openly challenging Freud on female psychology since the late 1920s.) Jokl thought that Freud was
influenced by other people, yet never by women. Jokl proposed
that Freud suffered "a shyness in approaching them to the
bottom."

I raised the example of Ruth Brunswick, as well as Helene
Deutsch, since they both were women in Freud's circle who
mattered to him intellectually. As far as Brunswick went, Jokl
maintained that he did not know what Freud had admired in
her, other than her having been a "diligent" and "believing"
pupil. Jokl thought that Freud had appreciated Deutsch "almost
as much" as Brunswick, and Jokl denied that there was any
jealousy between Deutsch and Brunswick. (On the basis of my
own contact with Deutsch I knew this to be untrue.) Brunswick
was "a good psychologist," although Jokl did not feel able to go
so far as to say that she was "as smart" as Deutsch. To Jokl,
Deutsch was more "the therapeutic observer," whereas Bruns-

wick was more "the psychologic observer." I took this distinction to mean that Deutsch was more concerned with clinical
improvements. (According to some reminiscences of Richard
Sterba (1982), Jokl had been clinically fairly crude and inexperienced as an analyst in the mid-1920s.) Freud himself sought
understanding, and in particular needed to have his own concepts comprehended. Brunswick was able to develop and adapt
Freud's ideas further than he himself could go.

Jokl specifically mentioned Karen Horney, who was another prominent woman in the movement around the time Jokl
entered it, but he never compared his own critique of Freud
with hers. Horney was originally "very Freudian." It was not
then recognized that she would in the end "go her own way,"
and develop an independent school of her own in New York
City. (Recently an International Karen Horney Society has been
founded; oddly enough orthodox analysts today are apt to cite
Horney approvingly, whereas her old ally Erich Fromm remains
on the list of unmentionable psychoanalytic classics [Roazen
1995a].) To Jokl, Horney was personally "very Bohemian,"
whatever that might have meant. Only in 1994 did I appreciate
how prescient Jokl had been (Paris 1994). Horney was also
"somewhat in competition" with Helene Deutsch, or more so
than with other women within the movement.

Hermine von Hug-Hellmuth was still another of the early
women analysts; Jokl did not think she had ever been analyzed
herself. He knew that it was her nephew who was responsible
for killing Hug-Hellmuth (MacLean and Rappen 1991, Roazen
1975). (It became an international news story.) Another "blow"
had been that the diary she published, as the work of a young
adolescent girl, was not "original" but rather Hug-Hellmuth's
own set of ideas. Freud had done what he could to protect her;
she did not mean the book as a "falsification," but simply wrote
about her own experiences with children. The book was not bad
for its time, but she should not have said that it was an authentic

diary. (In Britain it was withdrawn from print.) Because of the scandal over the book it was going to be a long time before the other members could be "reconciled" with her. She was a "rather naive person," who had good relations with small children. But she was "too simple" in her approach, and not really psychological enough, working more according to her feelings than any sort of well-thought-through position.

Jokl also mentioned Theodor Reik among the prominent analysts of the time. Jokl had liked him in Vienna but not later in America. Jokl thought he had been writing "fantasy instead of psychology," and had become more novelistic than scientific. He had become "aggressive" even against psychoanalysis, which is how Jokl understood Reik's book, *Listening With the Third Ear*. (Reik had a lot of trouble with New York City analysts; he was first of all nonmedical, and his former intimacy with Freud aroused substantial jealousies.) In Vienna Freud had liked Reik, and Jokl considered that Reik "deserved" to be one of Freud's favorites; Rank too was especially favored, as was Federn.

I mentioned Rank's first wife, since I had met her and thought her place in the history of psychoanalysis unduly obscure. (Even though she, just as someone even more famous like Bruno Bettelheim, had had no formal training, they both became prominent in the field of child analysis [Roazen 1990b, 1992b].) I said that I thought Mrs. Rank's situation must have been "very difficult" once Otto and Freud had had their falling out. Jokl understood that Mrs. Rank had not "diverged" from the psychoanalytic viewpoint. Jokl smiled wryly about how she had been "very clever," and "never really broke" with Freud. Mrs. Rank had a "good relationship" with Anna Freud, and that proved a key source of help. In discussing Mrs. Rank, Jokl intimated that he understood her story quite well.

Jokl explained his reluctance to see people who were interested in the history of psychoanalysis. (He had made an exception in agreeing to see me. I think my being, then, a young faculty member at Harvard and my having written to him on university stationery must have helped me get my foot in the door. My academic appointment at least gave me the courage to try what I might otherwise not have attempted; I had been authoritatively warned, for example by Eissler, that people would not talk of their contact with Freud.) Jokl felt that it was unusually difficult in this field to be sure of the "facts"—so many people saw the story very differently. As Jokl reflected on it, he proposed that the contrasting impressions of various people was all that one could hope to get. He thought it a legitimate inquiry to reconstruct what those who experienced the early era felt about it.

Within the Vienna Psychoanalytic Society, scientific work and private life were not just parallel, but they embraced each other. At this point Jokl gestured with his hands interlocking to indicate how it was impossible to separate professional and personal matters. Analysis was in those days "very isolated," and he thought that that still remained true. Only slowly after World War I did the profession become more widely recognized.

I asked Jokl how he had first heard of Freud. Jokl had been studying at the Burghölzli Clinic in Zurich, at a time when Eugen Bleuler was still heading it but no longer allied with Freud. (Bleuler left psychoanalysis before the falling out between Jung and Freud; Jung had once been a prominent student at the Burghölzli. But whereas Jung had left the Burghölzli to join up with Freud, Bleuler had remained in charge.) Jokl's training had been as an internist, and he had studied at a clinic in Prague before World War I. He had not yet graduated, although he had finished his formal requirements, when he went to Bleuler in Switzerland. The head of Jokl's clinic in Prague had wanted to establish a neurological division; at that time neurology was a part of internal medicine and separate from psychiatry. Jokl was therefore sent to Bleuler on an exchange basis, and it was under Bleuler's influence that Jokl became interested in psychiatry.

In 1914 or early 1915 Jokl went back to Prague and formally graduated. Then he returned to Bleuler. Jokl was "invited" (called up) to join the army as a doctor. And Bleuler told him that when he went to Vienna he should not forget to visit Freud. In 1918 Jokl was taken a prisoner in Italy, where he met a son of Stekel's who was also an Austrian officer. Jokl knew only a little about Freud; when Jokl went to Vienna, he visited Stekel not knowing of the break between him and Freud. (It seemed to me typical that no matter how momentous the pre–World War I controversy like that between Freud and Stekel might have seemed within the charmed circle of psycho-analysis, it took years for the outside world to perceive the full scope of the breakup.)

Jokl told Stekel of a letter that Bleuler had given him for the sake of introducing Jokl to Freud. Stekel told Jokl not to delay about visiting Freud. Even as late as Stekel's emigration to London in 1938 he was still trying, without success, to get reconciled with Freud. (Stekel was, Jokl said he later found out, "a charlatan," for many of his cases were his "invention." Stekel's ideas were not so bad, but his cases were "not true," and Jokl considered him "a story-teller," a "swindler." I regret that when Stekel's widow contacted me by mail in 1969, I failed to rush to interview her, for within a matter of days she died.) Thanks to Stekel's encouragement Jokl had gone to see Freud, and that was the beginning of his relationship with him. Jokl took his psychiatric residency at the University of Vienna under Wagner-Jauregg and Otto Pötzl; although Wagner-Jauregg, as the professor of psychiatry in Vienna, remained critical of Freud, Pötzl, eventually Wagner-Jauregg's successor, became a member of the Vienna Psychoanalytic Society.

I asked whether Freud's circle was like a royal court. Jokl first questioned what that might mean, and then quietly conceded that the point was a correct one. He thought it had already been so described, perhaps it was Adler who had done so. Jokl mentioned the irreverence of his acceptance of the royalist imagery by expressing uncertainty about what sorts of emotions might be thought to underlie such a court—would it imply "respect," something more than "esteem," or even "anxiety?" Not everyone, he held, thought Freud was "half a God," although maybe some did.

Jokl insisted that "we" never failed to tell Freud if a disagreement arose. According to Jokl, it happened that Freud "gave in once," with Jokl, over the issue of female genitality. Jokl did not believe in the form of the Oedipus complex that Freud supposed took place in women. Jokl repudiated the idea that castration anxiety in men equals penis envy in women. Jokl did not believe in Freud's own original formulation of the differences between the psychologies of the sexes, and Jokl claimed that Freud later "corrected" himself. Jokl thought that the basic psychological conflict was the same in men and women, and not dependent on anatomical differences. Freud did not exactly "give in," but he changed slowly, accepting the generality of the Oedipus complex.

For Jokl this issue was a central one, and relevant to the question of the nature of creativity. A woman has a natural tendency to be creative, which a man does not, while in men there is a "competition complex," a feeling of being incomplete, which has to do with not being able to bear children. Jokl found it always difficult to talk with Freud about this matter. For he always defended "the creativity of man," not woman. And this was so even though it is impossible for a man to bear children. Men therefore have good reason for "envy"; years later Freud "adjusted," Jokl claimed, and no longer contradicted the position Jokl held.

There was nothing he could not speak to Freud about; Freud never reproached or contradicted him. Only if there was

no possibility of bringing two views together did Freud insist on
one position rather than another. But Jokl agreed that Freud
could be "very rejecting," and if one had an original idea, there
would be a need to be able to prove it. In general Jokl maintained
that there were very few quarrels in the psychoanalytic world he
knew. (The absence of conflict may have been at a terrible price,
for I think analysts were apt to be unduly intimidated, and then
when differences did occur they too quickly mushroomed into
major ideological divisions.)

Jokl's curious-seeming contention about the absence of
quarrelsomeness made me wonder whether Freud had ever
spoken of his difficulties with Adler and Jung. These early
heretics came up extremely "seldom." But the word *bitter*,
which I proposed to describe Freud's feelings about Adler and
Jung, seemed the right one to Jokl. Evidently Freud did not feel
anything like that about Bleuler, for Bleuler had "never really
left" Freud. Bleuler always respected Freud, and so did his
psychiatrist son Manfred. At the time I was interviewing Jokl he
was reading at his desk a new article by Manfred Bleuler.

It occurred to me that it might be threatening for a man to
be dependent on Freud. Jokl conceded that some were conflicted, for example Rank. Yet Freud did not like it if someone
were "too dependent." Federn might have tended that way, but
then he had some of his own ideas. Rank was the one who was,
in Jokl's experience, so "threatened." Heinz Hartmann and Paul
Schilder did not have such problems. Hartmann admired
Freud—"that was his way of being dependent." Yet Hartmann
was not so important in Vienna, for he developed his own ideas
in America. Ernst Kris may have been more prominent than
Hartmann in Vienna; Kris's concepts about art were considered
interesting and valuable in Europe but no one really understood
them. (Kardiner thought that Hartmann and Kris had formed an
alliance in America and deliberately published together partly
for political purposes; the third member of this publishing

triumvirate was Rudolf Loewenstein, but he was never considered intellectually important in the United States, while in
France—where he had been Jacques Lacan's analyst—he has
been mistakenly treated as one of the founders of ego psychology [Roazen 1991b]. Hartmann, who lived until 1970, had
become in effect the prime minister of psychoanalysis, with
Anna Freud as the reigning monarch.)

Jokl considered himself distant from Anna Freud. He
claimed never to have especially admired her. For example, Jokl
found her book *Normality and Pathology in Childhood* (1965)
"very flat." Within the world of psychoanalytic terminology
depth has always been a word of praise, while *flatness* was one
of the worst means of dismissal.

Jokl was convinced that Freud's book *Beyond the Pleasure
Principle* (1920) was "very dependent" on Freud's "condition," implying that Freud's cancer, which was diagnosed in
1923, helps explain how Freud could have proposed the existence of a death instinct. Although Jokl was clearly off-base here
historically and confused about the date of Freud's illness, he
was trying to say that there was something "personal" or
subjective about Freud's hypothesis of the existence of a death
instinct. There were always "two groups" over the question of
the death instinct, and Freud "never asked" his followers to
believe in this particular theory. Jokl thought that Freud used his
conception as a compensation for his own medical "trauma,"
and that it had been a "good" means of handling his problem.

While Edith Jackson had been unable to think about what
in Freud's theories was affected by his personality, Jokl's discussion of the death instinct led him to propose that the part of
psychoanalytic psychology that was traceable to Freud's character, and therefore not objective, was his view of women. That
was where Jokl thought that Freud was "biased." But Jokl also
said he "dared" not think what species of "unconscious homosexual idea" might have been behind Freud's concepts of

women. Jokl stood back from the way he thought Freud had of "defending men" in his theorizing. Women should not be looked on as "a second kind of human being," lower to men. In Freud's conviction man was the "dominant" figure, and the female the dependent one. To be sure, Freud had female friends. But if a woman was more than a friend and became sexually dependent on him, then Freud lost respect. Jokl thought that Freud's wife Martha "did all the work for him," while he did not do much for her. (I did not challenge how anachronistic Jokl might have been about Freud's family life, which was established in the late nineteenth century. And I had not attempted to discuss the unconscious fears people may have had of quarreling with Freud; Silberer's suicide, like that of Tausk, seemed to symbolize what could happen if one lost Freud's favor.)

I did try to inquire about Freud's sons. Jokl dismissed Martin Freud as without "deep thinking," and supposedly Freud did not like him very much. Jokl even used the word *contempt* to describe Freud's view of Martin, but then worried that perhaps that was too strong a term. Freud may have "liked" his son Oliver, but Jokl thought he was "indifferent" to his youngest son Ernst. Jokl explained Freud's attitude toward Martin on the grounds that he had not been "spiritual enough." He was not highly intelligent, and had no interest in psychological problems; Martin was "a nice" person but "superficial." (I found that all Freud's pupils, including Jokl, tended to underestimate the extent of Freud's commitment to his biological family.)

I had first heard the story in Los Angeles that, besides the closely held secret of Freud's having analyzed his daughter Anna, he might have analyzed his own sons as well. Jokl thought that Freud did try to analyze his sons. Jokl said that the "rules" of a later generation were not then "valid." Earlier even, in the famous case history of Little Hans, one cannot find a "classical" analysis. Jokl maintained that it was "only later" that Freud became aware that one should not analyze relatives, parents and children, or married couples. (Freud's treatment of Hirst and his late relationship with the Brunswicks do not support Jokl's attempt to mythify the past.) Jokl thought that Freud's son Ernst had been analyzed first by Freud and then later was treated by Alexander, and that Martin had been analyzed by Hitschmann. I have not come across any evidence yet to support such claims.

Jokl's discussion of what he thought of Freud's analyzing Ernst, which Jokl felt had not gone well, led me to tell Jokl some of the evidence I had accumulated about Freud's having analyzed Anna. What I told Jokl came as news to him, and yet it was at the same time not unexpected. He was struck with how she had explicitly denied to him having been analyzed by her father. Around 1930 he met her on a walk in the evening. Anna was "depressed"; Jokl said that he teasingly told her, "You need more analysis!" Her reply was in effect, "Oh, I have had enough of that." Jokl then openly asked her if it was with her father. She denied it, and said it was with a woman, but Anna had not said exactly who. Jokl at the time had had his suspicions that she had not been telling him the truth.

In Jokl's opinion Freud did not have much therapeutic success with Anna. It was "not normal" for her to have failed to marry and to have remained so tied to him. Jokl said he had known she was very close to Lou Andreas-Salomé, as Freud had been also. And Jokl even heard that she had also been analyzed by her close friend Dorothy Burlingham. In Jokl's view Anna remained much "too dependent" on her father. There was a paradox here, in that Jokl thought that Freud did not usually like people who had to lean on him too much; in fact, Jokl went so far as to say that Freud had "a certain contempt" for people who were too dependent on him. But this generalization did not apply to Anna, since for his work he "needed" her.

Since Jokl was someone who had come to Freud from within medicine, and was clear about the professional differences between the fields of neurology and psychiatry in Central Europe at that time, I asked if Freud had had trouble, given his own narrow training neurologically, in diagnosing psychoses. Jokl thought that "they all" had that problem, since less "was known then" about psychosis. And therefore as a "reproach" against Freud such a point (the difference between neurosis and psychosis) would "not be justified." Jokl thought that Freud could "devote" himself to patients whom he did not like as people. (Perhaps David Brunswick would fall in that category.) Jokl mentioned A. A. Brill, whom Jokl claimed Freud had analyzed, even though Freud did not "trust him," and Jokl thought Freud had been right. (Brill's papers have been embargoed, but I think that once they are released he is going to come across as an unusually attractive human being, underestimated in the role he played in forwarding Freud's cause.)

Since there had been so much professional rivalry between Brill and Jones as leaders within the international psychoanalytic movement, it was easy to move from discussing Brill to talking about Jones. I discovered there was a family relationship between Jones and Jokl—Jokl was a cousin of Jones's second wife. In Jokl's view Jones and Freud had liked one another and had been impressed by each other's respective talents. Jones "tried" to be "objective" in his biography of Freud, which Jokl considered excellent, "by far the best" study on Freud. Even though Jokl was emphasizing the mutual respect Jones and Freud had for each other, I pointedly asked why Jokl thought Jones had accused his own former analyst, Ferenczi, of having suffered a psychotic breakdown toward the end of his life, which Jones used to account for Ferenczi's falling away from Freud during the final phase of Ferenczi's life. Jokl knew that Jones was not reliable on Ferenczi's alleged mental deterioration, and maintained that Jones's motivation could be considered "vengeance" for Ferenczi's having once been Jones's analyst.

The more Jokl and I talked, the clearer he thought he was

obliged to be about distinguishing between Freud as a person and Freud as a scientist. The line between Freud's personality and his contributions to psychology was one that Jokl sought to make clear-cut, for he argued that Freud as an individual was "not so important," and that each observer necessarily could only see him "subjectively." Supposedly psychoanalysis as a science was something different, in that it could be considered neutral and independent of the perspectives we might bring to bear on it. But I wonder if Jokl was not engaging in a bit of wishful thinking here, in that the more he talked about Freud as a human being, the further he illuminated the nature of what Freud's contribution was. I do not mean to imply that anything Jokl told me about Freud's character served to discredit the independent validity of Freud's ideas, but rather that it is in principle impossible to understand what Freud amounts to apart from understanding his ideas in the context of his own most idiosyncratic characteristics, as well as his own cultural era. (Jokl was rather better on Freud's individual psychology than in exploring the peculiarities of the society Freud sprang from, which Hirst had been so explicit about.)

As an analyst in good professional standing Jokl was obliged to maintain discretion. So when I asked him whether it had been customary for the children of analysts in Vienna to be themselves analyzed in the 1920s and 1930s, Jokl said that he did not want to be indiscreet. Although it was not "customary," many of his colleagues did send their children for analyses. Freud "certainly" did not disapprove of their actions, but "in most cases" Jokl doubted if Freud would have been explicitly asked whether it was a good idea to send children into analysis.

Jokl could not be in a position to say much about how Freud had treated him as a patient, other than to indicate the reasons why Freud had thought it advisable to keep Jokl in analysis for only a short period. But the example was in itself in stark contrast to Edith Jackson's experience, or that of the Brunswicks, where one might well wonder why Freud continued seeing them. Still, I regarded Jokl as a valuable source about the Vienna Psychoanalytic Society. I inquired about how Freud felt about the Vienna group, as opposed to his followings in Berlin and Budapest, for example. Jokl seemed to me remarkably honest when he said that there "were some doubts" in Freud's mind about his Viennese disciples, as opposed to those he had attracted elsewhere.

At the same time Jokl was unwilling to concede that there was any great distance between Freud's Viennese followers and Freud himself. Jokl talked about how often they met informally at Freud's consulting room; although he said it was "every week," I know it would be more correct to say that these meetings took place about once a month. Federn was the one put in charge of choosing who would attend. On those occasions it was possible for the Viennese analysts to discuss "many things" with each other, not just psychoanalysis but politics as well. The ten to twelve people who met regularly at Freud's place were indeed "rather intimate with each other," which from historical distance would have to be judged as an understatement on Jokl's part. It would be hard to imagine people knowing more about each other's most intimate lives than these early analysts, even if they necessarily were apt to invoke psychopathological terminology more often than would be the case among the general lay population.

Since Jokl had brought up the fact that these analysts talked about political matters, I inquired what Freud's views had been about the developments in Germany during the 1930s. Freud did discuss the changes that took place in connection with the rise to power of the Nazis. He showed "some concern," although he did not believe "completely" in the reality of what was happening. Freud would hardly have been alone in being relatively unaware of the momentousness of Hitler's ascendancy. In Jokl's view, and this was at odds with how Mark

Brunswick perceived the situation, Freud had "little respect" for Dollfuss. Jokl saw Freud as "closer" in political convictions to the various socialist parties. Although I tried to find out whether Freud might have had any opinions about Roosevelt's New Deal, Jokl thought that in those days little was known about American developments in Vienna.

I explored the nature of Freud's curiously negative attitudes toward America. Jokl did not consider Freud's anti-American prejudices as preposterous as they were bound to strike someone like myself who was raised in America. I rather thought, from Jokl's slight smile as he considered Freud's reaction to America, that Jokl somewhat shared Freud's own convictions against the New World. "Free love" should not be taken as the essence of psychoanalysis, which is how Jokl thought that Freud's work was characteristically misunderstood on this side of the Atlantic. Getting a divorce, or taking a new sexual friend, was hardly the substance of what Freud had stood for. Freud "hated" the way his work was apt to be vulgarized in America, and he disdained the many possible "commercial" uses of psychoanalytic thinking within American culture.

I also talked about various of the less well-known members of the Vienna Psychoanalytic Society with Jokl, if only to enlighten myself for the sake of further interviews that I might conduct with early Viennese analysts, but I emphasized clinical issues. I asked Jokl why Freud never wrote about the problem of countertransference, although Freud had mentioned the existence of such a concept. Jokl thought that Freud had in fact talked about countertransference, in the sense that Freud had discussed how an analyst can himself be "infected" by the "dangerous material" that arises in the course of an analysis. Here is where the analogy Mark Brunswick had raised with early x-rays came in. But Freud had never explored the subject of countertransference at any length.

Ferenczi was someone who was much more apt than Freud

himself to see the relationship between the patient and the analyst as a two-way street, in that Ferenczi eventually went so far as to advocate what he called the "mutual" analysis between client and therapist. I wondered whether, in Jokl's opinion, Freud's pronounced preference for Ferenczi, which lasted until the late souring of their relationship, could be understood as one way of Freud's handling his femininity. Jokl thought this was in reality the case, and that Freud's female friends were the same "use" to him as his male followers. These women, though, did not mean anything to Freud as females; in general, Jokl repeatedly insisted, Freud was not "accepting" of women, or at least he had "difficulties" in tolerating them.

I wondered whether Jokl thought that it could be possible to connect Freud's problems over femininity with his dislike of music. But here Jokl drew the line, and said that the answer to my question had to be "no." Jokl reported that Freud had liked to quote the humorist Wilhelm Busch in saying that "music is mostly felt to be disagreeable because it is combined with noise." (At one point Freud kept some of Busch's books in his waiting room.) With the exception of Mozart's *Don Giovanni*, Freud simply did not hear music. Jokl insisted that Freud's lack of musicality was not "a defense," that he had no relation to it, and therefore never missed it. (Jokl would have taken issue with Mark Brunswick's understanding of Freud and music.) Jokl pointed out that Freud could not successfully imitate the right tune. But this in Jokl's opinion was "a defect" in Freud and not "a nervous matter." Freud's lack of interest in music was "not a neurotic inhibition." Jokl thought that one should "speculate" about Freud's personality only if the proof is available.

Once again I tried to bring to bear Freud's character on the way he conducted his clinical practice, and so I asked if Freud's problem with femininity, which Jokl made so much of, had come up in connection with his clinical cases. Jokl did think that Freud had "more difficulties" in treating women than men.

Freud "had a blindness to certain typical feminine attitudes." After Freud stopped collaborating with Josef Breuer, Freud treated more men than women while previously his studies on hysteria had been conducted on females. (Edith Jackson would have contradicted Jokl about the nature of Freud's clientele.)

Jokl agreed with me that in his clinical practice Freud had not liked dealing with addictions and alcoholism, and regarded them as "not accessible" to psychoanalysis. Jokl added that "as we now know" that is "not really" true. Freud had in practice referred more women than men to Jokl as patients. And this was because, in Jokl's opinion, it was easier for Freud to reject a woman for treatment than a man. "Even in his private relations, Freud was more shy and retiring with women than men."

And yet, I pointed out to Jokl, by the end of Freud's life he was effectively surrounded by women. Jokl smilingly agreed that there was an irony to how events had worked out. But Jokl thought that the presence of so many women around Freud in his last years could also be considered "the work" of Anna Freud. For Jokl thought she was largely responsible for the way Freud ended by having so many women around him. (Jung, who had a rather different outlook on women, also had a remarkable number of them in his final circle of disciples.)

I wondered how, if Jokl were right about Freud's attitude toward women, Ruth Brunswick could ever have become so important in Freud's world. Jokl replied that Freud had respected her for "her knowledge," and not as a woman. It was not known then that she took drugs, although Jokl had since heard that it was true. Drug-taking was, Jokl acknowledged, a particularly disastrous symptom to have from Freud's point of view.

But Jokl attributed Ruth Brunswick's problems to the same "tragical circumstances" that had surrounded Silberer. Ruth had the feeling that Freud did not like and understand her. And that "may have" had to do with her taking drugs later. When "Professor" spoke of her, he did it always with "much esteem," but she was not convinced. I proposed that Ruth's dilemma seemed rather like that of Tausk, and Jokl thought that it was true that there was "a certain similarity." Tausk, too, "felt rejected, and yet was not." In contrast Silberer was in reality repudiated; "one could see it openly." In his behavior Silberer was "a little bit feminine," and he was "a bit too dependent." Perhaps Freud did not like "too much subordination." On the other hand Jokl also knew that Freud did not like it if a student were "too independent" either. (Stekel had written to Jones in 1912: "You will learn sooner or later that from time to time Freud has to sacrifice a friend. He only has use for people who confirm. Pagodas who say Yes" [Paskauskas 1985, p. 337].)

Jokl claimed that many people around Freud succeeded in being "highly independent" and yet in good contact with their leader. Jokl mentioned Hartmann, Waelder, and even himself. (But Jokl published relatively little, and was not as widely known as the others.) Jokl never felt he was being "subordinate." But with people possessing "feminine qualities," Freud was suspicious, as he would be with females "in general." Jokl repeatedly emphasized the significance in Freud's world of conflicts having to do with dependence and independence.

This issue persisted long after Freud's own death. Jokl mentioned how someone in Los Angeles had written a psychoanalytic article on Freud, and that it had been sent on by the journal to Anna Freud. Once she disapproved of the piece they did not proceed to print it, and the author in question was "very offended." When I mentioned something similar having happened to Felix Deutsch, in connection with an essay he had written about Freud's illness, that Deutsch too had gotten in trouble that way, Jokl seemed to have known about it. (But Deutsch was not personally taken aback, and instead his wife Helene was.) Erik H. Erikson, who had published about Freud to Anna Freud's displeasure, was in Jokl's mind not as vulnerable as others, for Erikson had such "broad horizons" that he could withstand Anna's disapproval. Erikson was, according to Jokl, not trying to claim that his concept of "identity" (Roazen 1976) was a psychoanalytic one, but intended it to be social as well; therefore Erikson remained better protected than other analysts might be.

In general Jokl was substantially disaffected with Anna Freud, which I found was also true of others who had direct ties, not going through her, to her father. When I told him how Anna had selectively arranged for material to be edited out of the first published edition of Freud's letters to Wilhelm Fliess, Jokl saw it as "a falsification." When I volunteered that it was "unanalytic" so to tailor the truth, Jokl went further and maintained that she had behaved in an "anti-analytic" manner. For early analysts that term, *anti-analytic*, was the ultimate in condemnation.

I asked if Jokl had known any of Freud's famous cases. Jokl said that he had only known Little Hans when he came back to see Freud as a young man in 1922. Jokl viewed the way Little Hans had developed as "very much a triumph" for Freud. To Jokl, Little Hans was at this time "an extremely healthy personality."

I also inquired whether Jokl had ever discussed any novels with Freud. He mentioned only Wilhelm Jensen's *Gradiva*, about which Freud had written. Jokl himself did not think much of the novel, and thought that Freud had "made the meaning out of it." Jokl considered that Freud's study of *Gradiva* was "a good poem" as opposed to its being "a scientific paper."

When I asked Jokl which was his favorite book by Freud, he mentioned both *Beyond the Pleasure Principle* and *Civilization and its Discontents*, even though Jokl thought that it was because Freud was endangered by his physical condition that he became so preoccupied with the problem of death. As I have mentioned, Jokl proposed that to "compensate" for Freud's own death anxiety he began to talk about the existence of an inner psychological concept of death. As early as in *Beyond the*

Pleasure Principle, Jokl considered that Freud had "contradict-ed" himself, for he took a quality of life and made a drive out of it. Dying therefore became an instinct according to Freud's description, and this was "helpful" to Freud's own death fear. (The inevitability of aggressiveness, turned either outwardly or inwardly, was a centerpiece of Freud's argument in *Civilization and its Discontents*.)

Even though Jokl might be mistaken, as I have suggested, about his dating of Freud's cancer, I think some credence should still be given to his firm conviction that Freud possessed "a neurotic fear of death." Jokl proposed that the anxiety Freud had must have been based on "guilt feelings." The fears Freud had about death had been present in his work much earlier than his proposal of a death instinct, and could be related to his well-known anxieties about traveling. Jokl felt that unconscious guilt would lie behind any such emotions in Freud.

I tried to get Jokl to think psychoanalytically about Freud's parents, since Jokl seemed willing to try and interpret other features to Freud's neurosis. Jokl thought that Freud was "very dependent" on his mother, and that much of Freud's tendency to anxiety could be traced to his inner reliance on her. Freud's mother was "very small, nice, and dominating"; she had had a family "court" around her. Jokl's first wife had been close to her; Freud was "the apple" of his mother's "eye." Jokl saw her as domineering; when I asked if she had behaved something like Freud himself toward the circle around him, Jokl replied "yes," although he had not made the connection before. She was treated by those in the family "almost the way he was in his own circle." In spite of Freud's lack of time, he visited her "almost every day." As I expressed some skepticism about the frequency of Freud's seeing her, since nothing I had ever heard could substantiate it, Jokl reverted to insisting that Freud had been occupied with his mother's health "all the time."

As Jokl viewed Freud, he was both "very dependent" on his mother and had "a rather exaggerated respect" for his father, who was "a somewhat primitive person." The regressive elements here can be linked, Jokl maintained, to Freud's inclinations to anxiety. This would be the core of Freud's own "oedipal conflict." The identification of women in general with his mother put them in the category of the "forbidden," and therefore led Freud to distance himself from them. Freud's conviction that women were "inferior" could be understood, in Jokl's way of thinking, as his defensiveness, explaining why Freud was "shy."

While Freud, like his own mother, was domineering in his professional circle, at home he was rather neglecting as a man. Jokl repeated that Freud's wife did "all" for him, while he had "little" contact with her. He had more to do with his wife's sister Minna. I asked whether Jokl thought there was a "split" in Freud's love life, in that it looked like he separated off a sexual object of affection, his wife, from someone like Minna, with whom he was on close human terms. Jokl cautiously said that he remained "unsure" about such a "split," which Freud wrote about psychoanalytically. Minna was "helpful" to Freud's work, as his daughter Anna later was. His wife Martha could not take that part, for she was "too simple."

Although Jokl had such a short analysis with Freud, it retained a decisive impact on his career; Jokl's experience does indicate that even at such a relatively late stage of his practice Freud thought it worthwhile to see a patient so briefly. For an orthodox analyst Jokl was relatively disaffected, and therefore reasonably open-minded, about what Freud had been like. Perhaps Jokl's geographical distance from Europe helped to account for how free-thinking he could be; compared with how sectarian others of his generation were, Jokl seemed remarkably independent in his views.

6

Cultism: Kata Levy

Budapest may have once been only a short trip from old Vienna, but interviewing Kata Levy, an analyst originally from Hungary, brought up a series of names and associations that did not arise in my speaking with Jokl, or any other of Freud's non-Hungarian patients. I interviewed her in the summer of 1965 in London, England, where she had emigrated in 1954. She lived near Anna Freud's house, which was at 20 Maresfield Gardens in Hampstead; Anna had in fact installed some steps at the rear of Levy's garden, so that Levy could walk through Anna's backyard in order more easily to get to meetings at the clinic for children that Anna then ran.

One of Levy's first gentle questions to me was how I had managed to find her. The answer was simple: there had been a letter to her and her late husband that had been published in a general collection of Freud's letters edited by Freud's son Ernst, and the editorial description of Levy as a psychoanalyst in London was all the identification I needed. Levy remembered the particular letter of Freud's, which she called "very touching," and therefore understood how I had managed to track her down.

I thought Kata Levy was a lovely, charming old lady, but I was surprised to find her described in print recently as having once been "beautiful" (Appignanesi and Forrester 1992, p. 380), since in 1909 Ferenczi referred to her in a letter to Freud as "a very rich, ugly girl" (Brabant et al. 1993, p. 111). She lived until 1969, when she finally passed away at the age of 86. My seeing her involved a set of entirely different considerations from any of the interviews I have recounted so far. It was not just Levy's physical proximity to "Miss Freud," as Anna was then known, that created a special problem. It was in truth intimidating to try to be independent and free-thinking without being tactlessly offensive. I did not get to see Jokl until almost six months later, by which time I was more emancipated about what I felt able to ask. My timing was fortunate, because while Jokl could be critical about some of Freud's key concepts, and held himself at a considerable distance from Anna personally, Levy was then living at the center of what can best be described as a cult. Anna had already invited me to attend weekly sessions at her clinic during one summer I was staying in London. I saw Levy in attendance at those meetings, and she seemed completely enmeshed in the world around Freud's youngest daughter. (When Lord Acton said, "Power tends to corrupt, and absolute power corrupts absolutely," psychoanalysis could translate that maxim into the seductions of being infantilized. The Chicago analyst Heinz Kohut was strikingly absorbed by the intricacies of Anna's doings as late as into the 1970s [Cocks 1994].)

The rooms of Levy's house that I saw seemed filled with

Freud momentos. She had a collection of Freud photographs and more than one bust of the founder of psychoanalysis; she had also managed to leave Budapest with a number of books connected with the early history of psychoanalysis in Hungary. But entirely aside from these physical signs of her involvement with the beginnings of Freud's movement, I could not fail to note the extent to which Levy remained emotionally caught up in Freud's own feelings. At one point, for example, when I asked about Freud's grief over the 1923 death of one of his grandsons, which came up in that published letter to Levy and her husband, her eyes had tears in them as she thought back on what had once tragically happened. And in terms of her own writings, copies of which she gave me, I had to take notice of how Anna Freud had written a short introduction to one of Levy's pieces, just as her father before her had given his own favorites prefaces to endorse their works (Levy 1960; cf. Levy 1949).

Her husband Lajos Levy (1875–1961) had been an internist who was exceptionally well read in European medical literature. That is how he had happened to come across Freud's name in the first place. He became head of a well-known Jewish hospital in Budapest. Lajos had, according to Kata, never been analyzed. This piece of information flies in the face of innumerable occasions in which it has subsequently been stated in the literature that Lajos Levy was analyzed by Ferenczi (Molnar 1992, Young-Bruehl 1988). This myth may have arisen because Lajos was Hungarian, and Ferenczi was the most important analyst in Budapest. (It is likely that Lajos Levy on occasion consulted Ferenczi about his problems, but Ferenczi regarded him as a "friend.")

Kata thought her husband had been the one responsible for introducing Ferenczi to psychoanalysis. She held that Lajos Levy had first given Ferenczi a copy of Freud's *The Interpretation of Dreams*. Lajos was verifiably one of the five founding members of the Hungarian Psychoanalytic Society in 1913. Lajos had also originally sent Melanie Klein to Ferenczi, when Lajos decided her medical complaints were neurotic.

But it would be anachronistic to think, as one scholar has recently written, that Lajos Levy was ever a "psychoanalyst" (Gay 1988, p. 392). Historians ought not to suppose that membership in an early psychoanalytic society automatically meant that someone was a practicing analyst. While being such a member nowadays would make that true, at the beginning of Freud's movement it was a different story; such nonpracticing members were thought to give weight to the fragile group of pioneering analysts. Lajos's picture did appear in a famous book of caricatures connected with a psychoanalytic congress in 1924. But Kata was definite that Lajos had "never" practiced psychoanalysis. An exceptionally knowledgeable old Hungarian analyst, Sandor Rado, spoke to me of Lajos as an "internist," which is how Kata (and Lajos's official obituary) described him.

Lajos Levy was reported to have mattered to Freud because he was unusually brilliant. He was said by Michael Balint, a Hungarian analyst then living in London, to have had a "really superior mind," and to have written "wonderful" articles for a medical journal. Lajos was evidently good for patients who needed a certain kind of reassurance. Although for understanding a case he could not have been better, Balint thought he would have made a "terrible" therapist. Freud relied on Lajos, among others, for medical advice, and Lajos also became Ferenczi's physician. Balint suspected that Lajos had to be held responsible as Jones's source for the malicious story about Ferenczi's final days, but Lajos sent letters to people denying that there had been any truth to Jones's account. (Kata Levy read only volume one of Jones's biography, and then selected parts of the rest; she regarded Martin Freud's book as the best one on "Professor," and when it came out she sent it to others as a gift.)

It would have been impossible for Ferenczi's name not to loom extraordinarily large in discussions with anybody associated with the beginnings of psychoanalysis in Hungary. Ferenczi remained, right up until his death in 1933, the predominant figure in Hungarian psychoanalysis; he was recently honored by a society founded in Budapest in his name. But he is probably most notable for the way defenders of orthodoxy stigmatize any approach they disapprove of by identifying it with the sort of work Ferenczi represented (e.g., Malcolm 1992). Only since 1992 has the full correspondence between Freud and Ferenczi begun to be published, and the final text, which will come to three large volumes, will demonstrate the full intimacy of the friendship between the two men; Freud was remarkably relaxed as he confided in Ferenczi by letter, often several times a week over the course of many years.

Kata Levy accepted the proposition that toward the end of Ferenczi's life he "started to go like Rank and Jung," moving, she thought, "away from" what she tactfully called Ferenczi's true "convictions." The most well-known dissidents in the history of psychoanalysis have established a revolutionary tradition, which acted as a lure for anybody who might start to disagree with Freud. Freud's pre–World War I denunciation of Adler had had the result, besides driving Adler out of Freud's movement, of turning Adler into a celebrity, and Freud regretted how he had contributed to giving Adler's views publicity. (Heresy-hunting inevitably results in creating martyrs.) The tradition of looking for traitors in psychoanalysis has meant that it has taken over sixty years since Ferenczi's death for some of his ideas to receive the objective assessment they merit. Until now it has been too easy for people to brush Ferenczi off as another psychoanalytic malcontent. And thanks to Jones's version of Ferenczi's death, Ferenczi has been thought by some prominent authorities to have died mentally ill (Roazen 1975).

Kata Levy knew enough to realize that toward the end of Ferenczi's life he had not been well. But she thought he was suffering from pernicious anemia, although she reminded me that she was not a doctor. When I reported to her that Freud had written, in his obituary of Ferenczi, that he had contracted pernicious anemia, that instantly settled the matter for her, and she thought that there was no further need to "speculate" about it. For Levy, Freud was—to put it mildly—a souce of unchallengeable reliability. I wonder now what she would have said had she known that Freud had written privately to Jones referring to Ferenczi's "paranoia," and proposing that "the slow process of destruction . . . expressed itself organically in pernicious anemia. . . ." Freud said he wanted Ferenczi's "sad end" to be kept a "secret" (Paskauskas 1993, p. 721).

Ferenczi was, in Levy's words, a "very kind" and "very sentimental" man. He had been in love for many years with an older married woman with two daughters who was herself overly "soft" and "too sentimental." Both she and Ferenczi were "the same way." The Freud–Ferenczi correspondence, when it is finally complete, will contain all the details of the long romance between Ferenczi and his future wife; eventually she divorced her husband, and according to Levy he killed himself when she remarried. After the First World War Ferenczi briefly became the first professor of psychoanalysis. There were two postwar Hungarian revolutions, one bourgeois and the second Communist; it was during the first upheaval that Ferenczi was appointed to his position, but it took effect only during the brief period when the Communists were in power and pro-psychoanalysis. Levy thought it "astonishing" that afterward Ferenczi was not killed, or that he did not need to emigrate; there were, however, some permanent professional problems that he faced within Hungary.

Levy knew that at the time I was seeing her Ferenczi's reputation was still under a cloud, attributed largely to Jones's slanted account of the difficulties between Freud and Ferenczi. In Jones's published account, these difficulties arose because toward the end of his life Ferenczi had been mentally unstable if not psychotic. (I had learned that Ferenczi had also been in love with one of his future wife's daughters, and that she had gone to Freud for an analysis; Jones's knowledge of this complication was inside information that, I believe, restricted Balint's ability to defend Ferenczi publicly.) When I asked Levy why Jones had done what he did to Ferenczi, her immediate response had to do with "brother jealousy," which referred to Jones's envy of Ferenczi's special position with Freud. But she also thought that Jones's jealousy may have extended to Freud himself.

Like so many others who had known Jones, Levy said she had not liked him. She and her husband had visited Jones once in the country while he was writing his biography of Freud. And then, when the celebration for the centenary of Freud's birth was held, at which a plaque was unveiled at 20 Maresfield Gardens, the house in which Freud had died, there was a gathering in the garden and Jones sat down to have a long chat with Lajos Levy. She knew that "Professor" had thought well of Jones, and that Anna could not "forget" how Jones had made it possible for the Freud family to come safely to England. But Kata Levy felt standoffish toward Jones, who even if he had been more likable as a person would still have aroused resentment among those who relied on their personal memories (rather than his books) for knowledge about Freud. With the mass of primary documents Jones had at his disposal it was all the easier for him to dismiss the reminiscences of others as less than fully reliable. And Jones, for example, brushed aside the idea that Lajos Levy had first given Ferenczi *The Interpretation of Dreams*.

Kata Levy had legitimate reasons for thinking that she had solid grounds for trusting her own personal understanding of Freud. Her brother Anton von Freund, who was known as Toni, had a sarcoma and was very worried about a recurrence of the malignancy. In addition, he had what Kata described as "some difficulties." (Others told me that Toni, who already had children from two marriages, was newly involved with a woman, an analyst not his wife.) Lajos suggested that Toni go to Freud, and in 1916 he first did so. Freud had promised Kata's brother that if the cancer did in fact recur, Freud would tell him the truth.

Kata's father had owned a large brewery, but Toni was only "half" involved in it. He compromised by becoming a chemist and getting a doctorate in philosophy. When it so happened that Toni made a lot of money on beer, at first he had not wanted to take it; then people said to him "why not" accept the money and do with it what he wanted. Toni was following the model of the Copenhagen brewery, where he had studied, about what could be done with profits earned from that sort of business. Toni used the money to found the international psychoanalytic press in Vienna, and also to create a psychoanalytic clinic in Budapest. He was also selected the Secretary of the International Psychoanalytic Association.

At the time of the Budapest Congress of Psychoanalysis in September 1918, Freud stayed with Kata's family in Hungary. The reception from the city of Budapest amounted to a turning point in the history of psychoanalysis. (Kata recalled Simmel in his military uniform, and Tausk too; Tausk took sick and vomited—"it created quite a stir.") At the time Toni was in analysis with Freud; he told Freud that he knew it would not be proper for Freud to stay in a patient's house, so he moved away, while Kata and Lajos remained. The whole Freud family had been invited, but only Anna and the "Professor" came. That was when Kata's friendship with Anna started.

According to how Kata Levy later remembered it, in the beginning she had been a model for Anna. Kata wrote her:

> From the start I was much older. I was "dear old Kata," and you asked once in a postscript whether you were to me a daughter or a sister. For a while you were only concerned with being grown-up, something that I—appar-

ently—already was. Then for a time we were like sisters, with all the accompanying jealousy. I was a "straight little oak" tree and . . . you seem to have felt at that time like the rich girl who, on account of her money, fears to be loved or, more precisely, to get married. You seem to have felt, for example, that my interest in you was really an interest in your father. . . . But then you started to march forward in seven-mile-a-step magical boots; you were in the Society, you worked for the publishing house, you became grown-up, learned a great deal of scientific thinking (from Lou Andreas-Salomé, too). During our summer visits, then, I always had the feeling that I was superfluous. And we didn't notice it at all when it came: you became the *older* sister. Via detours through social work and sculpting, I finally did find my profession in psychoanalysis; and I had a great deal to learn about it from you. [Young-Bruehl 1988, p. 195]

Since I met Levy when she was in such a dependent relationship to Anna Freud, it was a bit hard to imagine how she had ever been a "quasi-maternal companion" (Young-Bruehl 1988, p. 79) for Anna.

At the start of the relationship between Levy and Anna on the occasion of the Budapest Congress in 1918, Freud probably arrived in July, and Levy remembered that he was correcting some manuscript proofs there. The house itself was located in a district of factories; all the breweries were located in one section of town. A horse and carriage was placed at Freud's disposal. Food was then scarce in Vienna, as the war was coming to a close, but there were lots of fresh fruits and vegetables available from the Levy's garden in Budapest, and Anna with Kata spent some time putting up preserves.

Freud's wife also briefly came to the Budapest Congress; at

one point they stayed in the bungalow of Kata's sister. I asked whether Freud's wife had let him use analysis on the upbringing of their six children. Kata paused a long time before answering, and then responded, "Mainly the younger ones." But she said she did not want to speak about it.

In another context, however, I may have learned something of what Levy had had in mind, for she told me that Freud spent a month with them that summer in Budapest. She recalled Freud's interest in wild strawberries and mushroom-hunting. Freud had suggested sometime then that Levy might want to start an analysis with him. (After all, she told me, she was Toni's "favorite" sister.) She said that she had replied to Freud, "Surely, Professor, you are on vacation," and would not want to have patients, a response that seemed to me entirely in keeping with Levy's modesty. But Freud had in fact wanted Levy to be in analysis. For he said that he was starting to analyze Anna then, and he would like to have more than one patient to analyze. Anna herself had to leave Hungary before the Professor, since she was teaching school in those days. Levy remembered that two of Freud's sons, Ernst and Martin, had visited him in the Tatra Mountains toward the end of World War I; the war games of children made Martin turn pale, since a pretended ambush was too close to reality for him.

But it was in the course of Levy's thinking back about what the circumstances of her starting an analysis with Freud had been like that I first concretely learned, in a way which it was impossible to challenge, how Freud had in reality analyzed his own daughter Anna. I still cannot be certain whether this was part of what Levy had meant when she said that Freud's wife had allowed him to use analysis mainly on the younger of their children. Levy did not seem to think she had let the cat out of the bag by talking about Anna having been analyzed by Freud, although there was as yet no hint of it in the literature, and it came as startling when I finally published it (Roazen 1993a).

Then later Levy had gone to Vienna in the last months of Toni's life; he died on January 20, 1920. First he had been staying in a boardinghouse, and then later went into a sanatorium; Professor visited him there every day, "sacrificing his afternoon nap in order to do so." Lajos Levy had told Toni that he could get deeper x-rays in Vienna than at that time in Budapest. Others remarked to me on how exceptionally charming Toni had been, and the way everyone liked him. Kata herself had sailed down the Danube to see him, since that was the best way then to reach Vienna. Freud "of course" went to the funeral, and also wrote an obituary, which curiously disguised the exact nature of Toni's father's "industrial undertaking" (Freud 1920, pp. 267–268). And Kata never hinted to me at the existence of any scandal after Toni's death; he had left money to his Gentile mistress, Dr. Margit Dubovitz, which the family thought they had to try and fight.

Then suddenly Freud's middle daughter, Sophie, was snatched away by influenza. When Kata Levy went to see the Professor, she was "very disturbed" over Toni's death. As she put it, Professor was a father to him really. On that occasion Freud had said to her: "I don't know whom I am mourning now for, Toni or our Sophie." Supposedly there was only "one day" (actually five) between the two deaths. Freud subsequently wanted to have Martin Freud's son named after Toni, but Freud's daughter-in-law would not budge, so the grandchild got Anton for his middle name; the Kris son was also named for Anton. It was after Toni's death that Kata arranged for her analysis to continue with Freud a few months later. She told me that there were "interruptions" in her seeing Freud for treatment.

Kata's family had once been immensely rich, and her brother was one of the most notable early benefactors of Freud's movement. It had been Toni's idea to have psychoanalytic training institutes, with clinics attached to them to make treatment more accessible to the public. And he gave the equivalent of what was then worth over $300,000 to set up such an institution in Budapest; just after Toni died, the Berlin Psycho-analytic Institute opened its doors. Toni had also handed over "a relatively smaller sum" to Freud for "the foundation of an international psychoanalytic publishing house" (Freud 1920, p. 268). Because of the changed political conditions in Budapest, only the press came into existence in Vienna.

When I knew Kata Levy she was living in modest, middle-class-London circumstances, but she made it clear that her family as a whole had been impoverished by the coming to power of the Communists after World War II. The Communists rendered them "paupers," "robbers" made them "beggars." It would be in keeping with Anna Freud's loyalty to Levy as a member of a family who had early on backed the cause of psychoanalysis for Anna to do as much as she clearly did to help Levy when her financial circumstances were so different. It also turned out that Freud himself had analyzed Levy without charge, even though this was a practice that he argued against in his written recommendations for other analysts. (I found out that Levy's analysis was free only at the end of our interviews, when she asked me for a written record of what she had told me. I took that occasion to ask her about Freud's fee, and she wrote in my notes that there had been none, along with some minor corrections to the text I had constructed.)

Levy recalled that while she was in analysis with Freud, Ludwig Jekels, a Pole she thought of as an exceptionally nice man, had something critical to say of Freud in her presence. Jekels knew she was in analysis with Freud, and gave her permission to repeat what Jekels had said. Freud laughed when he heard what Jekels had done. Jekels was so kind that he made it easy for Levy by relieving her of the conflict he had put her in by speaking so openly about Freud in her presence.

Levy had played cards with Freud during the summer in

the Tatra Mountains. She thought she had "an anti-talent" for card-playing, and supposed he could not have enjoyed the games with her. I failed completely to draw Levy out about what sort of cardplayer Freud was; he seems to have relaxed by playing cards. It was in 1917, in the Tatra Mountains, that Kata had turned to Freud "very early" for advice about the bringing up of her son. There was a conflict in her mind between "educating" a child and "analysis." Lajos Levy was reported by Balint to have been "an unhappy man" because of Kata. She told me only that she thought that there ought to be grounds for occasions to say "no" to a child, but her husband wanted just to say "yes." As Kata phrased it to me, there is a necessity for supportive controls; if you do not help a child to internalize the standards that set limits, he will develop great anxiety about his own drives. Supposedly Freud was in agreement with the point of view she put forward.

Kata acknowledged that she and Lajos were having trouble with their young son. It must have been another source of tension in the marriage that it was Kata who had the money. One has to wonder, when she wrote Anna about the feelings of "the rich girl who, on account of her money, fears to be loved or, more precisely, to get married," whether Kata was not providing a grounds for her own identification with Anna's position. Kata's immense wealth had to play a part in her relationship with Freud; critics of his within the psychoanalytic movement (including Mark Brunswick) held that he had an excessive admiration for money, not for its own sake but for what it could do in promoting Freud's cause.

Kata thought that Lajos had spoiled their son too much, yet they did not want to send him away to a boarding school. Kata went to Anna Freud for advice, and she recommended that he be sent to August Aichhorn. Aichhorn, although not solving the problem, hit it off so well with the boy that the boy went to live with the Aichhorns, becoming the third child in the Aichhorn family. In effect, then, the Levys' problem was resolved by having the son live away from home. Aichhorn encouraged the boy to be a sculptor, instead of a doctor. Vilmos, the boy, was later known as Peter Lambda and he became a resident of England in 1938. At the end of Freud's life, when Kata spoke of him as being "retired" (perhaps this was after he stopped seeing patients), he allowed Peter to sculpt a remarkable bust. Freud had always liked the boy, ever since he appreciated his natural-ness as a small child in the Tatra Mountains, and honored him in 1939 by sitting for the bust.

Kata's sister-in-law Rozsi, Toni's second wife, was living in the 1960s with Kata in London. Rozsi had also been analyzed by Freud. After Toni's death she "broke down," and it had to be decided what to do with her. She had two children with him, and he had one child from his previous marriage. Even though Kata served me supper one night, when there were some clinical home movies to watch at Anna Freud's clinic, I could not get to meet Rozsi. It was a mild source of frustration to me that Kata would not allow me to interview Rozsi.

At one point, when I was asking Levy about the names of some writers that Freud may have mentioned during her analy-sis, she could not think of a Swiss short-story author, and she went out to ask her sister-in-law's help. The name turned out to be that of Conrad Ferdinand Meyer, who was someone Freud had liked very much as an writer. Levy read Meyer's stories knowing that Freud appreciated them.

I had asked Levy whether she remembered Freud's having mentioned any novelists or philosophers. She recalled that she had been reading Dostoyevski's *The Brothers Karamazov* during some portion of her analysis. Freud asked her, "Did you notice anything?" meaning he was looking for any resemblances to himself she might have found in the novel. It would be like Freud to try to extract elements of transference feelings. Levy thought that the old monk, who was more clever than all the others in the book, reminded her of Freud. (Father Zossima was also Ludwig Wittgenstein's "ideal of psychological insight" [Monk 1990, p. 549].) Freud was quick to spot the possibilities of her ambivalence, and he teased her that after the priest died he was "the one who stinks!" It was a little joke between Freud and Levy; she might not see Freud negatively yet, but perhaps later on she would. He had maintained that Dostoyevski was a master novelist, and that the book itself was the most beautiful in all world literature. (Levy also remarked on how much Freud had liked to be entertained by the *diseuse* Yvette Guilbert, although one might expect a woman's singing to irritate him.)

During her analysis Freud had once lent Levy a book about archeological excavations in Crete, referring to the Minoan culture that formed a deeper layer under Greek history. Levy knew that in one of Freud's later writings he referred to how Minoan civilization was like a more fundamental level of the mind. (It was in Freud's 1931 essay, "Female Sexuality," that he wrote: "Our insight into this early, pre-Oedipus, phase in girls comes to us as a surprise, like the discovery, in another field, of the Minoan–Mycenean civilization behind the civilization of Greece" [p. 226]. In 1908 Ferenczi had mentioned in a letter to Freud Gerhart Hauptmann's description of his travel to Greece, and "the layers over the Mycenaean" culture [Brabant et al. 1993, p. 9].) When Freud had loaned her the book, he looked at her as if to say, "Every book is so precious." She had reassured him about her commitment to returning it to him.

Book lending was clearly not part of ordinary orthodox psychoanalytic technique,[1] but Levy was aware that Freud had

---

1. Although in later years New York analysts might refuse the gift of a book from a patient, on grounds of the neutrality befitting an analyst, Theodor Reik once met Freud in the street in Vienna, and he said: "What a nuisance this is. A patient gave me a book and now I have to look for a book to give him." In

been exempt from "strict rules." By 1910 Ferenczi wrote Freud
that Ferenczi had discerned Freud's "newest principle . . . that
technique has to direct itself according to the uniqueness of each
case. . . ." (Brabant et al. 1993, p. 163), but then one has to
wonder, if that were really so, what Freud's vaunted technique
could really add up to. In Levy's treatment with Freud she
encountered some of his other "allowances." She was under
great pressure at the time. He said that he had to be strict, in that
she did not have an endless amount of time like the Americans
did. She claimed that he had not meant this comment to be a
denigration of those in his practice from America. But she was
aware of my own nationality as an American, and once she
found out that my father's family were Russian Jews, she
graciously talked about Yehudi Menuhin, and how cultured
Russian Jews could be. Although I appreciated her tact I did
discount her version of Freud's feelings about America. He had
been trying to tell her that she had to bear special problems,
unlike the Americans, since they might have years in analysis,
but that was impossible for her, since she had to get back to her
family.

Levy was in Vienna long enough to get acquainted with the
American patients who were with Freud "at that time." She
specifically mentioned Edith Jackson, and quoted Freud as
having said that such "Americans can have the luxury of staying
five years," while Levy could come only for half a year, and then
later for another half a year. In all probability I think Levy was
richer than Edith Jackson, at least when Freud first met her, and
it may have been just that Budapest was closer to Vienna than
the United States that made it possible for Levy to go back and
forth. This is what she meant when she had said that her analysis

---

other words, you could accept a small gift, and thank the patient
and also get his associations as well (Freeman 1971).

had "interruptions," for it stretched over a period of some years.

Nonetheless Levy was permitted to be at the formal psychoanalytic meetings, and later she took part in all the possible seminars at the Training Institute. I had asked her if she talked about the analysis with other patients of Freud's, as Edith Jackson had for instance, but she said no, that Freud had known who would not "abuse" the analytic setting in which he was seeing her. He had specified that when she was in analytic treatment with him, she would have to sacrifice contact with the Freud family for that period of time.

I inquired about Freud's attitude toward women, but Levy took mild umbrage at this question. Later on, when I was seeing Jokl, it was he who arranged to spend so much of the interviewing time referring to the matter. But I think Levy misunderstood my meaning, for she replied to my probing as if I were implying some possible sexual hanky-panky on Freud's part. "No one," she said of Freud's relationship with women, "queried Freud, and there was no reason to query it." She was thinking about Freud's habit of spending vacation time with his sister-in-law. Freud, she claimed, liked the high mountains, but the heights "disturbed" Frau Professor. So he went instead with her sister Minna, who was, Levy thought, not as "soft" as Freud's wife. Levy made it plain that when she knew Freud he was "a very respectable old gentleman." Freud had liked "tidiness," and there was nobody "Bohemian" in the immediate family.

In 1965 Levy was still going with others in a tiny group, on several occasions during the year, to visit the crematorium where Freud's ashes were deposited. They went, for example, on Freud's birthday (May 6), and on the anniversary of his death (September 23). Levy would go along with the Viennese analyst Willi Hoffer, Dorothy Burlingham, Anna's housekeeper Paula

Fichtl, Freud's grandson Ernst, and of course Anna Freud. Lajos's remains were in the Freud family place, and Mrs. Hoffer's ashes were around the corner. So a visit to the crematorium for Freud was simultaneously a family matter for the others as well.

Under the Communists in Hungary Levy had been able to practice analysis, but she could not advertise the fact. After World War I Freud had commented to her that the Communists were as bad as the Fascists. The Nazis were in Vienna long before they took over in Budapest; Levy did not encounter anti-Semitism until World War I, but it had been different in Vienna. After the Second World War, some old patients came back, and she got some new ones, too. She had first officially joined the Hungarian Psychoanalytic Society in 1928; we spent a good deal of time poring over the old membership lists of the society, as I hoped to stimulate her memories about what the group had been like. Professionally Levy had qualified as a teacher of defective children, and pedagogy remained the special area of her central interest. From 1935 to 1936 she was a counselor of education in a girl's school.

Most members of the old Hungarian Psychoanalytic Society had been Jews; there were a handful of Gentiles, one of whom became president when the organization could not be headed by a Jew. The Hungarian Nazis dissolved the psychoanalytic group, and during that time physicians in Hungary turned away from psychoanalysis. When Levy was first a member of the society about twenty people attended meetings. Within the society there had been two sides over the issue of "female castration anxiety." At first I had not realized that Levy was referring to the hypothesis of Freud's about penis envy, but she explained that she had taken "the Freudian" position while others (and not only women) took the opposing side. (Jokl in Vienna evidently was in the opposing group on this matter.)

A speaker in Budapest had once referred to the existence of Mrs. Levy's "group," and that of Wilma Kovacs, who had been analyzed by Ferenczi and was the mother of Alice Balint, Michael's first wife. Kovacs, like Levy, was not a physician; she was an "ethnologist." Levy thought that in retrospect there was some sense in thinking of there being two such groups within the society, although at the time it was first proposed she had repudiated the idea. She thought of herself as having been part of a group of lay analysts, mostly women, who loyally "kept" to analysis—and mostly they were child analysts.

I could not resist asking what Freud had thought of Hungarians. "Not badly" was her very rapid response; the immediacy of her reaction, as opposed to how she otherwise hesitated to answer some of my questions, led me to think that she may have had some inner doubts about what Freud truly thought of Hungary. (I knew that he was patronizing about Italians.) The main difference between psychoanalysis in Hungary and in Austria was that in Budapest there was "no Professor." The Hungarian society was altogether "smaller," and in Vienna they had more gifted people like Hartmann and Kris. Although the "second generation" like Nunberg had already been analyzed, there was also an older set in Vienna that had not been analyzed, and this group included Federn, Jekels, and Sadger. In Budapest, Ferenczi himself represented the pioneering generation.

In Vienna Levy once had made some notes of a small meeting held at the Professor's place. At the time she had made them just for herself, but by 1965 Eissler already had them for the Freud Archives (Levy-Freund 1990). At the meeting she attended Paul Schilder had given a paper on "character." Marie Bonaparte was there too and was able to date the meeting; of course Anna Freud attended also.

I did not succeed in getting very far with Levy in inquiring whether there were any cultural differences in the kinds of neurotic symptoms that Hungarians displayed. It would of course not be in keeping with Freud's doctrine to want to acknowledge the significance of national character in neurosis. But Levy wanted me to understand that in Hungary psychoanalytic patients were mainly Jews. While the Hungarians have "easygoing ways," and like to drink and enjoy life, it is not, she thought, in the Jewish character to take to alcohol.

Geza Roheim figured in Levy's memories of the prominent members of the Hungarian society. He had been interested in "primitives," which is the way Freud looked on nonliterate peoples, and Roheim undertook the first psychoanalytic anthropological field work. Marie Bonaparte had made it financially possible for him to go on an expedition with his wife to the "deserts" of Australia. Roheim had, Levy said, an immense knowledge of data, but when he lectured he just "threw it out" at the audience, and the information by itself was "too much." (I thought that was the way he wrote, too.)

Roheim had something of "the tribesman" in his appearance and ways. He had once been rich, and grew up in a big villa; but that was before the changes that made such wealth "go poof." His wife was kind, charming, and very devoted to him; she was a Gentile (he was Jewish). Because he came from such a wealthy family he had "every opportunity" to study and learn, and he used it.

Levy did not know for certain who had analyzed Roheim, but suggested that Ferenczi might have done so; she was certain that Roheim had not been analyzed by Freud. It went without saying that being a patient of Freud's put one in a special category, one that Levy could not be mistaken about. (It turned out that Roheim had first been analyzed by Ferenczi, and then later by Wilma Kovacs.) Roheim first came to Professor's attention at the Budapest Congress. Levy had the impression that perhaps people, including Freud, were "a bit disappointed" with the anthropological results Roheim brought back from Australia.

Levy mentioned at length a patient she had inherited from

Roheim, when he went to Australia, which seemed to be telling about how much she could extend herself for someone. The patient was a psychotic who slept under bridges, and she remembered what a "mess" his life was in. At one point he threw all his papers into the Danube, except she later found out that he had saved his passport. She went to Edward Bibring for a "control" (supervision), since she did not consider herself trained to treat psychotics. (I did not think to challenge her about why she would turn to Bibring for such a case, since he was not a physician either.) Later the patient turned up in London for nine months, coming back to "haunt" her. She arranged for him to get compensation for pulmonary disease and psychological troubles, since he had been in a concentration camp, but he "could not let himself succeed," and later moved to another country.

Federn was a more obvious person than Bibring for Levy to have turned to for help with her patient. Federn was known as the "King of Abyssinia" because of his physical resemblance to Ethiopia's Emperor Haile Selassie. Levy, like others, singled out Federn as a "kind" man, and she volunteered that among others he had analyzed Aichhorn. Federn was "the forerunner" of ego psychology, but she found it so "difficult" to understand his ideas. It came as news to her that Freud, too, had found it hard to follow some of them (Roazen 1975). Because of her son Levy had a special interest in Aichhorn. She had watched him interview delinquents, and was "very impressed." Her son did a bust of Aichhorn, without any training, when he was just starting out as a sculptor. Aichhorn had played cards with Freud, along with some of his "pre-analytic" friends like Professor Rie. Aichhorn dressed "unlike" anybody else. Eissler was a student of his, although Levy was not sure if he was analyzed by him. (To Levy, and to others of that era as well, having an analyst went without saying, like having had parents; it was Sterba who told me he had been Eissler's analyst, but it would not have been unusual for Eissler to have had more than one.) Aichhorn was "in another circle" besides the Freuds that the Levys had to go to when they were in Vienna.

Since Melanie Klein had started out married to a bank director in Budapest, Levy had a long-standing knowledge of the development of her work. The dispute between Klein and Anna Freud had dated from the 1924 congress, when they each read papers on their respective ways of treating children. Of course Levy was a partisan on behalf of Anna Freud, so it was not surprising that she thought that the influence of Klein's ideas (which she characterized as "vivid fantasies") had prevented analysis in England from "reaching its proper level." She thought that both Jones and Abraham had been "fascinated" by Klein, and knew that they had helped smooth her way. Levy was not astonished to hear from me that Klein had analyzed some of Jones's children. Levy's place in Anna Freud's world could be indicated just by the unusual photograph of Anna that she had in the house. Evidently, like her father, Anna had not liked to have photographs done without her permission beforehand. Levy had in her study a copy of Anna Freud's latest book, but it did not have any personal inscription in it. According to Levy, Anna did not publish that much, but had to be encouraged by others to pull her ideas together.

Since Levy was so regularly at Anna Freud's clinic, and I saw them both there, I inquired whether Levy could imagine the Professor having worked in such a setting. She smiled, and seemed quietly amused by such a thought. Then she answered yes, in that Freud was in favor of analysts working with children, and had encouraged Anna to go on with it. The staff in Anna's clinic was not chosen haphazardly, and the students were "carefully selected." But still Levy smiled at the idea of Freud's being involved in some such clinic. Her mind was already prepared for dismissing the "common misconception" that Freud was hard to get along with. But I think her amusement about the thought that he could work like Anna Freud did may have stemmed from a combination of the idea that he could have had the patience required for treating young children and the unique place Freud continued to occupy in her thoughts. I have no doubt that Anna Freud, too, put Freud in a separate category. Still, it was striking to someone like Michael Balint what a great success Freud had had with a woman like Kata Levy in keeping her in a dependent relationship to him.

7

"A Fine Thing for Normal People": Dr. Irmarita Putnam

Dr. Irmarita Putnam stands out in my mind as a representative of American upper-class manners and discretion; she was elegant and controlled yet outspoken and forthright, and all her obvious good qualities, including conscientiousness, combined to make Freud enthusiastic about her. After her analysis Freud wrote approvingly of Dr. Putnam to other analysts in Boston, even if some of them remained mystified by the changes that Freud thought he had started to bring about. It would be hard to imagine a patient of Freud's giving him a higher set of evaluative appraisals as a therapist.

In contrast to Kata Levy, who was a close member of Anna Freud's entourage and a participant in what appeared like a quasi-religious sect, Dr. Putnam struck me as one of the most unusually detached and brainy of all the former patients of Freud's that I ever met. Edith Jackson had implied as much about Dr. Putnam, as she drew a contrast between what Freud would have discussed with Dr. Putnam as opposed to what he talked about with her. Although Dr. Putnam had once been a practicing analyst in Boston, by the time I had met her she was 71 years old and living in a quietly elegant New York City apartment; unlike what I saw within Levy's stuffy-looking old-fashioned rooms, Dr. Putnam had absolutely no Freud memorabilia around. She had earlier retired from her practice, not because of age but out of personal preference. I found her, as I came to believe that Freud too had thought, one of the most intelligent commentators on Freud's clinical approach.

She had once been married to Dr. Tracey Putnam, a physician who was a nephew of Freud's early Harvard supporter James Jackson Putnam. It may seem odd that psychoanalysis should have had a special appeal for New Englanders with their Puritan heritage. As a family the Putnams went back to seventeenth century Massachusetts. But straitlaced Puritans were also deeply introspective and soul-searching, and in their conception of God they had a means of enabling them to come to terms with the unknowable and the unpredictable. People could get along without the concept of the unconscious because they had religious systems to explain the same phenomena. Nineteenth century transcendentalists transformed the old Puritan convictions about the supernatural world into special feelings about the character of nature (Roazen 1968). So it may not have been surprising that Freud received such a degree of support from someone with the impeccably correct social credentials as James Jackson Putnam. Freud, who was eager to see that his movement was not confined solely to Jews, went out of his way to cultivate Putnam.

As a young woman Irmarita Putnam (known as Irma) had become "great friends" with James Jackson Putnam's daughter

Marian (or "Molly"), whom we have encountered as a close acquaintance of Edith Jackson's. Irma and Molly went through Johns Hopkins Medical School together. After their first year at Hopkins, Irma had come to Harvard Medical School for the summer of 1917, and then again in 1918. Both times Irma had lived at the big Putnam family house in Cambridge, Massachusetts. Molly's father was then working on the lectures that he later gave at the Smith School for Social Work. He did not speak about Freud to Irma, and in fact she and Molly were not particularly interested in psychoanalysis at the time. Putnam was, Irma reminded me, a good friend of William James's. Molly later started out as a pediatrician at Yale, where she helped recruit Edith Jackson, and she subsequently became a child analyst in Boston. (I found that intellectually Irma was head-and-shoulders above Molly's capacities.)

At Hopkins Irma Putnam had studied at the Phipps Clinic with Dr. Adolf Meyer, a Swiss who was then the most prominent psychiatrist in North America (Roazen in press-b) But at that point psychiatry could not have been less important to her. She wanted to learn about brain anatomy; no one had tried to make use of the great laboratory that Phipps had given to Meyer "in order to get him to Baltimore in the first place." Meyer seemed "so strikingly European"; he came into class wearing a formal morning coat. He was very famous throughout Europe,and remains probably the single most influential psychiatric teacher in twentieth century American history. It was after this contact of hers with Meyer, when she took her course in psychiatry with him, that Dr. Putnam now felt an obligation to care about the subject. Although Meyer's formality tended to put students off, it was her contact with him that had really aroused her psychiatric interest.

Dr. Putnam decided, however, not to do her internship in psychiatry. The field was then operating at purely a descriptive level. There seemed "no feasible way to help" the patient in

those days. Lawrence S. Kubie, who later became a famous
psychoanalytic psychiatrist but whom Dr. Putnam knew as a
personal friend ("Larry"), reacted the same way she did, and did
not go into psychiatry at first either. (Later he was analyzed in
England by Edward Glover. While for a time Kubie was a leader
of orthodox New York analysts, the coming of the émigré
Europeans, which he had helped orchestrate, led to his subsequently being displaced from power. In later years he became
notably independent and free-thinking in his professional
views.)

Dr. Putnam had gone to work in China from 1921 to 1923,
pursuing her interest in brain anatomy. Her husband was a
neurologist and brain surgeon. After living in China, they had
moved to Amsterdam to pursue further work on brain anatomy
in 1923 to 1924. A friend of Tracey Putnam's from Boston, Dr.
William ("Bill") Herman, was in Amsterdam then, too, and he
asked a colleague named Ariens Kappers about finding him a
psychoanalyst. Kappers selected J. H. van der Hoop, who had
been a student of Jung's before his break with Freud. Irma
Putnam started an analysis with van der Hoop then, too, and she
and Bill Herman persuaded Tracey Putnam to do it also.

Her analysis with van der Hoop lasted six or eight months.
Although in retrospect she considered that he had been "unin-
spired" as an analyst, still she thought that he had "given them
all something." None of them regretted having gone to him for
analysis, and they had the greatest respect for him. But she
would not say "now" that he had been "a great man."

Van der Hoop had mentioned that Jung would be holding
a meeting at a tent in London, so she decided to go there to see
him for herself. As it happened, she had to sit in the first row.
Jung noticed her, and asked someone who that Chinese woman
was who was sitting up front. That he should have spotted
something Chinese about her bearing or looks fitted in with his

mystique about his intuitive abilities; he was very pleased with himself over the insight, so she and he became "friends."

Although Dr. Putnam felt at home in New York City where I saw her, she had lived for years in Boston and knew all the early analysts there. In 1932 she had been a member of a three-person constitutional committee of the Boston Psychoanalytic Institute, and in 1932 to 1933 she had been the first Chair of that organization's Educational Committee when training facilities were being set up; she was therefore one of the pioneers in Boston analysis. (For years the Educational Committee remained the most important single body at the Institute.) Dr. Putnam was so conscientious and upright that before my interview with her she had gone to the trouble (which she laughed about afterward) of rereading a book on the creation of the Boston Psychoanalytic Institute that had been occasioned by the twenty-fifth anniversary of the organization in 1958 (Hendrick 1961).

When Dr. Putnam and her husband returned to Boston from Amsterdam in the 1920s, they had both worked in Dr. Harvey Cushing's famous laboratory. Then a young woman came to Dr. Putnam to be analyzed; evidently she had been to every other analyst in Boston except for Dr. Isadore H. Coriat, who was for years, Dr. Putnam thought, the one Freudian successor to James Jackson Putnam in Boston. This patient was insistent about getting analyzed, and she seemed to be "a healthy person." So for the "amusement" of both of them Dr. Putnam tried her best, although she was "of course" largely "imitating" the way she herself had been analyzed by van der Hoop. Then the young woman's husband also wanted to be analyzed; he had been to a female analyst in New York City, who was one of the two women there who had been translating Freud's works. They were both "famous" as analysts, "everyone" knew them; one of them died, bequeathing the patient on

her deathbed to the other one, who moved to Boston. But the
young man had not got along satisfactorily with her, so he went
to Dr. Putnam instead.

"It seems so ridiculous," Dr. Putnam maintained, but this
is how many people got "dragged" into becoming analysts. She
had been visiting someone, for example, who had had a baby;
and the nurse said, "Oh, you must see so-and-so, who is having
a postpartum problem." Since Dr. Putnam felt she did not know
what she was doing in the field, she decided that she must go
back to Jung for some real training. First she went to consult
with Dr. Macfie Campbell, a Scot who was then working at the
Boston Psychopathic Hospital; he had been an assistant of
Meyer's, and looked on psychoanalysis benevolently. Dr.
Putnam had gone to see Campbell in particular because of her
uncertainties about what to do with a very disturbed woman
who was having postpartum problems. He thought it a fine idea
to take the patient to Jung. All Jung said, though, was how lucky
the young woman was to have Dr. Putnam as a therapist; he
refused to make a diagnosis. In 1925 Dr. Putnam spent not quite
a year in analysis with Jung; the patient she had gone to him
about in the first place never got better and wound up institu-
tionalized at McLean Hospital in Belmont, Massachusetts.

Thinking back on her contact with both Jung and Freud,
Dr. Putnam thought that "one could not have imagined any two
people more different." She said this with great emphasis,
conviction, and animation. (It requires historical distance, I
think, to highlight how much Jung and Freud had in common;
all curative techniques have to be understood, and made rational, within the belief systems of past time. Very little is known
about Jung's own clinical practice, compared with the literature
about Freud's; the only mention in print of Irma Putnam comes
up in the course of a recent biography of a Jung patient,
Christiana Morgan [Douglas 1993].) In Dr. Putnam's considered
opinion the "big man" in the field was Freud, not Jung.

When she returned to Boston, after having been treated by Jung, she spoke with Dr. Ives Hendrick, a Boston analyst who had himself been trained in Berlin. (Although she did not know even by the time I saw her that Hendrick was epileptic, and could have seizures during analytic sessions, she thought he was "very neurotic.") Hendrick had made it clear to her that she had been missing a lot up until then. What she had read of Freud "never touched me at all," and she had not been able to imagine that it was in any way connected with herself. Hendrick pointed out what Jung had not "brought into the picture" in the course of his analyzing Dr. Putnam. Hendrick, who was a prolific writer, "never knew" how his talking with her had been convincing, but it was then she decided that she would have to go to Freud.

Kubie, "a lifelong friend" of hers as well as a classmate from medical school, suggested that before she went to Vienna she should get in touch with the Educational Committee of the New York Psychoanalytic Society, so she would be registered as an official candidate abroad before she left. Abram Kardiner, who had himself been analyzed by Freud after World War I, said then that the rumor was that Freud was "senile," and that the great center for training was now in Berlin, not Vienna. (By the time I knew Kardiner he was blaming the Berlin Psychoanalytic Institute for overdeveloping the significance of libido theory.)

I asked whether she had told Freud about Kardiner's comment, when she had had her analysis with him, which was "approximately" in 1930. She had indeed informed Freud of Kardiner's remark, and "everyone knew" of it. It became a "standing joke" in Vienna. Edith Jackson, who was Dr. Putnam's "great friend," was in analysis with Freud at the time. Dr. Jackson said she would not be staying with him if he were senile, and besides, he was the "keenest" man she had ever met. (I had found that Kardiner, an original thinker, could be exceptionally sharp-tongued, and she agreed. He was the only patient of

Freud's ever to mention the existence in Freud's office of a spittoon, which he used. To be fair to Kardiner, he not only wrote some remarkable books, but helped found the Psychoanalytic Institute at Columbia University's College of Physicians and Surgeons.)

Dr. Putnam had somehow understood that Freud did not like to take people into analysis who had once been treated by Jung. So Edith Jackson "sounded out" Freud for her. (When I asked Dr. Jackson she could not recall having performed this service.) Marie Bonaparte was leaving for Paris "the next day," and she was accustomed to going back and forth from being analyzed in Vienna. So it happened that Dr. Putnam took Marie's time with Freud. But in hindsight Dr. Putnam was not sure if Freud had cared at all about her once having been in analysis with Jung.

At this point Dr. Putnam felt she could learn about the "psychodynamics" of personality, the explanation for motivation. She felt Freud was very attentive, as if she were his "first patient." While she was in treatment with Jung, he had wanted to talk primarily about what he was interested in, and with Jung she had wondered where she herself fitted in with all his ideas. (Others confirmed how, in contrast to Freud, Jung could be clinically self-involved.) Freud was "different"; he talked about "everything under the sun"—but he "analyzed" her, "too." He got on so well with her that he once joked about himself in the third person: "Everybody tells you things, even Freud."

Freud talked about his dealings with Ferenczi. There was give and take in the analysis (unlike the account that David Brunswick provided me of his own analysis). Although the analysis itself was never lost sight of, a great deal else came into the picture. He spoke about Communism and opera, for instance. I was surprised by her mentioning Freud and opera, and pursued that point in connection with what I had learned from Mark Brunswick. She thought it was not so much the musical side of opera that interested Freud, but the revolutionary aspect of something like Mozart's *Marriage of Figaro*. Freud was interested in the symbolism of the plot of another opera she attended, also. I asked about *Meistersinger*, but Freud never talked about it with her. She thought that Wagner was not performed that season in Vienna.

I must have mentioned David Brunswick to her as well, and she had known him "very well." He got her interested in the subject of Gestalt psychology. But she did not know he was in analysis with Professor; she reminded me that there was a separate entrance and exit from Freud's consulting room. (It would be fitting that David Brunswick kept his head down about his involvement with Freud.)

In connection with the figures Dr. Putnam did encounter in Freud's world, she mentioned that Franz Alexander had been in Vienna once for a day, on his way to Boston to become a training analyst there. Freud was "very worried" that Alexander would not be cordially enough received in Boston. So she wrote many letters back home about Alexander, but she thought that none of it had been "necessary" at all. (Presumably Alexander and the local analytic community spontaneously appreciated each other.)

Thinking back over clinical matters that arose during her year in Vienna, she mentioned how Frank Fremont-Smith, who was another good friend of hers, had an epileptic patient, with an accompanying neurosis, who was looking for an analyst in Vienna. Freud got "terribly excited" at this prospect, for he feared that the public might think that psychoanalysis was trying to deal therapeutically with epilepsy. He suggested that Dr. Putnam consult with Helene Deutsch about the patient. They all "hashed it out" for a long time, although the three of them never met together. The patient finally came to Vienna. She understood that it was her neurosis, which went along with the epilepsy, that was to be treated. She was "very grateful" for

being sent to Deutsch; afterward the patient came to see Dr.
Putnam and thanked her.

Dr. Putnam thought Deutsch was "fabulous." I had already
mentioned Federn, and she replied, "You may ask about Federn,
but she [Deutsch] was tops! Oh my," she exclaimed. Deutsch
was "certainly" the highest ranking analyst in the view of the
Americans going over there. If you could not go to Freud
himself, then one tried to get her. Deutsch's seminars were held
one evening a week, and she also conducted control analyses.
Dr. Putnam remembered how remarkable it was that at public
meetings Deutsch could pick up the various "threads" of a case,
recalling all the details of the patient the analyst was reporting
about. (Deutsch retained her capacities into her eighties and
nineties, when I knew her.) Dr. Putnam said Deutsch gave
"astonishing performances."

I suggested that perhaps Deutsch had "identified" with
Freud. But Dr. Putnam disagreed and insisted that Deutsch had
remained herself. Freud had been "timid," for example, about
the epilepsy case, but Deutsch was not. She would not undertake the analysis without having heard everything he had to say
about the case, but in the end it was her decision, and she took
the case. Deutsch's husband Felix was "greatly respected," but
he was not doing much in the way of psychoanalysis itself. Yet
of course he came to all the meetings.

Dr. Putnam took for granted Freud's unorthodoxy of
technique—what Kata Levy had termed "allowances." As Dr.
Putnam understood Freud's attitude, why should she not get to
meet all the problems that are bound to arise in the course of
being an analyst? By then it was clear she was going to practice
analysis herself when she returned to Boston. It all "happened
naturally." Freud never tried to justify how he proceeded. The
analysis was not kept isolated from life, which would be a
danger associated with adhering too closely to Freud's written
recommendations. Yet the analysis was undertaken in the

"strictest" fashion; there was nothing "social" about it, and only what was relevant got introduced.

She was struck by how Freud gave her commissions to undertake when she got back to Boston; for example, he wanted to be sure that a percentage of the dues of the Boston Psychoanalytic Society went to the psychoanalytic publishing house, and for a time that was done. She was also to see families of patients, to tell them things he had not wanted to put in writing. Freud obviously had a special confidence in Dr. Putnam, for he never entrusted such missions to someone like Edith Jackson; I have to assume that Dr. Putnam was pleased by this special confidence he placed in her. And I think that Freud was satisfied with the way he could allow someone like her to surrender to him; she was worthy of being an extension of himself. Freud had the unique pride of the solitary person who is reluctant to give of himself and is passionately concerned with preserving his own liberty, and yet he could permit himself to ask people to be his emissaries (or, if one wants to introduce a harsher view of him, his servants).

Dr. Putnam knew that Freud had been disillusioned with his early analyses, which had once looked successful but had turned out not to be. He talked about having become skeptical himself, especially about the therapeutic value of psychoanalysis; such loss of faith in the efficacy of psychoanalysis on Freud's part could become a self-fulfilling prophecy. When something happened in Dr. Putnam's analysis that was "classical," he would say, "Didn't I tell you that psychoanalysis was a fine thing for normal people," and he would laugh. In private Freud could be ironical about what he had achieved. (In later years Anna Freud tended to be defensive when anyone pointed out that if a patient could fully comply with the demands of an analysis, and was healthy enough to put up with what was expected, then the individual did not need that form of treatment in the first place. Freud himself, at least with someone he

got on with as well as he did with Dr. Putnam, had little
difficulty accepting that only exceptionally healthy people were
suitable for psychoanalysis.)

Dr. Putnam herself was concerned that in accomplishing
successful therapy, an analyst has to "break into" a complex of
emotions that the analyst cannot hope fully to understand. Yet
the analyst must proceed in spite of this necessary limitation and
inherent inadequacy. She felt that such complexities were being
dealt with much better in later years, but such an optimistic
conviction on her part was not based on her having kept up with
the literature.

There was one point where clinically Jung had it "over"
Freud, at least at the time that Dr. Putnam was in contact with
them both. Freud thought that he had just to analyze a patient's
problems through rational insight, breaking conflicts apart, and
then leave the patient to resolve them on his own. But if it is a
serious case, the patient cannot do on his own what Freud
expected. (Dr. Putnam never discussed the unspoken suggestive
impact Freud could have, perhaps because it was less with her
than with others.) If a patient were badly off, then analysis
would not be enough, which is why Jung emphasized the
necessary help the analyst had to give in lending a synthesizing
hand to the patient. (In future years the trend of thought called
ego psychology [Roazen 1976] would try to incorporate,
without always acknowledging Jung, this particular insight.)

Dr. Putnam felt in the course of her own analysis that
everything was her own responsibility, and she did not resent
what Freud expected of her. Before she saw Freud it had never
occurred to her not to "project like other people," seeing in
others her own weak points. The lesson she took away from her
psychoanalysis with Freud was that you should not find faults
elsewhere, but rather be preoccupied with what you yourself
are doing. Even if the other person was in the wrong, what
counts is what you are able to do with the situation. She had the

healthy-minded conviction that "anything can be made some-what better or worse."

Dr. Putnam thought one could not use this same attitude in dealing with children. In Anna Freud's seminar on child analysis at the time, this identical approach, appropriate to adults, was taken toward children as well. But Jung in those days put the responsibility for the child's welfare on the parents. Dr. Putnam thought that Anna Freud's ideas about treating children must have changed since 1930. Even then someone was capable of pointing out, "But the child has a sadistic mother!" When Dr. Putnam was in Vienna such a point was still apt to be ignored. External reality, and not just the fantasy life of the child, has to be taken into account.

Jung's placing the responsibility for the child on the par-ents therefore put in proper perspective the role of the patient's environment. Freud's essential contribution lay elsewhere; even if someone else was at fault, Freud focused on how you are going to deal with it, not how you are going to make the other person deal with it. Freud taught that the patient should be confronted in such a way that he or she could learn how to improve a situation, whatever it was.

(As Dr. Putnam talked about children and what was appro-priate in their treatment, I did not yet know about a terrible tragedy in her life. I later learned that her only child, a daughter, had killed herself during adolescence, at the time that the Putnam marriage was coming apart. I do not know what self-reproach Dr. Putnam might have felt, or the implications of this event for the rest of what she told me.)

When she was in Vienna, supposedly "nobody" then thought of applying psychoanalysis to psychotics. When I asked about Jung, and whether his own psychiatric hospital experi-ence was not relevant to the therapy of psychoses, she said that Jung had in truth "started out" by treating psychotics, but not by psychoanalytic methods. Later, when he was leading his own

school, he took no psychotics in treatment; his patients were
mainly doctors themselves. But Jung's concept of the collective
unconscious was a way of including the environment, which
was characteristically left out in Freud's own approach, in
understanding the life of patients.

Erich Fromm had successfully stressed the significance of
environmental factors, which seemed absolutely vital to Dr.
Putnam. She was not as aware of it when she was in treatment
with Freud, for she was then so interested in pursuing the new
point of view that Freud stood for. But she thought Fromm
deserved full credit for having put the sociological emphasis "on
the map." (She had raised Fromm's name with me; I had already
recognized his genuine stature in intellectual history [Roazen
1990c]. But Fromm had been deemed such an outsider within
orthodox analysis, despised almost as much as Jung, that it was
a tribute to Dr. Putnam's independence that she so readily
acknowledged Fromm's contributions, which even today are
underrated. It was, alas, in keeping with psychoanalytic sectar-
ianism that Fromm himself took a harsh view of Jung.)

Intellectual issues, rather than personalities, dominated my
discussion with Dr. Putnam, and she could easily move from
talking about Fromm to answering questions about how the
treatment of psychosis differed from that of neurosis. Federn,
she conceded, when I raised the subject, may have been interested in the therapy of psychotics, but Freud "never, never." He
thought a great variety of things could be done with treating
neurotics. But when I pressed her on the point of just how broad
a conception of neurosis Freud had been working with, she
conceded that the word *neurosis* meant many more things then
than now. It really was a "wastebasket," and it could be too easy
to put problems in that one category. (I regret that I did not raise
the issue of what, in terms of diagnoses, it meant to be poor. For
I believe that the richer one is, the more likely a diagnosis of
neurosis, which is more hopeful, will be applied.) Recently the

term *disorder* has become fashionable, without much consideration to the implied propriety of the metaphor of stability; and thanks to psychopharmacological advances, *depression* is too loosely being invoked today.

Freud had conducted Dr. Putnam's analytic treatment in English. He had asked her which language she preferred, German or English; she had some German at school much earlier, but chose English. When I mentioned how Freud had behaved with the Brunswicks, she first said that Mark had been living in Vienna, which presumably might justify Freud's insistence on German. But I think that Freud liked working with Dr. Putnam, and that might help explain why he left the choice of language up to her. Also, she thought that by the time she saw Freud perhaps he had learned something from his earlier experience, and changed on this point. (Freud did not rap on the couch in Dr. Putnam's analysis, as he had done with Edith Jackson and some others.)

Freud's English was "elegant"; he had encompassed "all the slang." As for his pronunciation, one would have thought he had lived in England for a long time. (After World War I, as English-speaking patients were pressing for his time, Freud took some lessons; his written English remained fractured.) By the time Dr. Putnam knew him he already had so many American patients that he did not speak a particularly British form of the language. His speech like his mind "covered everything"; he never lacked for a word to express something. Yet he did not talk like he wrote; he was never as elaborate as in his writings.

Dr. Putnam was full of admiration for Freud's scope, and the extent of his insight. She was also impressed with how self-critical he could be. For example, Freud once asked her in the treatment what she thought would "last" in psychoanalysis. She thought he remained "his own best critic." At the same time, she also thought that Freud was a man of "great compassion."

When I mentioned all the notable controversies in the history of psychoanalysis, such as those with Adler, Jung, and Rank, Dr. Putnam agreed that Freud could indeed be "cruel." That aspect of him had to be acknowledged. But she thought he was not easily aroused to anger. (Jung, on the other hand, was reported by others to have been quick to explode, and easier than Freud to get over it.) But when Freud felt that unrealistic motives were instigating criticism of his work, then he could be "angry." However, if he felt that the criticism was sincere and honest, he would never be upset.

In fact, Freud once upbraided Dr. Putnam, saying, "Now look, right here you are losing your critical faculties." Supposedly, in terms of the theories Freud advanced, he was an advocate of the advantages of regression as an inevitable and desirable part of the psychotherapeutic process. In practice, at least with Dr. Putnam, he was suspicious of signs of regressive credulity. On the occasion when Freud had chided her for giving up her detachment, she thought that it was "true," and that "right at that moment" she felt for the first time she had dropped her critical approach. (She never showed any signs that I could detect of having been interested in arguing with Freud merely for the sake of arguing.)

Dr. Putnam was exceptionally intelligent, and I thought it showed good taste on Freud's part that he took her so seriously. She said that she never felt that he was bored, or not listening to her, or that he was "relaxing" during an analytic hour. (My hunch is that her capacities enlivened Freud.) He always seemed interested in her, but she qualified this by modestly saying that she did not think it was because of her personally. She had enough organizational savvy to appreciate the way in which her future role played a part in Freud's reaction to her. She was going to be able to do something for his cause when she returned to the United States, and there was also the Putnam association that mattered to Freud. As with Kata Levy and the von Freunds, and even Hirst with the Eckstein connection, Freud built his movement by maintaining the continuities of historical ties.

Freud knew of the other people in the Boston analytic community then. But he had never met Ives Hendrick and did not know any of the other early Boston analysts, so he did not express an opinion about them. The commissions Freud had asked Dr. Putnam to fulfill when she returned to the United States had nothing to do with Boston analysis, and must have concerned patients elsewhere, most likely in New York City.

Dr. Putnam had paid Freud twenty-five dollars an hour, which in those days was a great deal of money and the highest fee an analyst got at the time. In addition, Dr. Putnam later sent some financial help to Freud for the press, which was one of his main hopes for the future.

Freud was very interested in everything Dr. Putnam said about the younger people she met at psychoanalytic meetings. Grete Bibring was "outstanding," and her husband Edward was too—a "very clever fellow." Dr. Putnam had a seminar with him. She also knew both Jenny and Robert Waelder in those days, but she thought the respective positions of all these people were probably best revealed in their standing at international meetings.

When I asked who was Freud's "chief favorite" in those days, Dr. Putnam's unhesitating response was Ruth Brunswick. "It was quite obvious." She had "access" to Freud; she was essentially part of the Freud family. She had a "courageous" mind; she was free in a sense to think whatever she wanted. She was not "restricted" the way most people were. She dared to "stick her neck out"—but "not playfully." She would change her mind tomorrow, but today she could think. She had the courage to behave that way with Freud because she could trust him not to take anything she said as final. Few people brought that same "freedom" to him. Ruth recognized that he was great; yet she was not trying to identify with him or to aggrandize her own ego by being with him. It was "pure pleasure on both sides." (Dr. Putnam was making essentially the same point as David Brunswick had, but she offered a different slant to it.) It was not that Ruth lacked pride in the relationship she had with Freud, but that did not constitute the point of it. Dr. Putnam said she had been "good friends" with Ruth, and felt very congenial with her, but she never went to any of Ruth's seminars in Vienna. Van der Hoop was in analysis with Ruth then; when Dr. Putnam first came to Vienna, she thought she might have to go back into analysis with him, which did not give her any "pleasure." But Edith Jackson had explained to him that it would not be good for his own analysis for Dr. Putnam to come to him again. So he said fine, now we can "play" together, and they went to the opera and so on.

If Helene Deutsch and Ruth Brunswick were ever rivals, Dr. Putnam had never seen signs of it. Yet once I raised the possibility, she thought they might have been jealous of one another. (Dr. Putnam had helped Deutsch get settled in Boston in 1935, putting a car at her disposal for example.) She knew that Ruth was especially interested in the psychoses, but that Freud did not think that area was one of the "applications" of psychoanalysis. Ruth never seemed to her to be "pathological"; perhaps she was "too free," but it did not cross her mind to think so at the time. She never saw Ruth except in Vienna, where Ruth lived in a splendid house. Dr. Putnam had heard about her American family but did not get to meet them. Ruth's second marriage, to Mark Brunswick, was so "extraordinary"; Mark had been to her first wedding, and said then that he would marry her someday. "And he did!" (I regret that I failed to pursue a line of questions about Ruth's interest in psychosis, and how unusual was the encouragement that Freud had given her on this subject.)

I asked whether Freud had ever spoken about the early history of psychoanalysis. She said that while Jung had spent "a great deal" of time criticizing Freud, Freud himself did not bother with Jung by then. She did not think that the feelings in Freud about Jung had "died down," but that it was not a very important issue to Freud any more. He once said that perhaps it would have been better not to have used the concept of sexuality to cover so much, but that the subject had needed all the notoriety that it got for the sake of securing the "discoveries" themselves. Freud never spoke about telepathy or thought-transference, but Jung would have been interested in it. As for the Jones books about Freud, they just did not picture the man she had known.

But Freud had not particularly gone into these historical subjects. He would say, for instance, that he used to think that women should have the same sexual freedom as men, but that he had changed his mind subsequently. He thought it was necessary to guard against such eventualities as the possibility of pregnancy; in those days, of course, contraception was more difficult than now.

Freud thought that Adler had played up one aspect of psychoanalysis, the concept of *inferiority*, which Freud thought was too much of a simplification. Adler had taken a piece of Freud's work, and others of Freud's students might do the same. (Freud never discussed Rank with her, but it must have been "a great blow" to lose such a gifted man.) Dr. Putnam remembered Helene Deutsch commenting that despite the contrasting underlying conceptions, the Adlerian school for children was still the best one in Vienna. Freud "never forgot" that what he had proposed were theories. And Deutsch reminded young analysts that Freud had said not to ignore how "the man with the syringe," or what turned out to be modern psychopharmacology, was "right behind them" in psychoanalysis, and that they had to hurry.

As a physician Dr. Putnam was interested in the mysterious issues of how the mind and the body interact, and she mentioned that Kardiner had once had a patient that he sent to a neurologist, who could not find evidence for a tumor, but the neurologist did not say that it was not there. Later Kardiner sent the same patient back to the neurologist, and this time the tumor could be found. The patient was telling Kardiner that there was something organically wrong. (Although the subject did not come up, Dr. Putnam must have known how Gregory Zilboorg had missed the fact that George Gershwin, during his analysis, had had an organic brain affliction.) Kardiner, although clearly brilliant, was not a reliable source about Freud during the period when Dr. Putnam knew him.

Dr. Putnam never saw any signs of symptomatology in Freud himself. She looked for such indices of neurosis, as one does "naturally" in the course of an analysis. (With someone like Kata Levy I would never have dared pursue any such line of reasoning.) I surmised that Freud must have been very well defended, and that some of his conflicts would show up better in his correspondence than they did in daily life.

I inquired, since she was an American, whether Freud had made any cracks about the United States: "Oh yes," but they were not exactly "cracks." He might comment that if only Dr. Putnam had been younger or managed to live longer, then the course of psychoanalysis in America might have been better. (That observation tallied precisely with what Edith Jackson had reported.) Freud made the "blanket statement" that American analysts would "repudiate" his work. He had no confidence in them at all. Yet he still was struggling to get Dr. Putnam's help in preventing analysis from going wrong in America.

In her mind Freud's attitude toward America fell into the category of his "distrust"—and there were grounds for such suspicion. It was so vast a country that he could legitimately fear that there would never be an organization capable of controlling the "fanaticism" of a few, and anyone could just hang out a sign as a psychoanalyst. It alarmed him that psychoanalysis could not easily be controlled in America. Yet in Boston there had not been a real problem with "wild analysis"; either these questionable analysts stopped practicing eventually or they came for more training.

Dr. Putnam felt that there was an underlying distrust on Freud's part about America, and not just because of the difficulty of organizing psychoanalysis there. American intellectuals were very different from European ones. She was impressed by how the Europeans, who emigrated to the United States during the pre–World War II period, had "fructified" American intellectual life when they came over. She was thinking, for example, of an institution like the New School for Social Research in New York City, and how a wave of émigrés sparked by the threat of Hitler had helped make it an illustrious place.

Since Dr. Putnam was not politically naive, I inquired about Freud's feelings about Communism. Freud had thought there was an "essential" jealousy between people that would always result in a situation that was incapable of being equalized. He was enough of a skeptic to be confident that a shortage of bread would not be resolved by a mutual sharing of a scarcity.

I asked Dr. Putnam if she thought she had been helped by her therapy with Freud, and her answer was unequivocal: "Definitely." He had considered her "normal," but she of course, like everybody, had "problems." Yet he did not expect her to stay on for five years or so. She began around Christmastime and wanted to be home by the next Christmas. The following year he agreed that she should go. I thought that her account of how the analysis had gone with Freud was rather like the way Hirst had described his own treatment. For she said that the analysis had set her on the road of learning more about herself and taking responsibility for everything that happened to her. Unlike Hirst, she was more mature when she came to Freud, and therefore did not credit him with having so large a part in the way she had turned out. But after the analysis she felt she was "on her way."

I asked whether there had already been difficulties between Melanie Klein and Anna Freud in those days, and Dr. Putnam thought there had been "a bit" of a conflict but she did not concern herself with it. I considered it very naive of her to observe that Klein, who was such a bitter enemy of Anna's, was "hardly ever quoted" in Anna's seminar on child analysis. She thought Anna, who was the only child of Freud's that she knew, was "a great woman," and she considered Anna's book *The Ego and the Mechanisms of Defence* (1936) to be a classic. Everyone felt that Anna was a "very important person," with an "independent greatness" to her, for she was out to cover a new territory. Although Freud did not think too much of the possibilities of exploring the psychology of young children, Anna "went her own way."

Dr. Putnam's 3-year-old daughter was with her in Vienna. At one point she was interested in the possibilities of visiting a child analyst, and took the child to Edith Sterba. I asked what Freud had thought; he said that it "might be interesting." But the child had no problems according to Edith Sterba, and she would not take her into treatment on the grounds that she was "too normal." (Since the daughter later killed herself, it left me with a permanent skepticism about the significance of the predictive value of diagnosis.)

Freud's attitude toward child analysis was a complex one. It was not that he was going "to turn it down"; he was too interested in his own children. But he learned about them not through his talking to them but by observing and listening. Freud considered that the obstacles in analyzing children might be insurmountable. And she never asked him for advice about her child. He made "a great point" about there being no psychoanalytic pedagogy, and she remembers that whenever she hears the ambitious claims of some analysts.

During the time she knew Freud, his illness was not at all apparent. He had an operation while she was there, and he was "out" for a week or ten days. But the fact that he was suffering from a sarcoma never came into the clinical picture, unlike with Mark Brunswick, who thought that the fact that Freud was dying was a constricting factor in Mark's expressing himself. Although the illness in Dr. Putnam's view did not disturb Freud's speech at all, it did affect his eating habits. I wondered whether it had had an influence on his not attending public psychoanalytic meetings. She thought that more significant than Freud's illness was his feeling that he could easily become an intimidating factor in the discussions that took place; young analysts might refer to him to settle differences if he were present at their discussions. And she thought he could easily have turned into an inhibiting force in their proceedings.

Dr. Putnam had such an immensely favorable attitude toward Freud that the way I inquired about battles he had become engaged in was to ask what people meant when they said that he was "intolerant." On the one hand he would ask, "I wonder what will last?" But, at the same time, if somebody proposed something destructive to these same ideas or rejected a part of the psychoanalytic framework Freud would be considered intolerant. Freud would not refuse to listen, or to reconsider something; he was always interested in anything proposed at the society. The feeling that he communicated was that "today" he felt strongly that this was so and this not so.

It was probably indicative of Dr. Putnam's independence that whatever letters she had received from Freud had been lost. She could not read his German Gothic script, although she could understand other people's script. In Boston she would take Freud's letters to his disciple Hanns Sachs, and have him translate them for her; even Sachs could "scarcely" read them himself. The letters from Freud were not very "interesting"; they were always about what he wanted her to do for him.

Dr. Putnam knew almost nothing about Freud's family life. She supposed that his wife must have been "the most wonderful person," in that she had been able to keep her equilibrium in the face of everything that happened to Freud's career. Freud's wife seemed "the most contented woman"; Irma had never talked to her, but saw her over the summer months.

I again inquired in what ways psychoanalysis might have been knocked off-kilter by Freud's own personality. In contrast to someone like David Brunswick, of whom it would have been pointless to have asked such a question, Dr. Putnam said that "it must have been so, inevitable." She thought that one would look for "signs." Yet she never felt any lack of objectivity from him.

But some of the other accounts of analyses with Freud sounded "incredible" to her. Joseph Wortis's book (1963) about his own experiences with Freud seemed "really wild"; she mistakenly thought it must have taken place before she saw Freud. Wortis had had a "disgraceful analysis," and Dr. Putnam was "really ashamed" of it. She was most unhappy that people might think that such an embattled exchange had had anything to do with analysis. Yet she agreed that if a patient got off on the wrong foot with Freud, the analysis might end up being all fouled up.

Thinking about Freud's possible personal difficulties, Dr. Putnam reflected back on how Freud had been "always" smoking, but otherwise he did not show any signs of neurosis, and she said she was looking for it. On the whole she had "a favorable attitude" toward Freud; her respect for this "old gentleman" stemmed from his willingness to explore and discover something new. She admired his open-mindedness, and how he was affronted when she showed evidence of not being critical. Then again, she did not constitute much of a threat to him. Maybe if she had stayed longer in Vienna there would have been difficulties between her and Freud, as there had been with Ruth Brunswick. Certain patients could have become threats to him, but Marie Bonaparte and Edith Jackson were not in that category.

Dr. Putnam could imagine someone easily constituting a threat to Freud—a person who was competitive from the beginning. There are people who enjoy fighting. It is possible to be more interested in the process of struggling than in what the struggle is about. And a psychotic patient might have been felt as a menace to him. My mentioning a question about Freud's possible "possessiveness" really surprised her. For he was doing "nothing" but giving his ideas out. He had his "treasures," to be sure, but he did not hoard them.

Also, as a woman Dr. Putnam thought she was no possible threat to Freud. There was so much that he wanted her to do, and she was willing. She laughed about the way she was supposed to collect money on behalf of his cause. Sometimes she thought he was not discreet about patients whose families she was supposed to see. Mainly he wanted her help in connection with the deficit that the publishing house ran. He would write and ask, for example, would she request Alexander to make a contribution, along with herself? It was a matter, she thought, of about a couple of hundred dollars, and these requests came once a year for awhile, and then they petered out. Sometimes the press was really in straits. Dr. Putnam did not know whether he had written similarly to Edith Jackson.

I inquired about any novels Freud might have mentioned. He maintained that he got all his ideas from the Russians, especially Dostoyevski. He was willing to grant that they had known everything. And he said that he had had Russian patients, and that they had taught him "all he knew." In a breath he could be "extravagant." Despite his comments about Americans and

Russians, Dr. Putnam had no knowledge of which nationalities he might have admired especially. Nor did she have any special thoughts about Freud as a Jew. He did not seem to her strikingly Jewish; she "never" thought of him as being Jewish, but then again she did not have much feeling for "such things." Freud did tell plenty of Jewish stories, which Mark Brunswick had commented on too, but somehow these tales never in her mind had anything to do with him, and she could not remember them.

When she was in treatment with Freud in Vienna, she was not seeing any patients then; she went to Freud six days a week. Later in Boston she saw eight patients a day. To get Sachs over to Boston, on behalf of the Boston Institute, she had had to guarantee him eight regular analytic patients. Helene Deutsch had later wanted the same commitment. Dr. Putnam was certain that it had not been "difficult" to find eight such cases for Sachs, but she had "sworn" never to do it again. They did not need Deutsch the way in which they had felt desperate about getting Sachs. They had at first wanted someone "violently" for training purposes, so she put herself out in behalf of Sachs. But even without a prior set of assurances Deutsch came over with a great entourage of patients accompanying her anyway. Sachs had been very happy with his practice in Boston. Dr. Putnam had not discussed picking Sachs with Freud; Bertram Lewin had suggested Sachs's name to her. She felt glad for some reason that she had not discussed the matter with Freud.

I ended the interview by asking if there was anything I should have raised that I did not. She told me then a story about how she had once been troubled very much about a patient. She had done this and that for the patient. She had given her money, undertaken lessons for her at Radcliffe College, got somebody to paint her portrait—in short, she had done everything an analyst is not supposed to do. Freud said, "Sometimes one has to be both mother and father to a patient." He was entirely sympathetic to all she had done for the patient: "You do what you can." This story seemed to her "a very important" one, for most people would find it hard to believe about Freud. He was capable of being "completely unorthodox" if he thought the occasion called for it. He would want to be sure that it did not mean some personal gratification for the analyst but was in the interest of the patient.

I then raised the matter of Freud having analyzed Anna himself. "Oh yes! How unorthodox can you be." Unlike Mark Brunswick and others who were critical of Freud, Dr. Putnam did not look on Freud as having breached any professional or human taboo. She had known about Freud's analysis of Anna when she was in treatment in Vienna. (Oddly enough the Viennese sounded regularly to be familiar with Freud's having treated Anna, while I did not meet any English analysts, even well-connected ones, who seemed to know about the story. It remains an open question whether even Jones knew for sure at the time, although I think he must have suspected the truth.) Dr. Putnam thought Freud could be said to have had "great success" with Anna, and she thought her "a wonderful woman."

Of all the interviews I conducted about Freud, the encounter with Irma Putnam is one of the easiest to reconstruct, because she was so orderly and at the same time unusually intelligent. Although Jokl could be critical about Freud's views on women, and the stereotype about him as a sexist has become commonplace, Dr. Putnam was an emancipated career woman who nonetheless got on unusually well with Freud. At times, for example, in connection with Freud's analysis of Anna, Dr. Putnam could have been more free-thinking than she was. But I believe Freud would have had every right to have been proud of her account of what her analysis with him had been like.

8

Between Father and Mother: Eva Rosenfeld

Eva Rosenfeld was very different from Irma Putnam. She was effusively expressive and incorrigibly individualistic, and she worked out a more ambivalent relationship to the creator of psychoanalysis. Rosenfeld got to know Freud and his family far more intimately than Dr. Putnam did. She was of Central European origins, and her approach to Freud differed from that of Dr. Putnam. Rosenfeld, too, became a practicing psychoanalyst, but she had no prior medical training and she never, as long as I knew her, retired from the conduct of the profession.

Irma Putnam came to my attention because I was at the time living in Boston, and therefore all the early local analysts, even though she was no longer resident in the city, inevitably mattered especially to me. With Eva, however, I got put onto her by a London analyst who singled her out as someone who could be counted upon to be outspoken and unusually frank. In London by the 1960s those around Anna Freud were apt to be like Kata Levy, loyal and discreet about everything connected with the early days of psychoanalysis. So that when I heard that Rosenfeld would be both knowledgeable and emancipated, I thought it would be worthwhile getting to know her. I found it a surprising judgment when I later read that "among the Vienna-based women who moved in Freud's and Anna's orbit, Eva Rosenfeld was, next to Ruth Mack Brunswick, Freud's undoubted favorite" (Appignanesi and Forrester 1992, p. 380). Still, Eva was someone of undoubted historical importance. Eissler had already interviewed her some years before I saw her, but that document will remain sealed until the year 2008.

In my first interview with Eva Rosenfeld I was struck by her willingness to talk to me about her analysis with Freud. While with others, such as Irma Putnam, I based my interviews on my interest in studying the general history of psychoanalysis, and approached the critical matter of their personal analyses only gradually, Rosenfeld was straightforwardly eager to pursue the details of her own therapeutic contact with Freud. She was curious to know what others of Freud's patients had been willing to talk with me about, as David Brunswick had been, too. She knew—at least from a distance—each of Freud's other patients who were still alive in England, where she herself then lived.

Rosenfeld stated at the outset that she did not care what I published about my contact with her, providing only that it came out after her death. At the same time she wanted to see "the" book I wrote about Freud's circle, and asked whether I would attribute comments to her personally. She told me she would show what I wrote to Anna Freud, as she did with the two historical papers that she herself had written. On another occasion, however, she told me that she wanted me to wait until after she and Anna were both dead before publishing all the material she gave me. As it turned out, she lived to see several of my books appear in print, and despite her not liking one of them, she continued to cooperate with me long after she knew that I had incurred Anna Freud's sharp disapproval (Roazen 1993a).

It quickly became obvious to me that Rosenfeld was a member of the inner circle of the old London analysts. She even offered to show me around the house at 20 Maresfield Gardens, since my visit there had been spent interviewing Anna Freud. During the time I first saw Rosenfeld, at the end of the summer of 1965, she thought that Miss Freud would be at her country home at Walberswick, or perhaps she had already gone with Dorothy Burlingham to the retreat they shared in Ireland; Anna had been especially "tired" that year. Although Eva had the authority to take me through Maresfield Gardens, still she referred to Anna Freud as "Miss Freud" and to Freud as "Professor." When I mentioned having seen Kata Levy, she acknowledged that Levy was "probably the oldest" of their circle whom I could meet in London. (Rosenfeld herself was then 73 and lived on until 1977.)

Rosenfeld said that her analysis with Freud started in 1929, and I discovered that like Kata Levy's it was free. But I doubt if she knew at the time I first saw her that Freud had not charged Levy either. While Freud had seen Levy because of her brother Anton von Freund, and found it unthinkable to charge someone whose family had been so important in helping to forward the early course of psychoanalysis, Rosenfeld had come to Freud through her friendship with Anna Freud, which started in 1924. By 1929 it had been Anna who suggested the analysis to her, saying that Freud would have the time and that it would be without charge. Rosenfeld joked with me that I should not tell anybody about her not paying for her own analysis, otherwise she would be "besieged" with people also asking for free analyses. (Pfister, a Swiss minister, thought his psychoanalytic practice a part of his pastoral work, and treated many of his patients without gratuities [Micale 1993].)

Rosenfeld started off her analysis having trouble saying anything that came into her mind, and therefore the rule of Freud's about giving free associations was not an easy requirement to fulfill. After all, he was "God Almighty" to her, and yet he was "a bit put out" by her reticence. She saw him six times a week for about two months; she later went to him once a week, on Sundays, when Dorothy and Anna went out together in the afternoon.

Her contact with Freud was informal enough so that sometimes Ruth Brunswick could call and say: "Do not come, Professor needs fresh air." (Rosenfeld was the only person who talked to me about telephoning the Freud family apartment; she thought the number was "a very famous one.") A drive in the country might sometimes be more suitable for Freud than time spent analyzing her. "We were a sturdy lot" was the way she spoke of the possibility of missing a session as opposed to later patients with whom it was necessary to spend "half an hour" about the loss involved in not seeing the analyst on an upcoming weekend. Rosenfeld knew Ruth Brunswick well, and understood that when Marie Bonaparte came to Vienna she would stay at Ruth's house. Rosenfeld's analysis with Freud resumed over the summer holidays, when she went to him "every day" again.

She reported having once complained to Freud about his own "lack of religious feeling"—a theme to which she returned. His answer one time was to go back to his consulting desk, from where he took out a little statue, indicating that those were "the gods I believe in." He "shortsightedly" saw religion as a "fraud," a "pack of lies," absolutely "an illusion." He did not think there were such deep feelings so "unkillable" that they must have a meaning. The give-and-take between Rosenfeld and Freud was such that she also could discuss with him her special interest in Leonardo da Vinci. He "made" her once look at a Leonardo print on the wall, and he said then that his study of Leonardo was his "favorite" book. But she reminded me that Freud did not talk too much in those days because of the pain that he always had in his mouth.

Rosenfeld was noteworthy for having helped run a school in old Vienna for children who were either in analysis themselves or whose parents were then undergoing treatment. The initial impetus for setting up the school had come because a patient of Anna Freud's, a young woman named Minna, who had been recommended to her for an analysis by the psychiatrist Pötzl, seemed to be psychotic, and Anna Freud had decided that she could not break away from her family while she was living at home. So Anna looked for some place for her to live, and Bernfeld had recommended Mrs. Rosenfeld's house. Minna made "a big success out of her life," and got along "famously" with Rosenfeld's daughter. Minna went every day to Anna for her analysis, and Rosenfeld never noticed anything odd about her. Minna lived with Rosenfeld for eight years, and was the inspiration for the creation of the school that Rosenfeld later ran with the help of Dorothy Burlingham and Anna Freud; Peter Blos and Erik H. Erikson were two of the prominent teachers (Erikson 1963).

Only later did Rosenfeld decide to start formal psychoanalytic training, which she undertook in 1931 at Simmel's sanatorium outside Berlin. That curious institution was designed to be an ideal psychoanalytic community; "everyone, even the nurses and janitors," was supposed to be analyzed. The interior was designed by Freud's son Ernst, who was an architect. Rosenfeld had a photograph of Freud and Anna on her consulting room wall that had been taken at Simmel's. The sanatorium lasted five years before going bankrupt; Rosenfeld's official training had taken place later in Berlin, where she had had the analyst Therese Benedek as her supervisor.

Rosenfeld's position within psychoanalysis remained a highly personal one. She had had the job, for instance, of finding summer homes for the Freud family. No matter how she might have aspired to a more exalted role within Freud's world, he continued to consider her primarily as an intimate friend of Anna's. She once had had a theory about the *Mona Lisa* smile, and sent it on to Freud, but he evaded answering her, saying he was glad that Anna would be telling her what he thought. She had first met Freud while talking with Anna late one evening in her bedroom, which was located in those days at the point of intersection between the office part of Freud's apartment and the private family living quarters. Freud had been walking between the two sections when Rosenfeld first saw him. Later, when she was living in Berlin, Rosenfeld would go to visit the Freuds twice a year; he became "frailer and frailer," more and more "ill," as the years passed.

I always wondered what these former patients of Freud's thought of Jones's biography. Rosenfeld liked volume one "the best," but found volume two "too burdensome." She could not really believe that people might actually be interested in "all that controversy" connected with Adler and Jung. Volume three seemed mainly notable because it recorded "so much suffering" on Freud's part, which Rosenfeld and others had to witness. She thought he was "displeased" that she was not more aware of what a big tragedy the events in Central Europe were during the 1930s. Freud had keen memories of earlier progroms, while Rosenfeld had her day-to-day troubles to keep her busy.

Jones had been the one to get her as well as others out of Berlin in 1936. She left Germany with her old mother and her son; her daughter, only 15 years old, had been tragically killed in a mountaineering accident in 1927. Anna had remembered that the year before Minna—the child who had been living at Rosenfeld's—had such anxiety attacks in the country that they had to leave. Anna wondered whether there was a "connection" or a "premonition" of what would happen, in this fear on the part of a "friend." Anna like her father had an interest in telepathy. I only learned from others that at the end of World War I Rosenfeld had also lost two small children to acute illnesses. But Rosenfeld mentioned not these losses but rather the "ruined lives" of her brothers as contributing to her interest in psychoanalysis; her brothers were not "bad," but "sweet," and therefore could be considered "sick." She met Freud in November 1924 after her brother Anton had died. She hypothesized that when she met Anna she must have thought "now I have got my brother back."

Rosenfeld then saw Freud four more times after he arrived in England. She remembered his remark, when she first saw him in his study in London, how "everything is here, only I am not here!" As she said about Freud in a broadcast she gave in Germany at the time of Freud's centenary in 1956, he will be here long after we are all gone. That year she also spoke over the BBC about Freud. According to her son's account, she "reminisced harmlessly about the Freuds. Anna's wrath was quite disproportionate to the offense. . . ." (Heller 1992, p. 46). I have read a draft of Rosenfeld's talk, found among Anna Freud's papers, and I cannot imagine what Anna took exception to. Perhaps Rosenfeld's son was correct in suspecting that Anna was apprehensive that if Rosenfeld could offer anecdotes publicly, perhaps someday she would release Anna's personal letters to her. (They finally appeared as an interesting book in 1992 ([Heller 1992; cf. Roazen 1993c].)

Rosenfeld spent most of her life involved with psychoanalytic thinking. She had first read Freud's *The Interpretation of Dreams* in 1911 and did not like it. But her fiancé "insisted" on asking Professor's advice about the desirability of their marrying, since they were cousins. Freud had said yes, that they should go ahead and marry. It was not uncommon for the women around Freud either to be unmarried or to have husbands who somehow did not count. Rosenfeld and her husband formally separated in the 1930s, and she did not even remotely blame, at least to me, her involvement with psychoanalysis for the failure of her marriage. Her husband had been "most generous" and "wanted" her to go to Freud. Her husband was one of the "first listeners" to Freud's lectures at the University of Vienna, and "never resented" Freud's place in her life.

Rosenfeld saw Freud as a symbol of truth-telling. While she was in analysis with him, someone in his circle had said how worried he was about Professor's stomach—forgetting she was a patient of his. (Anna was away.) Rosenfeld tried to hold back what she had heard, and he guessed what was going on in her mind. He then lectured her that neither of them had "the right" to do that. She thought that to have known Freud was "enough for a life to have meaning."

Given the timing of Rosenfeld's closeness with Freud, I asked her about Ruth Brunswick. Rosenfeld knew her as "an outgoing American," a woman who was "warm and explosive"; Ruth "always went on her nerves," and made "a big tum-tum around Professor," like a "whirlwind." She was charming and explosive, very intelligent as well as vivacious, and Freud liked her a great deal. Her first analysis had been with Freud before 1924, when Rosenfeld first came into contact with the Freuds; by then he had already had his first terrible operation, and was "established as a dying man." Rosenfeld knew a bit about Ruth Brunswick's daughter, who lived then in San Francisco and had just visited Walberswick. She also was aware that Mark Brunswick had remarried after Ruth died "prematurely." She understood that Ruth had slipped in the bathroom, and that the fall had killed her. She thought of Ruth as "quite an ill woman," who had a mysterious illness in Vienna, for which doctors "came and went." Probably her complaint was "psychosomatic," and she did not worry Professor about it. At one point she said Ruth had had a "slumbering psychosis," and came to a "miserable end." Ruth had a house in the suburbs of Vienna; she was a great friend of the Princess Marie's, and they shared a villa in the summer that the Nazi propagandist Goebbels later occupied. Hitler and the Nazis had "their taste" in summer places.

Ruth Brunswick was very strongly "attached" to Freud, as she had once been involved with her own father. But Rosenfeld knew nothing about Freud's "disappointment" with Ruth. According to Rosenfeld the Freuds would not speak of Ruth to her, for it would create "great troubles"; there was supposedly "no gossip" going around. She did think that Freud frequently became disillusioned with people; he "went out" too enthusiastically, and then felt disappointed. Processes of "idealization" preceded Freud's feeling that he had been let down. He did not have a "realistic" appraisal of people at first; he needed so much to find someone to look up to, and it can be so "hard" when "you are so high." Freud had become disillusioned with Rosenfeld too; she thought that one way of understanding how Freud could hate was by seeing the way his sense of disappointment with people could be so strong.

Unlike Marie Bonaparte, who was "one hundred percent devoted" to Freud, Rosenfeld was not that sort of "star" in Freud's world. Her son later wrote about "one great gash, deliberately—some would say provocatively—inflicted by my mother" on her relationship to Freud (Heller 1992, p. 44). For in 1937 she had decided to go for an analysis with Melanie Klein. Freud "abhorred" Klein and felt that Anna was attacked by Klein, which was "to a certain extent true." But Anna was "always wonderful under attack." Rosenfeld had once written to Freud, about her wanting to go to Vienna for four weeks to explain Klein's position to him, but he "gently said no," that she could not convince him and that he did not want to have to convince her.

Freud's letter to Eva has recently been published, and is easy to misunderstand.

There are other aspects of the matter to consider, one that could prove disagreeable for you, another that could prove disagreeable for me. You know what my attitude toward Melanie Klein's work is. I too think that she has found something new, but I don't know if it means quite so much as she believes, and I am certain that she has no right to use it to place theory and technique on a new basis. Our four weeks would naturally attempt critically to unravel what you have found in yourself to confirm the Kleinian theories. It is possible that I might bring you to another judgment of these things. Then you would go back to London and find yourself in opposition to the circle and direction of work when you would manifestly prefer to stay in tune with both. On the other hand, it wouldn't be possible for you to hide from the English group the influence that you have experienced through me, and that would kindle an antagonism I have gone out of my way up until now to avoid. [Appignanesi and Forrester 1992, p. 383]

Freud's old-world tact should not be mistaken for what his real underlying feelings were. It is remarkable how these people managed gently to skate over the hurts that took place; manners in old Vienna were sophisticated, and sometimes hypocritical, but this complicated side of things has not often enough been explored. So Freud could sound cautious when he was most certain.

The other possibility, that in four weeks you would convince me of the fundamental significance and correctness of Kleinian findings, I do not really think is a probable outcome. I think then that the piece of inner work that is now thrust upon you, the resolution of your intellectual allegiance as well as of your father or mother influence, is something that you will have to sort out without help, at least without mine. Because as always I take a lively interest in your destiny, I am naturally unhappy that such a problem should have posed itself, particularly for you. [Appignanesi and Forrester 1992, p. 383]

Appignanesi and Forrester (1992) think that Freud's words read "like an attempt to allow her to think the matter through clearly for herself and points her in the direction of Klein, a direction, he suggests, she has already decided on." And the letter is somehow taken to be "a telling reminder of Freud's impartiality, at least towards some of his friends and former patients" (p. 383).

Based on what Rosenfeld told me, however, any such construal of Freud's words is wrong. She underlined the way he took her interest in Klein as "an analytic matter," which is what he meant by referring to her "father or mother influence." Without saying as much, he thought she was using Klein as a resistance to himself. And Rosenfeld wrote Anna in 1947 about "how much I hurt you" (Heller 1992, p. 182) in the past. It would be impossible to dissociate Freud from Anna in his last days, if only because he was so physically dependent on her. He would not have cared enough about Rosenfeld to have felt exceptionally wounded by what he took to be an emotionally charged reaction against his own way of thinking. But he would have identified with Anna's sense of being abandoned.

In Rosenfeld's mature opinion Klein was not a genuine "schismatic," whatever Freud or Anna believed, for Klein "always explained" that if you proceeded along Freudian principles, you would arrive at her specific conclusions. (Dissidents as far apart from Klein as Jacques Lacan and Sandor Rado also adopted an identical line of reasoning on behalf of their own respective theories.) Mrs. Klein visited Freud in London during the last weeks of his life. He was "very much a gentleman" toward women, and he asked her what she was working on. When Eissler interviewed Rosenfeld, he wanted to know more about what Professor's attitude toward Klein had been.

I asked whether Rosenfeld thought that Freud had been impatient toward those he analyzed, and she said that it was true more "toward the end" of his life. Every word caused him "pain," and he was "not easy to understand." (Mark Brunswick had insisted that Freud had not talked less as he aged, but that his final relationship with Ruth had been wounded by his illness.) Rosenfeld thought it "amazing" that he could succeed in carrying on for so long. She had lost her daughter in the accident in 1927, the same year that Freud published his *The Future of an Illusion*; he dedicated a copy of the book to her with the inscription, "to brave Eva." She saw herself as trying somehow to soldier on.

Of all his pupils and adherents Freud got on "easiest" with the women. Among Freud's male disciples he had "little sympathy" for Federn. Jones played a special role in that Freud had "a soft spot" for the non-Jews in analysis, and Jones would fit into the line of Gentile disciples like Jung. (The Viennese political philosopher Sir Karl Popper, sharply critical of his fellow Jew Freud, shared a similar approach to Popper's own Gentile followers.) Freud had had "a real transference with Jung." Freud was not so disappointed with Rosenfeld because she did not matter much. Hartmann, who entered Freud's world after Rosenfeld, became "the blue-eyed boy"; his being Gentile, like Jung, was "the main attraction."

Yet as all-important as his work was to him, within the Freud household one could not hear the word *psychoanalysis*. There was never a vulgar joke or gossip in the family. Although they did not take themselves too seriously, they never made fun of something they believed in. The Freuds were very "prudish" about sexual allusions. Rosenfeld did not think Freud was ever unfaithful, because he held that sexual intercourse was justified by the wish for children. In his personal life there were many taboos, or things "not done." He loved stories about unfaithful women; what a "bore" it would be for them to be straight. But he would not have "allowed" such conduct in his own family.

So Freud never played with technical words or used the professional jargon at home. And he did not talk much about an issue like his attitude toward America. He was "like an emperor," and he knew that everything he said would be "taken up and used." The usual quietness of the analyst means that the patient listens keenly for what he might say. In his last years Freud did not talk "very freely," unless someone came to discuss a point on a professional basis. At the dinner table he was "almost always silent," and not particularly interested in food.

Rosenfeld knew about Bullitt's significance for Freud, but she had thought he was working on Moses and not Woodrow Wilson. She had been suspicious that he was "bragging," but it did not turn out to be so. She did not know whether he had been analyzed by Professor, nor how important he was politically, "although he acted as though he were." Bullitt prided himself that he was writing a book together with Freud. His daughter Anne, whom he "worshiped," was staying at Rosenfeld's home. Bullitt did not like Anna Freud too much, and she did not particularly appreciate him either.

Rosenfeld had been prepared for my asking about Freud's relationship with his sister-in-law Minna, since Eissler had earlier asked her if Freud had had sexual relations with her. (By withholding his interviews for years, Eissler was giving his interviewees a sense of increased self-importance.) Rosenfeld's view was that Freud had "hated disorder," and that the "discord of jealousy" that would have been entailed in such a relationship meant to Rosenfeld that it was "so impossible" for it to have taken place. Freud once asked her about his "famous love affair" with Minna: "You believe it too." But she thought he was offended, more for Minna's sake than for his own, that she did not think such a liaison had taken place.[1]

Freud's wife was not an uninteresting person. But Rosenfeld could not allow herself to get close to "Mama," as she was known. Frau Professor "never loved" Anna; it was "the tragedy of Anna's life." Her mother had not wanted her sixth child, and therefore her father meant everything to Anna. Rosenfeld would have been a favorite of "the ladies," Mama and Minna, if she had not "held back." Anna would have had to listen to them say, "See how Eva [Rosenfeld] does this or that." Mama was deprecated inside the family, "very much so." But not by her daughter Mathilda or her sons; the circle around Freud was responsible for that. Since she was such "a perfect lady," one could not tell how long the love lasted beween Mama and Freud, or whether she was jealous of Minna. Mama and Minna were "such Siamese twins." Mama was "certainly" jealous of Anna, for Anna looked after Freud, rinsing his mouth, at a period when Mama did not do anything any more.

Minna was the more literary of the two women; she once gave Rosenfeld on her birthday a basket of cosmetics with a note, "Civilization and its comforts," an obvious takeoff on Freud's title *Civilization and its Discontents*. (Rosenfeld was "a little bit adopted" by the family, and they celebrated her

---

1. Henry A. Murray told me that when Bilinsky's (1969) article first appeared, alleging that Jung once claimed Freud had had an affair with Minna, that Bilinsky had gotten it "wrong." Freud did have a complicated emotional involvement with Minna, which may have been briefly distressing to her. But Jung felt that Freud's inability to follow through by making his wife's sister into a sexual partner was a sign of Freud's own neurotic inhibitions, and testimony to Jung's emancipated superiority in lacking Freud's supposed sexual hang-ups.

birthday.) The children in the household suffered from the "double authority" of Freud's wife and Minna, for either the "two mothers" both sat on the children, or there was discord between them. The children's "jealousy" of Mama's and Minna's preoccupation with each other was worse than the emotions usually associated with the ties between mother and father.

Rosenfeld agreed that although Freud loved his sons he was disappointed in them. Ernst was his "brick," the pillar of his security. Rosenfeld never heard Freud talk about Oliver, who she thought of as a "strange" man, a "bore." She did not know why Oliver's daughter Eva "had to die" during World War II, and she correctly suspected that there was a secret about that (Roazen 1993a). Freud would never have interfered with Martin's extramarital affairs. Talking with him would have done "no good." He was "a scoundrel," and Freud could not "govern" him. A Don Juan has an "incurable oedipal tie," and out of feelings of being deserted by his mother deserts other women in turn, as an act of "revenge." Rosenfeld was uncertain whether Freud could be said to have "lost interest" in his sons, since it was a question if he even "cared" by then.

His sons had amounted to "nothing." She never discussed with him his possible disappointment in them. It appeared to her that the sons took after the mother's family, while the daughters were more like the father's side. He was a "fond father." She wondered whether he had really expected any more of his sons: "Or was he not too interested in himself by then?" He did not want any of them to become doctors; he would have wanted a successor, but none of his sons had the makings of one. Only Anna stayed in the apartment at the end; Mathilda lived with her husband "around the corner."

As with Hirst, Freud knew Rosenfeld's family; he had been "very fond" of her mother, who was "a fine, distinguished lady," the sister of Max Schiller, who was Yvette Guilbert's

husband. (Rosenfeld established the personal relationship between Freud and Yvette [Knapp and Chipman 1964].) Freud's
last public appearances were sitting in the "middle of the first
row" at Yvette's concerts. Rosenfeld would have dinner afterward with Anna and Dorothy Burlingham; they were all so
noticeably "not smart" in their dressing that the waiters could
tell these women belonged together, even when they arrived at
the restaurant separately. Freud admired Yvette's courage in
calling a spade a spade; she had a talent for expressing herself
through physical movements, and symbolized "the soul of the
French" with their inborn psychology.

Rosenfeld saw Freud in the context of cosmopolitan Central European culture. And unlike Irma Putnam, for example, she
had no difficulty in seeing Freud as a Jew. Those with Freud's
background had gone for a long time with no persecution. As of
1848 they were full citizens; Moses Mendelssohn had helped to
liberate them. Freud was to Rosenfeld a fruit of the emancipation from the ghetto; he was part of the "young sap" of all that
ancient civilization.

I mentioned Freud's father in this context, as I thought too
little was known about him. But Rosenfeld remembered that
Freud had emphasized how deeply his father's death had affected him. In those days the mother, not the father, had the role
of educating the children. Freud's father Jacob had been a textile
merchant, but was "very poor." After Freud was born, there
were five sisters, and then Freud's younger brother Alexander.
Four of his sisters, all those still living in Europe, were "gassed"
by the Nazis in 1942.

Freud had wanted his last child, who was Anna, to be a
boy; he did not send Wilhelm Fliess a telegram when he
discovered the sex of the child, for Freud had been planning on
naming a boy for Fliess. Freud's wife too was disappointed;
Mathilda Hollitscher had said Anna was a "difficult, deprived"
child. And yet with her birth Freud's practice improved. The
pleasure and devotion that Freud and Anna got out of their

relationship meant that "only by ordinary standards" could her life be considered "a tragedy." He called her his Antigone. Rosenfeld dissociated herself from the common view that saw Anna as having "lost" out because of her tie to her father, it having supposedly been a tragedy for him, too.

Fliess was important as a "contemporary" of Freud's. Rosenfeld saw Freud as a "slow developer," and to her it seemed that the Fliess period came "so late" in Freud's life. Those letters to Fliess were really "more important" than any other available document. The correspondence with Fliess sounded very much like Freud of the later period, but even though he would have "felt" the same then, he would not have "said" such words of warmth. He was much "warmer" than his children, and than Anna in particular.

To Rosenfeld, Freud had had "a mission." While hysteria represents a "mobilization" of all psychological forces, and has "a body" to it, he was much more obsessional in his last years. Anna also changed; once she had been a lover of poems, but by the 1960s she had grown more and more "rigid" in her ideas. (Yet in 1929 she had also been capable of writing Eva: "being good and being in analysis finally amount to the same thing" [Heller 1992, p. 112].) "Tante" Minna remarked on how Freud once had brought a pencil of Minna's to her room; it did not belong in his study, and he could not stand having it around.

Once, when the Freuds were staying at a summer house, it was found that the bookshelves were too small for his books; they had to be removed "immediately." Freud's "obsessionality" was expressed in all his being. He needed that immense amount of self-control and discipline in order to endure the pain. Minna thought that "any ordinary man" would have made an end to himself sooner. During the Fliess period he was much more disorganized in a creative sense, which was appropriate for his age. His theory of dreams did not after all "fall out" of him like from a machine. He had described psychology as his "tyrant," and that was hysterical of him.

As a psychoanalyst it was impossible for Rosenfeld not to conjecture about Freud's childhood; she was much freer in doing this than Jokl. She proposed that Freud's nanny had played a special role. Jones had made her take that point out of an article she wrote about Freud. But she had been impressed with how Freud had preached to his family after his nanny had taken him to church. She hypothesized that Freud had been disappointed in that it was not his God; he was therefore thrown out of religion, which was a"trauma" for him as it was for her own son, who also became a hater of religion. To Jones this theory of Rosenfeld's did not fit his own notion of atheism. But Jones had said to her, "You won't publish what Puner has written." (Puner's [1947] biography had been one Jones set out to counteract.)

For Rosenfeld, as for Puner, Freud was "ambivalent" about his Jewishness. Apollo can look nicer to us than we do ourselves. The ideal of beauty has to be related to the aesthetic pleasure we take in otherness. The contrast between classical models (like Apollo) and Renaissance ones (like David) appealed to Freud. Rosenfeld had been influenced by Kleinian versions of aesthetics in her Moses paper (Rosenfeld 1951). When Freud told that story about his own position on religion, and his sort of "gods," he meant that he believed only in something "tangible."

Freud had been preoccupied with the Moses theme and his Jewishness during the last period of his life. I asked why, with his sensitivity to anti-Semitism, he had not left Vienna sooner than the Anschluss? "There was an attitude that it cannot happen here." And then the Gestapo would not let him go. He was old and ill; losing his home at such an age was very hard. One of his "obsessions" was that anything out of the ordinary, unexpected, and not "guarded against" roused anxiety and discomfort.

Rosenfeld's knowledge of Freud covered the last fifteen years of his life. Dorothy Burlingham came to Vienna shortly after Rosenfeld first came in contact with the Freuds. Rosenfeld and Anna were already intimate friends by then. Dorothy's husband was manic-depressive, and she was afraid of him; she wanted "an ocean" between him and her four children. Theodor Reik was her analyst at first; she spent a few years in analysis with him, which was "unsatisfactory." Then Freud accepted her as a patient, and Anna took her children into analysis. In Rosenfeld's own analysis Freud referred to Dorothy Burlingham as "your rival!" Anna, Burlingham, and Rosenfeld were a trio of friends for quite some time. The idea of the weekend was an American notion, but Burlingham would take Professor out into the country in her car. Later she lived on the second floor of the building on the Berggasse where Freud made his home.

Rosenfeld was at some of the last seminar evenings in Vienna, which were held every month in Freud's office. Edoardo Weiss once presented a paper, and there was "silence" afterward. Freud was embarrassed that he had the effect of inhibiting others. He "disliked" the idea of his own "influence."

In general, Freud resented what he could not understand. That attitude helps explain his approach to music—Freud found it essentially "unfathomable," and he did not like feelings that were not rationally explicable. Part of his objection to religion came from the same sort of reasoning. "Frau Professor" did not take up religious practices after his death, although "certainly" she might have wanted to do so while he was alive. At her mother's funeral, Anna had a rabbi who spoke "very tactfully." Presumably the rabbi's presence meant that Anna thought her mother would have wanted it so. (Her aunt Minna was not cremated, unlike Freud's wife, most of whose ashes were added to Freud's own, "probably" because of Minna's traditional Jewish feeling, and was buried at Golder's Green, the crematorium.)

Freud had become, as many observed, a kind of rabbi himself, and I asked how he could stand the adulation. He had "difficulties" with all his students. He felt, "I am not obliged to return their feelings." He was pleased that they liked psychoanalysis, but did not want to make it include himself personally. He certainly did not want them as "pals." He was grateful, personally, to people like von Freund and Max Eitingon for their gifts of money. And Pfister was a Christian whom he liked very much. But Freud did not want any of them as "friends." He became "very aloof"; when he was ill, he did not want to eat with others around.

Although many analysts, following Freud's recommendations, thought of the couch as an essential part of the profession, I questioned the advantages of its use. Rosenfeld, too, like Freud, said she would find it a strain to have to face patients all day. It is true that psychotics need the reality of the analyst there, which the couch works against. And nonverbal communication was by then "all the rage," but it is easy to forget that Freud wanted to strengthen the ego by being able to say what feelings are. He was not treating psychotics, and did not want psychoanalysis to be "a handmaiden of psychiatry." He dreamt of there being university chairs of psychoanalysis. He also had hoped to win the Nobel Prize; his failure to do so was a "disappointment" to him.

Like Irma Putnam, Rosenfeld thought that Freud did not believe that this therapy would be good for psychotics. A neurotic in a transference looks for a "lost" love, but a psychotic searches for a missing self and projects part of his ego onto the analyst—not the same thing as a neurotic transference. Freud had in mind something "more cultural and more individual" than the treatment of psychotics. He wanted people to be something "higher" or better—a superman, in Nietzsche's sense. It was not the same thing as wanting to help somebody who feels an electric box is persecuting him, which was psychiatry in the old sense. He was interested in scientific progress in the treatment of psychotics but not in therapy with them. Freud was moving away from the medical aspects of the possibilities of "cure."

As a young man Freud had been interested in philosophy, not medicine, and I asked about his adolescence. Rosenfeld had not thought about it. He "must have been poor and proud," and his mother "adored" him. He thought of infatuation as "a pathological state"—Eva was "very convinced of" that. Freud must have been glad his courtship of his future wife was over, since while infatuated one was "not at one's best." He did not like infatuation in patients. During the course of his courtship he was "singleminded and possessive."

Rosenfeld could not think what Freud was not "possessive" of. He was that way about everything, in contrast to what Irma Putnam had thought. Rosenfeld remembered how "terribly nervous" he was once on a train ride until his luggage had been assembled. She traced these feelings back to his "trauma" of leaving home in Moravia as a small boy, and how his parents felt at the time they headed for Vienna. His "train phobia" in adulthood could be connected to how his parents had once felt, and he had picked it up, too. He was possessive of his children—possessive and generous at the same time. He was generous about money. For example, he gave money from unexpected consultations to Anna for charity. Anna explained this when she and Rosenfeld met; that is where the money came for the young woman Minna to stay at Rosenfeld's.

Freud smoked cigars constantly, and Rosenfeld took it as an essential constituent of his personality. When he had made some good interpretations during her analysis, establishing a connection between an adult problem and an early childhood one, he would get up and say, "Now I deserve a cigar!" She thought many scientists need to smoke when they are doing their best work. But in Freud's case she related it to his mother.

It "certainly" is not true that the tie between mother and son is as "perfect" as Freud liked to describe it; as we shall see, Rosenfeld thought that Klein was better than Freud in describing such emotions as a mother's envy or jealousy of a son.

Freud's analysis was a father analysis, whereas since his death post-Freudian psychoanalytic thinking has concentrated on the mother. Transference is now understood as so much more complicated and difficult. In his essay "Analysis Terminable and Interminable" Freud must have by then come across the "mother tie," which is "indispensable" to psychological understanding, and makes necessary a new "technique and assessment." Rosenfeld liked to say that Freud stood on the pier and "fished" for the mother relationship, but still standing firmly on the pier, whereas we are on the "sea" with our patients. She thought it important to remember that Freud did not treat children.

Rosenfeld linked the mother and the infantile with the unknown and music. Freud did not want to go further than he could solve. "In limiting your aims," he would say, "that's masterly." His attitude toward music was not discussed, but it was just taken for granted. There was his immense enjoyment of Yvette Guilbert, and the references in his *The Interpretation of Dreams* to Wagner. But their living quarters were so small, he was "afraid" the children might take music up, which they all could have. By and large he was simply not musical.

This was striking because of Freud's familiarity with the nonrational. As a teacher he had "a tremendous seductive power"; early in an analysis one is so "vulnerable." It is then that one discovers such surprising things about oneself. He wanted to promote the struggle to work this out into adulthood.

Rosenfeld thought she had not had the makings in her to be a good "disciple." (A number of other pupils of Freud made the exact same claim about themselves.) Freud wanted his students to be both independent and fruitful, yet he complained of them that "the goody-goodys are no good," but "the naughty ones go away." He was the most cautious of all his listeners, and as his own student he would not have enthused.

Freud had complicated emotions toward his patients and pupils, and I wondered why he had never written more on countertransference. Rosenfeld thought that was "a very big issue." The subject seemed "rather overdone" now. For Freud transference meant "an error," or at least erroneous feelings. Hence the essence of being a psychoanalyst was identified as being not in error, so there would not (or could not) be such a phenomenon as countertransference. But as for the unmarried women who became analysts, they did in fact seem to develop countertransferences; they needed brothers, sons, lovers, children. Rosenfeld herself thought she had never had a patient whom she could say "stood" for some figure in her past life.

I got much further with Rosenfeld in exploring Freud's analysis of Anna than I did with Kata Levy. As far as its being a secret went, Rosenfeld maintained extravagantly: "All Vienna knew!" Lou Andreas-Salomé was Anna's analyst later on, yet subsequently Anna tried to deny having ever been analyzed by her (Roazen 1993a). When Rosenfeld met them, Andreas-Salomé and Anna were already "declared friends." A book of Lou's was dedicated to Anna. I asked how could he analyze her. "He just took the liberty!" Rosenfeld cited the Latin maxim: "What is permitted to Zeus is not allowed to an ox." Technically he was quite unorthodox. He wrote his works on technique, but these recommendations were not for himself. He did not ask his students to "obey the rules" either. He wanted them to be good understanders; he was too wise to be dogmatic about technique. The rules were there for everyone—but not for the ruler. Although I inquired if Freud grew more arbitrary as he aged, Rosenfeld thought he always took great freedom in what he did. For his pupils, and the world, he laid down his precepts. Anna Freud once wrote to Rosenfeld that "one must be an exception-

ally good analyst in order to be allowed to modify analysis''
(Heller 1992, p. 161).

There was the rule, for example, concerning "abstinence."
Supposedly a moratorium was imposed on making any major life
decisions during the course of an analysis. But then an analysis
lasted in those days for some six months. The longer a period of
time people chose to stay in analysis, the more impossible this
sort of abstinence became as a rule. Interruptions in an analysis
were not so easy in the 1930s, for patients were too much in
"awe" of the analyst to break off treatment. In Rosenfeld's early
years as an analyst one did not send out bills; patients kept track
of how much they owed.

I tried to fish around for anything else Freud might have
done in "unorthodox" directions. Rosenfeld brought up the
way in which they "all" went in and out of the family. She
herself lived in the Freud house during the summer, while she
was in analysis with Professor. She reported that story about
how worried they were about Professor's stomach trouble to
Jones, because of how it showed Freud was committed to the
truth. But Jones told her to make sure that the part about living
in the house when it happened got left out. As Loe Kann, Jones's
common-law wife, once wrote to Freud about Jones: "I wonder
why he is such an incorrigible fibber (to put it politely!)"
(Appignanesi and Forrester 1992, p. 238). When Jones (1955)
wrote of the early "dissident" Stekel that "he had no scientific
conscience at all" (p. 135), it does sound to me like the pot
calling the kettle black.

Rosenfeld remembered that one time just before a session,
Aunt Minna had handed her some medicine and a spoon, saying:
"Make sure that he takes it!" He did swallow what she gave him.
She then spun fantasies about having poisoned him. She felt that
going to his consulting room was like being called to the
headmaster's at Eton's. (Ruth Brunswick, Mark thought, would

not have been so close as to have handed him medicine, but would have been apt to have sent him to some doctor for a consultation.) Rosenfeld thought that Freud liked the "warm nest" of women around him; he would not have liked it if male colleagues were there. When Rosenfeld first arrived on the scene, Rank was already effectively out of the movement; Abraham in Berlin was still then thought the most highly of.

Freud wrote heaps of letters to people like Rank and Abraham; Rosenfeld thought Freud was better with his followers on paper than in person. For an artistic person, any letter is written half for oneself and half for the recipient. As time went on Freud became even further "withdrawn." Irma Putnam never saw him over an extended period of years, or within the family setting. At the dinner table Freud could take "a few bites of his food," then put the plate down for a dog. "Everyone winced."

His physical frailties seemed to heighten the impact he had on Rosenfeld. One of his interpretations to her from her analysis still rang in her ears: "Your bad luck is that I am like your father." This notion must have borne later on his observation about the conflict in her between the father and mother influence, when she told him about her interest in Klein's ideas. Freud had acknowledged that perhaps he, like her father, had expected "too much" of her. He was also implicitly recognizing the problem of an analyst being in reality too much like a past figure in a patient's life.

Anna was the youngest Freud child, just as Rosenfeld was in her own family. As the only girl Rosenfeld was the "favorite." One of Freud's earlier interpretations to her touched on this point; she was looking at a light fixture made up of six bulbs and noticed that one was different. Freud then said, "You mean you are a special favorite, like Anna." Then he got up, and saw that it was in reality a special bulb. But the interpretation was still accurate. Rosenfeld pointed out how his insights, especially some of the early ones, sometimes sank in ten or fifteen years later.

Freud had not engaged in speculative reconstructions of proposed early childhood traumas, like those Albert Hirst or his aunt Emma were accustomed to. Rosenfeld returned to how very difficult it had been at the beginning of her treatment. He was such "an Olympian god," and she was supposed just to free-associate, talking about such silly childish things, like ditties. She was so embarrassed, and he was "ruthless, ruthless." Once he said: "The intellect is like a solicitor," meaning whichever side pays, reason follows emotion.

Rosenfeld spent more time with Freud as a family man than in analysis as a patient. Once Simmel, when he was staying with the Freuds, said that if he had had such a wife, he too could have written all those books. (More than one of Simmel's wives was a former patient.) Simmel had emerged from the bathroom, saying that Frau Professor had put the toothpaste on Freud's toothbrush. Rosenfeld launched into a discussion of what so-called Victorian families had been like, and how different society was now. Her parents used to visit her grandparents every evening. Minna used to pour Freud's second cup of coffee—"He hardly ever had to touch a thing!"

I asked whether Freud could be dogmatic, and she thought that he would be so in behalf of what he considered principles of scientific truth. She recalled the struggle between Jones and Edward Glover over the significance of Melanie Klein's work, which started around 1938. Jones had retired to the country, leaving Glover to preside over the British Psychoanalytic Society. Klein's daughter Melitta, who was also an analyst, would say "terrible things" about her mother at the society, opposing her point by point, and Glover would "back her up." Glover had been "quite Kleinian originally," and could have been supposed only to have gotten inside information from his analysis of Melitta. It was odd how Freud, who did not like infatuations, should have so inspired them not only toward himself but within psychoanalysis as a whole. In the struggle over Klein, analysts were aware how Freud, in expelling Adler, Jung, and others, could be "extremely vengeful" and "angry."

Freud's cancer meant that he could no longer engage in such controversies, and he was careful about Klein. His illness meant he was already "very silent" when Rosenfeld first met him. By nature she considered herself "an outsider," although a "popular" one both in the Freud circle and in the Society in London too. In the years she knew him he was constantly moving his jaw and mouth because of the pain. He endured over "fifteen years in martyrdom"; he became "really difficult to understand." He alluded to this handicap in talking to Yvette Guilbert: "My prosthesis does not speak French." He could "just" manage to talk in English, which he had "always" spoken. He became "quieter and quieter," busying himself with the dogs, which was his "pleasure." How "angry" it made Frau Professor when he put his own food down for the dogs. (I doubt she much wanted the dogs around at all; according to traditional Jewish experience, dogs were used to patrol the boundary between the Gentile territory and the ghetto.) Rosenfeld thought that Freud had never discussed his cases with his wife or Minna, but she conceded that he had talked about his ideas with Minna. Frau Professor had a separate place as the "mother of his children."

In Rosenfeld's last years with the Freuds she had gone to look for summer houses outside Vienna with "Mama." According to Rosenfeld "the ladies" had been "terribly particular." The house had to be "scrubbed and prepared." They arranged for "green loden" for Freud's writing table. Freud could "not stand" one night not sleeping by his wife's side, even if it meant they had to do so in a "teeny room."

At the summer resort of Grundlsee, the Freud entourage

took five houses—for Marie Bonaparte, Ruth Brunswick, Dorothy Burlingham, Eva Rosenfeld, and Freud. Brunswick was then "the most intimate" with him; she had the "least inhibitions." She was immensely warm and forthcoming to him, demonstratively overriding the "rigidity" of Freudian manners. She was "like an American." But Rosenfeld thought Brunswick was "not up to" the talents of Helene Deutsch. In his "veneration" for the women around him, Freud was "re-creating" the situation of his childhood in which he had his five sisters. He did not quite know, according to Rosenfeld, what to make of her; she was "more courageous, aloof, and more feminine" than the others. Her "awe" of him was "a barrier" between them. Freud acted the same vis-à-vis Rosenfeld as Anna did. He respected whoever was first with Anna. Dorothy Burlingham was a rich American woman who could help Anna after his death.

Freud thought well enough of Rosenfeld that he gave her, as he did the other women around him, a ring. Freud himself always wore such signet rings. When Freud talked to his disciples, he would lick this gem. This was "a little tick" in Freud's makeup, and it disgusted an early pupil, a Russian named Dr. Kaplan. Freud also gave Rosenfeld another piece of jewelry. He had given Burlingham "a lovely brooch," which she lost in the snow; she was "heartbroken." But Rosenfeld found it and they were "mad with joy." Rosenfeld received the brooch from Freud that he was having made up for Burlingham as a replacement. Rosenfeld had lost her father when she was 15 years old, and she felt it was "terrible" until she had met Freud. Her first dream in the analysis could be understood as her saying, "now I have you back."

The analysis had definitely helped Rosenfeld, and she was "so responsive" to what he said. She "never forgot" his interpretations. Sometimes what he said became true after twenty years. He maintained that if her father had lived, she would have "hated" him; that was supposed to be "at the root" of her "troubles" with men. Freud had a great capacity for saying the right thing at the right moment. And she had "a gift" for responding to what he meant. He would have been less successful with someone not as Jewish as she, or with a Gentile who did not take suffering for granted; she thought he liked that trait in her.

Late in my interviewing of Eva, I read her two letters of Freud's that she had not known beforehand and that I had only recently come across. One was to Herbert Silberer, in which Freud told him he no longer desired personal contact with him. (I had not known about it when I saw Jokl.) The other letter was to Lou Andreas-Salomé, describing Freud's relief after Tausk's suicide. Rosenfeld knew that Freud had a way of "discarding" friends, and thought it "unavoidable" in life. In exactly the same way, she thought, he was "through" with her one day, and "nothing would have changed him." She lost him over Klein—he was "aloof" afterward. He was a "finisher"; this was a neurotic piece remaining from his relationship with Fliess. Rosenfeld chose to trace it back to when Freud was a child, and they "made him" not love his nanny any more. Freud repeated his disappointment over and over. He did not cease to love that nanny, even though they told him to stop and sent her away.

Freud was for Rosenfeld "irresistible," and he did not do anything intentional to be that way. Freud was convinced that a child must constantly "woo" his father; he thought that that was what "forms character." Again and again Freud implied: "Take better care, be better next time." This was the moralism in Freud that Mark Brunswick also commented on. Rosenfeld once showed Freud something she had written. He turned the pages, saying "so short," which was, for her, a criticism. He nipped her writing "in the bud." She never dared to come to him again with anything. (He once said, "You must write only when you have to write, not when you want to write.'') Freud sought to get the best out of people; Anna too could work all the time and not notice her exceptional diligence.

Was he like a flame, with moths around? (I was thinking of Silberer, Tausk, and Ruth Brunswick.) But Rosenfeld felt he *"was"* a flame, and the rest were moths. There was nobody for him to share anything with. His anxiety about others stealing his ideas, which played a big role in the famous controversies in his life (and was only hinted at by Hirst on the subject of cocaine), was "over" by then. He was so far above anybody else. In his later years he was quite hard and not malleable, but when he was young, he was trying to find an equal.

I wondered whether Freud had enjoyed fighting too much. Rosenfeld thought he was "belligerent," and so was Anna. Someone so independent and courageous was likely to be pugnacious. He could be "wise," but he could not be "unaggressive." During his engagement he had been jealous of his future wife's mother. "A genius does not want to share, and when he tries, it turns out wrong."

Rosenfeld could not really be turned out by Freud, because she was never really "in." Marie Bonaparte was "the darling" to the end. Marie and Ruth Brunswick "stuck it out" together as friends, whatever Freud's changing inner feelings about them. Brunswick had her money and American connections; he was "a simple man," still the son of "a poor textile merchant." Rosenfeld herself was for Freud "a dead end." What could he be "through" her? "Analysis was his everything"; she thought that he had "overrated" her intelligence.

Freud's moralism was such that *worthless* could be "a great word" for him. The people who could be helped by psychoanalysis were those who truly were somebody. Analysis was "a moral medal"; he had become a preacher, even if of the anti-Christ. The neurotic was a pioneer of a future standard of ethics. One had "deserved" to be healed by psychoanalysis; it was not a medical affair in Freud's eyes. As far as long analyses went, he regretted them, but if the patient could afford to pay it was all right. After a ten-year analysis, and if Freud thought well of the patient, he would let it turn into a friendship.

Could Freud be considered paranoid? Rosenfeld deemed "all this" getting angry in the end with people as "paranoid." A great man is so from within, and cannot fight everything all the time, but he can see everything. In Klein's terminology, Freud could not be depressed, nor could Anna, at least not the way someone can who has overcome what Klein called the paranoid phase. Then one would think, "What have I done to him?" instead of dwelling on what he has done to me. Characterologically these paranoid types are the less valuable people; he would not admire this in others. But his pessimism, his poor view of human beings, was inconsistent with a depressed person, who would never think of people as worthless as such. Pessimism is "a hidden paranoid trait." Freud devaluated people—just as he repudiated religiousness.

Sometimes Rosenfeld told him things in her analysis that she had heard from her grandmother. "All right," he would say, we must call her a "pioneer" in psychoanalysis. She wondered why he had not encouraged her more, and concluded that it was because she went against some of his ideas. There was "something missing of personal greatness" in him. (After my book on Freud and Tausk came out in 1969, she wrote me of Freud: "I did not admire his personality, but you had to admire his work. . . ." I wrote her back that "a great man is all of a piece, the good with the bad, one cannot have the one without the other." Even by 1973, when she was helping me identify people in a group photograph from the 1929 Oxford Congress of analysts, she asked me not to use her name, because "the Freud ladies"—meaning Anna and Mathilda—would be *very* angry with me.")

Compared with Freud her other analyst, Klein, was "not a

nice person at all" and "paranoid to an extreme!" Klein understood other people, even if she said things sometimes stupidly and clumsily. She had a secure handle on religious feelings—how one feels better when one is good than when one is not good. This is what she meant by her concept of "the depressive position." Freud did not want to be bothered by comprehending her point. Klein "misbehaved" against Anna at the Oxford Congress; Klein "and the whole English crew" became "a crowd" against his one young daughter. It looked "persecutory"; Freud took it as directed against him. It was supposedly her "first paper" before a congress, and Jones, with Klein, was "downright nasty" to her. Those who followed Klein did so "fanatically." In Klein's view mankind was "striving for the sun." It was an expression of idealism, but Klein was "her own first ideal." She was more "narcissistic" than Freud ever could have been.

I wondered what sort of analyst Klein was and how Rosenfeld would compare her with Freud. Klein was "a first-class analyst," though "not so stupefying as Freud." Rosenfeld could never forget his interpretations because he had "a sharp intelligence." It was not so with Klein. In "a fluctuating way," she was "always helpful," although her single interpretations were nothing. Rosenfeld's life was "shaped differently" after Freud. Following the analysis with Klein, things she had felt previously were "confirmed." Freud's "impact" was "immense," due to his "courage to say something."

Klein became "more and more cruel," and she experienced "terrible suffering" under her daughter's attack. Klein felt misunderstood, and the more she felt so, the more she became angry. But Klein was "never" angry with Rosenfeld—she was the only one Klein kept peace with. Klein would have loved to win her over from the Freuds. Rosenfeld ended up as a member of the so-called Middle Group in England, neither in Klein's camp nor Anna's. Klein told her: "You have sacrificed your analysis to the friendship with Anna." Rosenfeld just shrugged her shoulders as she quoted Klein, as if it were a secondary matter. Freud and Anna were "at first upset" that she went to Klein for that analysis, but Rosenfeld felt "so depressed."

Klein loved her male disciples—John Rickman and Herbert Rosenfeld, for example. She enjoyed them more than her female followers. Klein let herself be a bit spoiled by such men; they mattered as "fanatics." In her analytic views, Klein was nearer the truth than Freud. She understood that both mothers, as well as daughters, can be bad. In contrast, Freud kept to an idealization of the mother, which was combined with a certain unconscious devaluation of women. Freud was "a little bit afraid" of antagonism in a man, and more safe with women.

Rosenfeld understood the difficulties within Klein's own following. Paula Heimann, for example, who later became a turncoat from Klein and allied herself with Anna, struck Rosenfeld "dead" for twenty years because she was "unfaithful" to Klein. A baby is truly sadistic—whatever Klein wrote—only if the mother is taken away. Klein was not a successful mother, but she had the "frailties and weaknesses" of a woman. Klein's book *Envy and Gratitude* was Klein writing on Heimann. Klein could not take criticism from her followers, and Heimann was "envious."

Freud had not understood male envy of women, which is especially a problem in our century. After menopause a woman identifies more with her father. A man's envy is bound up in a changeover from a different cultural pattern that prevailed in the nineteenth century. Rosenfeld thought it was impossible to read Jung along with Freud in one lifetime, but that Jung would be good on this issue. A woman can make herself into a man, but not a man into a woman. Freud thought that Klein, like Jung earlier, was "unintelligible." That is what he meant when he wrote that he was sorry that this battle between mother and father had arisen in Rosenfeld.

Klein's own therapeutic results were "not good"; one can analyze depression and increase it. Paradoxically Freudians do not analyze depression and cure it. They help by making the personality "smaller and less aggressive." Kleinians, on the other hand, say, "Look at the whole prism of the world." They were mostly interested in psychotics, at the time I was interviewing Rosenfeld. Klein's results were positive in that she trained many analysts; there is great gratification in being a disciple.

Freudians aim to stabilize personality, while Kleinians want to make everyone into a Kleinian. They are "crusaders"; yet Freud was not a crusader. He was always sober and "never" worshiped himself. He "gave his life" for psychoanalysis, but never exaggerated "one millimeter of his success." He was realistic to the utmost. He was "a simple man with a great subject." Rosenfeld saw many modest moments in him, which was corroborated by Irma Putnam. He wrote cautiously to Yvette Guilbert about what psychoanalysis is and can do, and in writing to Einstein he did not want to play the role of the "wizard" or the magic man. He adopted a certain hardness about himself, analysis, and people who wanted to worship him.

The worst of the Klein controversy came shortly after Freud's death. In his old age Jones "went away" from Klein. Glover had "meant to do his best" by Melitta; he saw in her how she had been "damaged" by her mother. Rosenfeld was unsure why Glover had made his views into a "campaign" against Klein. Glover was "pretty nasty" to her. Jones and Glover were like "two fiends" to each other, "deadly enemies." This was already true by 1936, when Rosenfeld moved to England; the controversy became "frightful" even before the Viennese came in 1938. There were the old Freudians like David Forsyth, Grant Duff, Barbara Low, and David Eder. On the other side the leading Kleinians were Jones, Klein, and Rickman. Ella Sharpe and Nina Searle were "victims" of the struggle—Searle retired because she could not stand the fighting. Sharpe was "terribly English"; to Rosenfeld they were all very "worthy bores." Sylvia Payne was "a sober onlooker." Kate Friedlander was completely Freudian, while Paula Heimann quickly became Kleinian; both were from the continent. Joan Riviere was a devoted Kleinian who had been a patient of Freud's, one he took seriously. But Rosenfeld quoted Freud as having said of Kata Levy that she was "clumsy," and "a little fool." These comments about Levy came up in the course of Rosenfeld's analysis, when Levy was staying with her, living in her house. Anna Freud wrote to Rosenfeld in 1927 about "Poor Aunt Kata with her assiduously acquired pseudo-knowledge of analysis" (Heller 1992, p. 104). Levy had "food fads." (According to Rosenfeld, Toni von Freund's first wife committed suicide; she poisoned herself at breakfast and in front of her husband's eyes.) Later Anna Freud had "saved" Levy's life.

Anna remained a central figure for Rosenfeld, although the friendship was necessarily complicated. In Rosenfeld's view Freud had analyzed Anna because he was "deadly afraid" that someone might hurt her. Freud must have thought he could do it "loosely," without binding her too much. He was "happy" when she found Dorothy Burlingham, for she was then in "safe" hands. He was then beyond "caring." Anna was "a chaste virgin," and it was a "handicap" in her life. She was really "not flammable." She had been in love with Eitingon and confided in Rosenfeld that it was so; he was married to "a frightful woman." But she never got over "her last barrier of fear." Neither Anna nor Freud knew how afraid she was of her father. In 1927 Anna had written Rosenfeld, "I am so glad that you are no longer afraid of us" (Heller 1992, p. 104).

Anna played a special role in Freud's final years and at his death. I asked Rosenfeld whether they had waited too long at the end, before administering the morphine, and she said yes. Schur had told her "with great resentment" that the suffering had been excessive. Anna "wanted him to go on and on." He could not or would not take morphine. And Anna, because of her "respect for life," could not "allow" Schur to act. "Mama" in those days "did not count at all." Rosenfeld had seen him on his last birthday, May 6th, and he was "in frightful pain." The family had been "heartbroken" when he had kept his first operation in 1923 "secret" from them. When I raised the problem of suicide, Rosenfeld said that she thought "all his books would have gone for nothing" if he had killed himself. (Yet Freud's death was a euthanasia.) Until three days before he died, he could still read and take an interest; when he put his last book aside, that was "the end." Not many were told about the funeral after his death on September 23, 1939; however, there were "a fair amount" of people there.

In later years Rosenfeld went on to be a successful London analyst and supervisor. She scarcely mentioned this side of her work, which must have been gratifying to her, but years later I found out that her pupils were immensely fond of her. She was capable of inspiring a special sort of devotion—not one tied to any special doctrine, nor one that led to any partisan allegiance. As I tried to look at Freud through Rosenfeld's eyes, inevitably I missed seeing her own uniqueness in the round.

9

Bloomsbury: James and Alix Strachey

James and Alix Strachey were well known among Freud's British patients. Eva Rosenfeld, among others, had told me of Freud's admiration for the English, because of their "simplicity and lack of gushiness." Freud's half-brothers had moved to England when Freud's father had moved from Moravia to Vienna in 1859, and Freud kept in contact with his English relatives. After World War I some of Freud's American patients resented Freud's preference for his English clientele. Because his American analysands were mainly Jews, coupled with his desire to encourage his Gentile followers as well as his general anti-Americanism, Freud preferred to spend time with his students from Britain.

James Strachey was of special interest because he had been

the editor-in-chief of the multivolume *Standard Edition of the Collected Psychological Works of Sigmund Freud*. At the time I interviewed him, he had recently authorized a biography of his older brother Lytton to be written by a then unknown writer, Michael Holroyd. Strachey was delighted that Holroyd had been to Eton but had gotten no further in higher education—Strachey was rather puckish on that point. He gave Holroyd unrestricted access to all Lytton's correspondence. He thought the letters were too "racy and damaging" to people still living to publish, but he did not want the letters edited. He claimed he did not think that Holroyd's books would be very good. When Holroyd finished his drafts, he showed the manuscript to Strachey, who in turn wrote a series of snippy footnotes that helped immeasurably to liven Holroyd's (1971) text.

When I interviewed Strachey during the summer of 1965 he was actively concerned with disposing of Lytton's library and papers, along with portraits and a bust. There was even a letter from Freud to Lytton concerning Lytton's *Elizabeth and Essex*, which Strachey had not been able to find in time to be included in Freud's collected letters. (He never breathed a word to me about this book having been dedicated to himself and his wife Alix.) According to Strachey, Freud had missed Lytton's central points in the one book that Lytton had tried following Freud's ideas. As for Lytton's general attitude about Freud, he was "skeptical" about psychoanalysis, even though there are many parallels to be detected in Lytton's approach and that of Freud's (Roazen 1991d).

Alix had in fact argued with Freud, during her analysis, about Elizabeth, who Freud viewed as "a bad queen." When Alix protested Freud's assessment, Freud only budged to the extent of denouncing her further: "Anyway, she was a bad woman." Alix was "furious," since she thought that Elizabeth had been an exceptionally good queen, at one point sheltering Mary, Queen of Scots. Freud seemed to have what Alix considered a "romantic" attachment to Mary, rather than Elizabeth, on the grounds that she was the underdog.

Although James Strachey had reason to be considered especially prominent in his own right, I found that Alix Strachey was much more interested in the kinds of questions I was asking. This was surprising to me in that, before my interview, I had looked at her book on the unconscious "motives" of war and found it politically simplistic even if psychoanalytically correct. Alix was listed in the *Standard Edition* as having assisted James, but she seemed to me to "wear the pants" in the family. She allowed herself to show pride in having been one of the "old liners" in psychoanalysis, and was helpful to me in getting James to expand on certain points. She could instruct him to go off and bring me some recent photostats. And the interplay between their two memories was informative and instructive.

Both James and Alix had come from the highest strata of English intellectual life, which meant that my interviewing could proceed with no holds barred in terms of books and ideas. Alix was educated at Newnham College, Cambridge, while James went to Trinity College, Cambridge. James came in contact there with Frederick Meyers's Society for Psychical Research; although that organization had been interested in telepathy and the occult, it mentioned Freud's *Studies on Hysteria* long before anyone else in Britain. Alix thought that psychoanalysis "cut against" any belief in "spooks," but James held his ground about how he had first happened to read Freud's article, "The Unconscious," which he thought "sensible." (In 1912 Freud was asked to join Meyers's society, and he agreed; he also contributed an article for their proceedings [Hinshelwood 1995].)

It was characteristic of the Bloomsbury set of luminaries that they had Cambridge connections. (I myself had spent a year at Magdalen College, Oxford, which meant James Strachey— who had not been back to Cambridge for forty years, and

pretended to have some fantastic ideas about monstrous archi-
tectural changes that had supposedly taken place—could tease
me about having gone to "the other place.") It was tempting to
talk to the Stracheys about some of the famous friends they had
had, and how these people had reacted to psychoanalytic
teachings. Freud, I presume, would have appreciated the quality
of the minds that James and Alix had, and he surely perceived
something of their strategic social position.

Freud had given James Strachey a paper of his to translate
early in the analysis, and although Jones was appreciative of all
the translating work that James ultimately accomplished, there
are grounds for thinking that Jones, a relative outsider to the
establishment in Britain, was resentful of the special sphere
within British intellectual life that the Stracheys moved in.
According to one reliable source, the writer and anthropologist
Geoffrey Gorer, James and Alix had married in June 1920
because it was easier that way to get a visa to go to Vienna. Since
James and Alix were still living together it did not cross my mind
to wonder about their respective sexual preferences, but Gorer's
point about the circumstances of their marriage should have
tipped me off that it was less than a passionate sexual union. The
evidence that has appeared over the years would seem to
indicate that James was not as exclusively homosexual as his
brother Lytton, but when he first met Alix, and was delighted by
her, he described her approvingly in a letter as "an absolute
boy" (Meisel and Kendrick 1985, p. 23).

Neither James nor Alix had any medical training, yet Freud
later gave instructions to Jones that they both be made full
members of the British Psychoanalytic Society. Karin and Adrian
Stephen (Virginia Woolf's younger brother) never forgave Jones
for having insisted that they both go to medical school before
they became analysts. They complied resentfully with Jones's
demand. Quite aside from the standing that James and Alix
secured within Freud's world, they also had a place of genuine

eminence within British intellectual history. (Although I never thought of it at the time, I should have been more on my toes about who in Bloomsbury had been sleeping with whom.)

James and Alix lived in a nice country house in Marlow that once belonged to Alix's mother, who had been a painter; the Stracheys moved there in 1954 after Alix's mother's death, so that they could have the peace and quiet needed to finish the *Standard Edition*. Otto Fenichel had "wanted" the edition "very badly." At a meeting after the end of World War II, at which both Ernst Kris and Anna Freud were present, James Strachey had "boldly" offered to undertake the task. The others were relieved that one person, rather than a committee, would be responsible for doing it. (A French team has recently been laboriously at work bringing Freud out in Paris.)

At the time I was seeing the Stracheys the final volume of the *Standard Edition*, which was numbered as the first, had just been finished, even though it did not appear until 1966. (The index volume, prepared by one of James Strachey's collaborators, did not come out until 1974, by which time both Stracheys had already died.) In the days when the *Standard Edition* was still incomplete, buyers paid the publisher, Hogarth Press, for the complete set, and they received each volume when it was published. (I regret that I failed to ask James the exact royalty arrangements, but I doubt he ever got paid much for his translations; they were primarily a labor of love.) When I asked James what he thought Freud would have said of all his work on the *Standard Edition*, James clearly implied that Freud would have considered it so much nonsense.

James, who only lived on until 1967, was particularly proud of the job he had done on volume one, since it was unusually large and contained the reconstructed manuscript of Freud's 1895 "Project for a Scientific Psychology," which Freud did not care to have preserved. Freud had originally sent it to Fliess, and when Marie Bonaparte acquired Freud's correspondence with Fliess this manuscript was found too. Fliess's widow was eager to see that the Freud material succeeded in getting safely out of Nazi Germany, and by selling these documents through a bookstore for a nominal sum she succeeded in her objective. Freud had offered to reimburse Marie Bonaparte—whom the Stracheys accurately referred to by her proper royal title as "the Princess George"—but she resisted for fear Freud would want to destroy the material. "Though she had been analyzed" by Freud, James observed, "she was a woman, and resisted." I found him eager to be witty and clever, and—like his brother—savored *bon mots*.

"The Project" had been originally edited by Ernst Kris, but James thought Kris had done "a very messy" job. (Eva Rosenfeld had not particularly liked Kris, on the grounds that he was "very ambitious." At the outset "no one" expected Kris to become "a real analyst," because he had been a museum curator. Kris was first analyzed by Helene Deutsch, and later by Anna Freud.) There were some parts of the original version that did not make any sense to James, and he had had Anna Freud check the manuscript herself. James considered "The Project" very "up-to-date" neurologically, but then he had spent only some three weeks once studying medicine; to the upper-class English, doctors are apt to seem like lowly blood-letters, and nonmedical psychoanalysis has always flourished more in Britain than the United States. Freud's handwriting for "The Project" was almost illegible, there were often no periods, and Freud did not capitalize everywhere he should have, so James had to make paragraphs artificially.

In general James was a stickler about details, and apt to be unhappy with anybody else's editorial work. He thought that the German editions of Freud's were a shambles, and they undertook to translate his own notes and scholarly apparatus, as have the Italians. The task of translating and editing Freud turned out to be far more complicated a job than James ever anticipated, if only because Freud had interpolated so much new material into later versions of his texts. Freud also could excise certain earlier references. Strachey worked from the published versions of Freud's works, as opposed to the existing manuscripts, on the grounds that what counted was the version Freud had authorized for publication. In those days all the letters and manuscripts at 20 Maresfield Gardens had not yet been photostatted; James had to deal with Anna Freud to consult original Freud drafts, so it was convenient and self-preservative to reason that the printed text was what had been approved by Freud. (We now know, though, from the information Dr. Ernst Falzeder brought to my attention [see Chapter 3], that some papers of Freud's that appeared after his death were altered from the surviving manuscripts.)

I had many questions to ask both Stracheys, and their house seemed to overflow with primary documents about the history of psychoanalysis. But I could not help noticing how decidedly unusual if not eccentric these two people were. James, who was 78 and bearded, looked just like pictures of Freud in his later years. (I was told that for years James had liked to pose as older than he was, and as cut off from the outside world; growing old meant "catching up with himself," as one London analyst put it.) James claimed to be three-quarters deaf, due to a cold, and he was blind in one eye because of a detached retina, which they did not know how to cure when it happened. One glass of his spectacles was kept clouded because of his blindness. Then in 1953, before he had put *The Interpretation of Dreams* to bed, the retina detached in the other eye, and he could not see for six months. The *Standard Edition* project looked like it was in jeopardy, until he finally had a successful operation. Duncan Grant had done a painting of James in 1910, when James was 23; the large number of books around James indicate how scholarly he always had been. James and I sat for awhile talking alone in the sunshine seated in old-fashioned wooden lawn chairs.

The oddest aspects of James's and Alix's life became evident when they served me lunch. As far as I could figure out they lived entirely on tinned food. Alix served ginger beer with the meal, explaining that it appeared in Dickens. She told me that she had not seen the man she had been ordering food from by telephone for the last nine years. (I can certainly believe that Alix had "an erratic attitude toward food," and had once suffered from an illness resembling anorexia nervosa [Meisel and Kendrick 1985].) She took charge of washing up the dishes, but before doing so she tied a string around her waist to be sure her clothes got no water on them. It was then that I noticed that she was wearing a piece of string also as a watchband. The taxi driver who took me to the house from the local train station said he had rarely ever seen Alix, although from time to time James went alone on trips. Alix wore enormous shoes, and her thin legs were covered in brown stockings; her long face was etched with deep lines.

Both Stracheys were isolated from what one would think of as normal human contact, and the mail box was a mile away. It was hard to believe that they each had once been practicing analysts in London. For a time James had a heavy caseload; he was remembered by Kata Levy as having been "halting and shy." From time to time Alix still saw an "old patient," for the sake of "just keeping in touch," but she indicated some concern about whether she was still understandable. Although she lived on until 1973, after James's death she had some sort of collapse. I really could not imagine what sort of therapist he could have been like, for he was so detachedly bookish; I thought that Alix would have been better in human communication. But James had in fact written a 1934 paper, "The Nature of the Therapeutic Action of Psychoanalysis," which was famous, although it seemed to me most unlikely that he had been much good at what he had been writing about. For example, he wrote of a patient that "the best way of ensuring that his ego shall be able to distinguish between phantasy and reality is to withhold reality from him as much as possible" (p. 147). Such an approach might have its basis in certain of Freud's theories, but it is hardly consistent with Freud's clinical practices.

It was characteristic of James that he could quip about his predecessor as a translator of Freud into English, A. A. Brill, that he was a "very nice man" but had two flaws—he did not know German and he failed to understand English. Brill was by origin a Hungarian, which explained James's aphorism. By the mid-1960s it was notorious that Brill, who had been responsible for assembling the huge *Basic Writings of Sigmund Freud*, which appeared in the vastly influential Modern Library edition, had produced texts that were not thoroughly reliable. I was suspicious of James's possible anti-Americanism, when he smiled over what a shifting variety of reasons Freud had for disliking America; Alix thought that the United States had been unusually receptive to new ideas, and did not seem to have the more traditional British prejudices. (I did not know at the time that she was born in New Jersey, though had not been back to America since her infancy; Eva Rosenfeld too had an American birth.) Brill for years was the leading analyst in New York. With Freud's approval Brill substituted his own slips of the tongue for those of Freud. Brill had not wanted the Modern Library edition to replace Freud's individual texts, so Brill would here and there drop whole passages for the sake of preserving Freud's copyright.

While in the 1960s James Strachey's work seemed an essential corrective to what Brill himself had bequeathed, starting with Bruno Bettelheim's 1983 critique of Strachey's translations a new generation has become aware of how inevitably interpretive any translation is. Bettelheim blamed the

Stracheys for the medical monopoly on psychoanalysis that for so long has prevailed in the United States, and while it is true that the anti-religious bias of Strachey helped Freud sound more scientistic than the original German warrants, it would in my opinion be a mistake to ignore just how much Strachey accomplished for Freud (Wilson 1987). Freud's English was good enough for him to spot Strachey's considerable talents as a translator, and even when Strachey came up with a new term, such as *cathexis*, no matter how miffed Freud may have been at first he actually introduced the word *cathexis* into one of his German manuscripts (Freud 1926).

Freud's knowledge of different languages was considerable, and he had some experience himself as a translator. (Freud's translations were at least as controversial as those of Strachey or Brill. Freud inserted footnotes, for example, which made his teacher Jean-Martin Charcot unhappy. Freud was delighted with the work Strachey succeeded in doing, which is bound to make it more than a bit awkward for contemporaries to poke holes in Strachey's accomplishment.) James claimed not to have really known German when he went to Freud, who typically accorded a sophisticated latitude to those he approved as translators of his own work. The example of James in England could be fleshed out by different figures in other countries, and in languages besides English. In Italy, for example, Freud thought it was correct of Edoardo Weiss to substitute his own slips of the tongue for Freud's. These early translators were trying to forward Freud's cause, not to come up with something to use as holy scripture. It would be unfortunate, I think, if the inevitable limitations of Strachey's splendid edition were to lead now to a fundamentalist quest for the so-called true Freud, instead of our concentrating on a mature evaluation of the substance and validity of Freud's ideas themselves.

Strachey had not started out alone as a translator in

English, as Jones had made certain key decisions before him.
English-speaking readers should sit up and take notice how odd
it is, and an indication of French parochial preoccupations, that
there are in existence more than ten French translations of
Freud's short paper on negation. Jacques Lacan may have taught
that we can rediscover the genuine Freud through "the literal-
ness of the text," but surely that ought not to be taken as the
final truth of the matter. A French translating group has recently
revived the usage of words that have fallen into disuse for
centuries. One cannot take these critics of Strachey seriously as
long as they repeat the proposition that the new French rendi-
tions of Freud consist of "the text, the whole text, and nothing
but the text." The so-called "genius of the French language"
does not justify the use of neologisms. These translating co-
workers in France have proposed "a Freud in French that is . . .
[sic] Freudian." Improving on Strachey, a thoroughly worthy
objective, should not become identified with abandoning our
critical faculties for the sake of reifying Freud's works as gospel
(Roazen in press-a).

   Although the Stracheys have been accused of tendentiously
translating Freud, both of them were more emancipated about
Freud than some analysts today. Idealization of Freud can take
many forms. The Stracheys played a key part in the history of
psychoanalysis in Britain, in that they helped make it possible
for Melanie Klein to move there. Alix said she had been "very
instrumental" in getting Klein to England. Alix, after her analysis with Freud was over, was in Berlin with Abraham from
1924 to 1925; a book of the letters between James and Alix from
that period came out in 1985. Alix had not gone to Abraham on
Freud's suggestion; Klein was also a patient of Abraham's at the
same time. Alix wrote to James in London about Klein, and
James spoke to Jones. According to Alix "they were all" against
Klein in Berlin, and she could not seem to "get through" to

Freud in Vienna. Hans Lampl especially was against her, but then he was Viennese and that whole circle seemed hostile to her work.

Alix joked about how arbitrary had been the way Freud had gotten she and James into meetings of the Vienna Psychoanalytic Society; this was in contrast to how Freud had later waited to allow Edith Jackson to go to those sessions. (Alix said he must have "commanded" it.) The members met in a room, not a hall, and sat around a table. The Stracheys were both in Vienna for about two years. James thought that Freud had liked it that they stayed that long, unlike the way he reacted to the Americans who supposedly left too soon. (I could not succeed in explaining to him that it had often been Freud who broke off the treatment of his American patients.) Alix had decided that she needed more analysis, which is why she had gone to Abraham in Berlin; later in England she continued being analyzed by others.

It was not easy for me to probe with the Stracheys about the nature of their own clinical contact with Freud. I was inhibited partly by their famous names, but more by the kinds of eminent friends and associates they had. Virginia Woolf was simply "Virginia" to them. I considering myself lucky to have picked up what I could from the Stracheys, and they allowed me back, without wrecking my contact with them by being too intrusive. My questions were more or less built on the kinds of points the Stracheys were willing to bring up. (They had refused to cooperate with Eissler's oral history project; Mrs. Riviere had done so and James claimed the typist got the manuscript "all wrong." Had the Stracheys permitted a tape recorder, I might have appeared to be ahead in scholarly terms, but then maybe no genuine conversation would have taken place. The reader will remember how misleadingly tilted Eissler's contact with Hirst or Edith Jackson could be. And I knew that Helene Deutsch spoke differently when she was being taped.)

Since Alix spoke about having gone to Abraham, whom she

considered "a good scientist," it gave me an opening to discuss with James what Freud had thought of Abraham. James agreed that Freud had not personally liked Abraham, but that he respected him; Abraham was "very sane, even a bit dull." Ferenczi was, in contrast, "dotty," although James left it an open question whether in addition Ferenczi was "really dotty" (i.e., insane), which is what Jones's biography implied. Abraham's letters to Freud were "terribly long-winded." (Helene Deutsch said it had been shocking for her to see how infantile Abraham, her own second analyst after Freud, could be toward Freud.) James said that a very angry letter Freud sent to Abraham just before his death in 1925 had been "suppressed" in the published edition of the Freud–Abraham correspondence. (An unexpurgated version of these letters is only now in the works.) James was in favor of publishing "everything," but he thought it would be another fifty years before all Freud's letters were out.

According to James, Abraham had a much more balanced view of Jung and Rank before they left the movement than Freud himself. James rejected my interpretation that Freud may have been right, at least with Rank, in that Abraham (and Jones) may have made a bad situation worse through personal jealousy. While the Stracheys were in Vienna during 1920 to 1922, Rank was "the favorite." Freud had said that he could not invite the Stracheys to a Christmas party, for it would be an interference in their analyses, but Freud got them invited instead to Rank's Christmas party. The Stracheys knew and liked Rank's wife Tola, who enjoyed acting as a hostess for Freud.

While James regarded Adler as "trivial," Jung was treated seriously. Jung had had, according to Alix, "great access to the unconscious." She thought that Jung's autobiography should be "required reading" for all analysts; while parts of it were "gibberish," there was a "very good section on God." (It is now known, thanks to the research of Sonu Shamdasani, that there is in existence a second volume of Jung's reminiscences, which has so far been embargoed by the Jung family.) The autobiography allegedly showed "how sick he was at times," and how close he got to the "primary process" thinking of the unconscious. Alix in particular was critical of Georg Groddeck, especially since Freud had proclaimed that Groddeck's work was as good as Rabelais. She objected to the way Groddeck saw the unconscious everywhere; if "two trains were in collision," then it must be because someone "wished" it. She thought that eventually Freud had to read him out of the movement, although originally Freud had imposed him on a group that was unwilling to have him.

I asked whether Freud had ever changed, and James chuckled a bit and said no, as if Freud would have been the last person ever to do so. James saw him in London several times during 1938 to 1939. What the outside world did not understand about Freud, in James's view, was how "humorous" he was. (Freud [1905] in print used the example of a "cynical" joke that seems to me to typify what he might appreciate: "A wife is like an umbrella—sooner or later one takes a cab" [p. 110].[1]) The Stracheys knew Freud, which affected the translations in all sorts of intangible ways; the extent to which Strachey was on target is currently underestimated. Freud was not "at all" as severe as in his pictures; he supposedly "hated" to be photographed. And when artists drew Freud, they felt they had to make him took stern.

It was in keeping with James's own extraordinary exactness that he criticized Jones's biography for being "rather disorderly." In James's view Jones repeated himself too much. There was a huge pile of letters at the house from Jones, who sent James portions of the biography as it was being written. According to James, he often sent correct dates to Jones, but

---

1. Peter Swales has used this joke for different biographical purposes than my own.

frequently Jones transcribed the wrong material into print. Jones was very precise about facts and "always inaccurate." When Jones was in error, it was in an authoritative-sounding way; "all the details are off." He would write and ask for the correct information, and then would forget it. James's own volumes of Jones had the amended dates all there; it "wants" going through from start to finish. James also thought that Jones had a "morbid" interest in Freud's cancer, and spent too much time dealing with the sickness, rather "reveling" in all the "gory" details.

Jones could be "very tactless" at public meetings, tearing apart somebody else's paper. Strachey once gave a dinner party in the 1930s for Jones, who wanted to meet the Bloomsbury economist John Maynard Keynes. The evening was "a flop." Keynes told Jones all about psychoanalysis. "He liked to do that sort of thing, have dinner with an expert and then tell him all about it." In James's view Keynes did not know very much about psychoanalysis (cf. Winslow 1986, 1990). Leonard Woolf was there that memorable night, too.

James had given Freud a copy of Keynes's book on the Treaty of Versailles when it first came out. It was translated into German, but James gave him the version in English. Freud thought "very well" of Keynes's book. (Freud's attitudes toward male homosexuality, and his theory of perversion, have been off-putting to many British intellectuals, but evidently not to Keynes.) Freud had also liked a book that made psychoanalytic interpretations of Woodrow Wilson. Alix said she was skeptical about such "applications" of psychoanalysis, while James was not; yet she was the one who wrote not just about war, but the psychology of nationhood.

E. M. Forster was another of the Stracheys's Bloomsbury friends, but "Morgan" was not interested in psychoanalysis. Forster and Virginia Woolf feared that analysis might interfere with their creative powers. Alix thought there may have been something in their objections. Virginia's "voices" had "led her on.'' Alix thought it was in principle an open question whether she would still have had those "voices" after a "completed" analysis, although I do not know what that might mean. Any such notion of finality has to have been an unfortunate illusion.

I read through some of the letters Jones had written to Strachey while the biography was under way. Jones referred, at one point, to Freud's "idiotic" enthusiasm for Rank. There was an amusing letter about how the libel laws in England, as opposed to those in the United States, restricted the free flow of Jones's prose. Jones claimed he could not say that Jung had said such and such with a "sour" look. (Jung lived until 1961.) Jones might know that Freud never used the term *Thanatos*, but did not realize that this was because of Stekel's having cited it already. I was in particular interested in what Jones had written Strachey about the Freud–Bullitt manuscript on Woodrow Wilson. Jones had read it while writing the biography; afterward, he wrote Strachey that Bullitt was "manic" and "obstinate." Apparently the manuscript was "locked up" with a letter code; U. S. Marines were needed to put it back in a safe. Jones used very strong language; he thought the book would make a political sensation, hurt the Democrats, and do psychoanalysis no good among impartial historians. Mrs. Wilson was then 88, and Jones thought she would not hold out much longer. Bullitt believed that the Versailles Treaty had "caused" World War II; nothing had happened since then to change his mind. Jones mentioned that perhaps Strachey would include the Wilson manuscript in the *Standard Edition*, since after all he had included *Studies on Hysteria* co-authored with Breuer in volume two. (In both cases Freud believed in having chapters signed by the authors.)

I asked how Jones could have done what he did to Ferenczi in the last volume of the biography. James immediately raised the point about Jones having had a "pseudo-analysis" with Ferenczi. To Alix, Ferenczi seemed "a bit wild." James said that Freud loved Ferenczi because he published the untrammeled sort of thinking that Freud was prone to but controlled and did not put in print. Instead of seeing Ferenczi as a great pioneer in therapeutic technique, James thought that Ferenczi had only made attempts to shorten analysis; if a patient were reliving a relationship with the mother, then the analyst should act like the mother. Such techniques seemed to both the Stracheys "almost wild."

I wondered what effect on Jones, and on the British Psychoanalytic Society, the coming of the Viennese analysts in 1938 had. Alix could not stop talking about how the newcomers "mangled" the English language. It made meetings "very difficult." "How awful it must be to live abroad!" Somehow the Stracheys were used to American accents, even though James had never been to the United States. Six months later James and Alix were going for a well-earned vacation to the West Indies to celebrate the completion of the *Standard Edition*.

The issue of the arrival of the Viennese analysts in England raised the vexing topic of Melanie Klein. According to the Stracheys, the Viennese handled her "very stupidly" and intolerantly. Supposedly Freud would have gone Klein's way had he lived and still possessed his health. Mrs. Klein was "not a very good expositor" of her own ideas. But after she was a success she "came to believe in every word she had written," which was at odds with her previous "modesty" in Berlin. Alix had translated some of her papers. Only Abraham had not been against her in Berlin. (The Berliners always seemed more efficient than the Viennese, but Alix was not sure the papers were really any better there.)

Alix said that once Klein was established, and Jones did help her when she was in England, it was necessary to be more critical of her, since "she took all her ideas so seriously." Neither of the Stracheys seemed to know that Klein was an unknown in the United States in the 1960s. They were convinced she had been "domineering," especially when she was "on top." She could be "very stubborn" about how her books should be translated into English. Neither Strachey seemed to see that Klein was drawing on Freud's own heritage as a fighter. When Jones had come out in behalf of Klein, Mark Brunswick thought the whole Freud family turned against Jones, and that Anna Freud's dog Wolf was very perceptive in trying to bite Jones, since the dog knew what Anna and her father were feeling.

As far as Anna Freud went, the Stracheys felt they had underestimated her. In Vienna she had been "very charming," and seemed to do "a bit of embroidery." Alix did not guess that she had "the Freud brain." Anna's possessiveness about Freud's manuscripts may have been founded on "a fear of exploitation," and a desire to devote herself to the future of analysis. Of course Anna may have been "mistaken." But Alix thought that Anna was afraid of the attitude which might lead to a hunt for a drinking problem in Freud, on the grounds that such a frailty would be a basis for saying he was "human." That's the kind of digging Anna wanted to avoid.

Freud did have a weakness when it came to cigar smoking. Supposedly he smoked "very small" cigars, until the Americans started bringing him the bigger ones. When James visited him, after his analysis, Freud always offered him a cigar, and seemed to expect that James would want to smoke it. Freud was "always" smoking. Alix cautiously proposed that maybe "nowadays" doctors would attribute Freud's cancer of the jaw to his smoking. This was one of the exceptional occasions when James took over; he dismissed Alix's idea about linking the cancer to smoking as a "superstition," and Alix promptly gave in to James's objection.

The one issue on which I got absolutely nowhere with the Stracheys was Freud's Jewishness; they seemed even dimmer on this point than Irma Putnam had been. I confess that at the time of my interviewing it never crossed my mind to suspect them of

being anti-Semitic, but now that letters between James and Alix
have been published it is impossible not to notice that prejudice.
It even crops up in Virginia Woolf's diaries, although her
husband Leonard was Jewish. When I asked James about Freud
as a Jew, he simply brushed aside the point; people are individuals, that is all, James insisted. The one Jewish trait that James
spotted in Freud was the way he acted as head of the family.
When I asked whether Freud had extended that patriarchal sway
to the rest of the movement, James conceded that that was what
"people said," but James did not seem to like the general point
I was driving at. James even dismissed my question about why
psychoanalysis had arisen first in Vienna.

Alix thought that Freud's attitude toward money was a
distinctly Jewish aspect of him. She did not, like others, praise
Freud for his honesty about finances; on the other hand she was
not so put off by Freud as a Jew not to have admired him and his
work.[2] But she failed, for example, to find it was true clinically
that in order for patients to do well in treatment they had to
make a financial sacrifice. She attributed Freud's insistence on
the importance of such payments to his Jewishness. "They *are*
interested in money." (Both Stracheys had private incomes of
their own.)

When they had first written to Freud in 1920, he had said

---

2. In 1924 James wrote Alix: "I had a very tiresome hour
with Jones and Mrs. Riviere. . . .The little beast (if I may venture
so to describe him) is really most irritating. . . .They want to call
'das Es' 'the Id.' I said I thought everyone would say 'the Yidd.'
So Jones said there was no such word in English; 'There's
"Yiddish," you know. And in German "Jude." But there is no
such word as "Yidd." ' 'Pardon me, doctor, Yidd is a current
slang word for a Jew.' 'Ah! A slang expression. It cannot be in
very widespread use then.'—Simply because the l.b. hasn't ever
heard it" (Meisel and Kendrick 1985, p. 83).

he wanted them to use English currency. The charge was at first one guinea a session, then it went up to two guineas per session. Later on the fee became five guineas; at that point they could not have afforded to stay with him. They were in Vienna during the "devaluation," and were "rich" for "the one time in their life." Alix was also present during the inflation in Berlin.

Both Stracheys kept referring to Freud as a "social democrat," or some sort of socialist. They were not in Vienna, as Mark Brunswick was, when Freud supported Dollfuss against the socialists. The Stracheys thought Freud had been "on the side of the poor," and they maintained that he voted socialist; there was not always a Liberal candidate running. Alix was impressed by Freud's boldness in the social sphere; for example, he had said that the greatest benefactor to mankind would be someone who invented a sure and cheap contraception.

The Stracheys were convinced that Marxism had been no barrier to the acceptance of psychoanalysis in Britain, because it was not until the late 1930s that English intellectuals "went political." James singled out Frank Ramsey as an extraordinary Cambridge logician and metaphysician, "as brilliant as Bertie Russell," who had been analyzed by Theodor Reik, written a book on psychoanalysis, but died early (Monk 1990). The others in the circles the Stracheys moved in were "all too frightened" to be adequately receptive to psychoanalysis.

Even Leonard Woolf, Freud's publisher at Hogarth Press, took Virginia for treatment during her breakdowns to an eminent "quack, Sir somebody-or-other," who told her to "drink Ovaltine" three times a day. James had been reading Leonard's autobiography (I had been impressed with how unpsychological Leonard had been about Virginia's collapses); James knew Leonard before and after his marriage to Virginia. It was James who originally suggested to Leonard that he publish Freud. An attempt to produce an English edition of Freud's works in Vienna had failed, which is when Strachey tried to get it done in

England. The copyrights for the English versions were all snarled up. Jones had persuaded Freud to permit the "collected" edition to come out in the 1920s; Mrs. Riviere was "in charge" of that. In those days Hogarth was only bringing out "little pamphlets." Sir Stanley Unwin would not touch Freud's work except on "impossible" terms. James thought that Hogarth Press really got started on the money it made out of publishing Freud's work. Virginia Woolf even translated Freud's essay on Dostoyevski.

When I asked James and Alix whether their analyses with Freud had been conducted in German or English, they were genuinely not sure. Both Stracheys spoke in English, they agreed, but Freud might with one of them have started out in English, and then switched to German. Alix finally concluded that Freud spoke in German. She stressed the desirability of the analyst and the analysand speaking the same language. They each had a genuine love for words. I had said something complimentary about Hanns Sachs's book about Freud, since they were, like Kata Levy, enthusiasts in behalf of Martin Freud's reminiscences. Alix said she would read Sachs's volume; she was impressed by Sachs's knowledge of idiomatic English, except that he used idioms in "all" the wrong places. But Alix readily agreed that Sachs might well have been able to write well; it was likely, though, to be "sentimental," but James thought that was all right "as long as it was genuine."

Sadger was one who stood out among the "local" Viennese, along with Federn and Hitschmann. Alix thought that Sadger had a special interest in sadism. She said that he was the "kind of man" who did what he did out of "personal loyalty and devotion." Had it not been for Freud personally, Sadger would not have been interested in the material of psychoanalysis. (Freud had complained in a 1908 letter about Sadger's fanaticism, yet by the end of Sadger's career he was writing a book so heretical that Jones thought it warranted putting Sadger in a concentration camp [Roazen 1975]. Sadger did not survive the Nazis.)

In his analyzing the Stracheys, Freud had said that they were "the first couple" he had treated simultaneously. This was before Freud analyzed Ruth and Mark Brunswick. Alix thought that Freud may have been interested in the possibility of telepathy between her and James, but that nothing like that had occurred to them. When one of them missed an analytic hour, the other could have it. The first year they went six hours per week, the second only five hours weekly. There were desperate economic conditions then in Vienna, with begging in the streets. Alix recalled how "a black-coated man," a professional, had in 1920 asked at a restaurant if he could have the rest of her pudding, which she was too full to eat any more of. Such an incident underlines the frightful character of the conditions in Vienna then. Freud had wanted their money; they "daresay" he would have seen them on Sundays, if they had offered. James wanted his sessions to be not too late, so that he could go to the opera, and Freud agreed. In James's view Freud's waiting room and study office were both "stuffy" and very Viennese. James had read most of Freud before he went over. (In Vienna he and Alix used to go to the Cafe Zentral in order to keep up with the London *Times*.)

The Stracheys were both musical; when I saw them they had up-to-date stereo equipment, even though the cost was "ruinous." When James had asked Freud about Mozart, he had replied: "Oh, he is different." Alix maintained that an English intellectual is not supposed to like music, and by convention a Viennese was expected to love it. So Freud may have been posing about music, making "a parade" of his skeptical stance. (On the other hand they took Freud's remarks about death seriously, although such views were at odds with how he "enjoyed life" so much.) One of Freud's relatives claimed that he was terribly afraid that the children might take to music, and

that it would interfere with his work. Freud had been knowledgeable enough, or I thought a bit grandiose, to have said that
thanks to Gustav Mahler's "treatment" (consisting of them
walking together for four hours in Holland) his Tenth Sym-
phony, which was unfinished at Mahler's death, was better than
his Ninth.

During the second year they were with Freud, he sched-
uled their hour at a different time each day, so that there were
occasional sessions that would conflict with their going to the
opera in the evening. Sometimes she had to get up early, perhaps
for an 8 A.M. appointment. Alix thought, when she was always
hurrying to get to an appointment on time, that she may have
been the first woman to have run on a street in Vienna. Freud
was that punctual. He took an "old-fashioned" attitude toward
women. He thought they belonged "at home," yet he honored
them a "great deal" for having "finer feelings" than men. He
believed they were "weaker" and needed "protection." If they
turned out to have "a brain," Freud was willing to "give them
their head." (Alix confessed she thought that men have better
minds than women.)

Freud complained bitterly about the way they both mumbled during their analyses. And he objected to how he had to use
so much English with his American patients. The Freuds "all"
have big mouths, and articulate what they are saying clearly.
During the analysis the Stracheys lived in a pension at the top of
the hill of the Berggasse. Alix emphasized that they were
"students," and therefore did not have to cut all social ties to
the Freuds. Alix could still know Anna Freud in Vienna.

With James, Freud might rap on the couch in order "to
drive a point home"; it was no sign of irritation. James was a bit
proud of how if he got into difficult material that he wanted to
evade, he could always do so by bringing up an erudite subject
that would send Freud to looking it up in an encyclopedia.

The analyses of both James and Alix were conducted on a

sophisticated level. Alix said that Freud had cited Conrad Ferdinand Meyer, the Swiss writer he mentioned to Kata Levy, and
Freud used to quote Friedrich von Schiller. James also reported
that he once said that Dostoyevski was the greatest novelist, and
that Freud had heartily agreed. Freud thought Dostoyevski was
superb, but then Freud admitted in a letter to Reik that he really
did not like him. Freud, however, never mentioned Joseph
Conrad; James implied that Freud was not treating them on *that*
intellectual a plane, while Alix emphasized that they were there
more to learn than as patients.

James was expert on all Freud's texts. For example, James
had helped suppress a 1935 footnote to Freud's "Autobiographical Study" in which he withdrew his commitment to the idea
that Shakespeare's works had been written by the man from
Stratford. Based on a 1920 book written by someone named J. T.
Looney, Freud threw his allegiance to the Earl of Oxford (a
curious belief that Ruth Brunswick seems to have shared). James
had been "so much taken aback" that he wrote Freud asking him
to reconsider it, in the light of the "effect the note was likely to
have on the average English reader, particularly in view of the
unfortunate name of the author of the book referred to." Freud
was "forbearing" and allowed the note to get dropped in
England, but thought it could be retained for the American
edition since the same sort of British "narcissistic defence need
not be feared over there . . ." (Freud 1925, p. 64). James had
argued with him about the identification of a butterfly in the
Wolf Man case history, and Freud (1918) was convinced and
changed the name in all later editions. (Others, such as Sandor
Rado, reported Freud's having failed to make corrections to
literary slips he admitted having committed.) James's literary
taste was such that he remembered that Freud had thought the
fourth section of *Totem and Taboo* was Freud's finest piece of
writing, and so did Thomas Mann.

James proposed that the endings of Freud's books are all

"difficult," because he was just about to start another one; he had begun to express his thoughts in an elliptical form. James thought that *Group Psychology* was "simple," but James could not make "heads or tails" out of *Beyond the Pleasure Principle*. James especially liked Freud's last book, *The Outline of Psycho-analysis*, which was left unfinished at Freud's death. As for *Moses and Monotheism*, which was the final book Freud published, James thought it curious that Freud had withheld its appearance for fear the Catholic Church would not like it, when it was the Jews who were to be offended by its thesis. The fact that "historically" Freud's Moses hypotheses might have been all wrong did not seem to faze James a bit. Mrs. Jones had done a very hurried job of translating *Moses and Monotheism* in order to get the book out before Freud died. They were in too much of a hurry for James to have done the job properly. Jones's wife was originally Viennese, a relative of Jokl's, it will be remembered, and James was referring unfavorably to her work, in contrast to his own, when he reaffirmed the well-known principle that no one can translate into English when it is not the native language.

The Stracheys were among the most illustrious of Freud's patients that I interviewed. Although their credentials must have played a role in Freud's accepting them for treatment, he hardly appears to have been put off by their positions in Britain. Evidently Freud had started off with James by reading word for word Jones's letter to Freud about James. Jones had written: "He is a man of 30, well educated and of a well-known literary family (I hope he may assist with translations of your works), I think a good fellow but weak and perhaps lacking in tenacity" (Paskauskas 1993, p. 378). However Freud may have embarrassed Jones by that sort of indiscretion, it must have helped establish himself with James, getting the analysis off on a good footing. Both Stracheys remained devoted to Freud for the rest of their lives.

10

Conclusions

One of the central objectives in presenting my accounts of the therapeutic contact that these ten people had with Freud has been to show the range of the clinical situations that Freud found himself confronting. Opinions will differ about how successfully Freud was able to handle the complexities of what he became involved in. To an extent he aimed to evoke the kind of dependencies he then tried to overcome; yet he also inevitably was unaware of the degree to which his own personality, as well as the treatment setting he created, was having a regressive impact on his patients. As I traveled about interviewing his patients I sometimes heard the exact words being repeated; it was hard not to think that Freud's patients had been induced into lasting, quasi-hypnotic states. There is an important kernel of truth behind the famous aphorism of a contemporary of Freud's, the Viennese satirist Karl Kraus: "Psychoanalysis is that mental illness of which it believes itself to be the cure" (Timms 1986, p. 109).

It may not be too surprising that in his lifetime people easily misunderstood Freud's intentions. The confidentiality of psychoanalytic proceedings meant that it was hard to follow what had actually gone on in Freud's consulting room, and the propaganda Freud published about his new procedures was bound to be in its own way misleading. Even he himself could not always be sure about the nature of the conflicts he became enmeshed in; the human soul is bound in some sense to be unfathomable. Freud's ambitiousness could lead to diagnostic mistakes, and patients can fail to improve for a variety of reasons. Although Freud privately knew how often psychoanalysts could err, what he published put all the responsibility for things going wrong on the shoulders of the patients themselves. If someone did badly in psychoanalytic treatment, it was always possible retrospectively to say that they had not been suitable for analysis because of the "inaccessible" nature of their difficulties. Unfortunately the elaborate system of thought Freud created allowed too much leeway in terms of the possible excuses for therapeutic failures. But even today, with the huge literature about Freud that has already appeared, the import of the psychoanalysis he created remains highly controversial.

The issue of power is almost never discussed within the clinical literature. And this remains true even though in 1937 Freud thought it worth repeating "the words of a writer who warns us that when a man is endowed with power it is hard for him not to misuse it" (p. 249). Recently there has been a great deal of publicity associated with the sexual abuse of patients by their therapists, but the larger questions associated with the multiple occasions on which clinicians wield unchallenged power have rarely been examined. Transgressions, given the inevitably private nature of therapeutic practice, are hard to check; money is at least as troublesome as sexuality. It is no wonder that our legal systems are still struggling with how to deal with evidence provided by so-called psychological experts.

Freud had a special stature by virtue of his historical role in creating a new field. But he did not help to control the abuse of power by the attitude he chose to take toward the question of ethics and psychoanalysis. For Freud sought to distance himself from moral inquiry, as if examining such questions of ethics might threaten the scientific status he hoped to attain for psychoanalysis. He liked to think that what was moral was self-evident, and although he had originally been distrustful of bureaucratic training procedures for future practitioners, in the end his position relied on the training institutes, along the lines proposed by Toni von Freund, being able to supervise the quality and behavior of psychoanalysts.

However, the question of the sorcerer's apprentices remains a perplexing one; in writing to Jung, Freud compared himself to "the venerable old master" (Falzeder 1994, p. 173) of Goethe's poem. It was impossible for anybody else to make his system work as he did. Freud had been determined to found a school of his own, independent of regular university life. Therefore he set out to found a variety of training centers that were designed to be independent, at least to some degree, of his own personal direction. But the specific therapeutic procedures Freud had devised were highly personalized ones, and even when his students were privy to how Freud behaved in practice, they often chose to follow some of his written recommendations rather than the living oral tradition they knew about.

I take it for granted that it requires some historical perspective to be able to appreciate what it might have meant, in the day and age Freud was living in, to make the effort he did to understand the dilemmas that patients presented him with. These ten examples of individual patients' lives, based on their reports of how Freud treated them, should help make more vivid just how Freud was likely to have conducted himself. One does not have to be an apologist in behalf of everything Freud ever did, or a trade-union advocate in support of the cause of the movement he created, to appreciate how different a world from ours he was functioning in. We should not too readily impose hindsight on how Freud undertook to assist these people.

From a crass and ahistorical perspective, Freud may to some appear a charlatan, with the transference he talked about seeming to be like the "magnetic" rapport advocated in an earlier century by the followers of Franz Anton Mesmer (Darnton 1968). One of the greatest novelists of our century, Vladimir Nabokov, responded with glee to the publication of the Freud–Bullitt study of Woodrow Wilson. As Nabokov wrote in a letter to the monthly *Encounter* (February 1967, volume 28), which had published portions of the work: "I welcome Freud's 'Woodrow Wilson' not only because of its comic appeal, which is great, but because that surely must be the last rusty nail in the Viennese Quack's coffin" (p. 91). (Just as Nabokov suppressed Bullitt's collaboration in the book, an orthodox Freudian like Peter Gay listed that text under Bullitt's name first, although that reverses the original order [Roazen 1990a].)

To the extent that Freud's approach was curative, it was because he and his patients shared a common belief system, one that may seem alien to us today. According to Franz Alexander (1940) he was "not surprised to hear" from Freud "that according to his experience in the majority of successful cases the success is based to a considerable degree on the continued faithful attitude of the patient to his analyst even though he may never see his physician again" (p. 202). If the first-hand accounts of these ten patients of Freud's sound unlikely today, it is helpful to be reminded that "healing is only possible because the relationship authentically particularizes personal experience in symbols that are culturally and practically relevant" (Kleinman

1988, p. 137). The continued faithfulness that Alexander reported Freud's alluding to is only understandable, in terms of his own procedures, within an era that has now vanished. Freud was behaving rationally in the context of the enlightened expectations of his time, even if in retrospect he may look like a charismatic healer performing his cure within a quasi-communal setting (Micale 1993).

Freud's repeated claims of being a scientist have to be placed within the context of his social world. These pretensions to having made a neutral contribution to the so-called science of psychology tended to grow more pronounced as Freud aged and became increasingly disillusioned about his earlier hopes for having accomplished therapeutic gains. I think that it was tempting for Freud to mislead himself, in that devoted followers of his were eager to supply him with what he and they thought were confirmations of his alleged "findings." Part of Freud's problem was a historically conditioned conception of what constitutes science, and he made too sharp a break between theoretical preconceptions and "facts."

The suggestive impact of Freud personally and the tilted effects of the psychoanalytic procedure were such that he did not have to be alert enough to the extent to which, even though he might try to check his results, they were shot through with all sorts of self-fulfilling prophecies. People in trouble will believe almost anything, at least temporarily, if they think it will lead to making them feel better. So there were multiple incentives, entirely aside from the economic motives of self-interest among those who became practitioners, for psychoanalysis not to have the kind of built-in safeguards that one would expect of a scientific discipline. Patients like Edith Jackson who invested a small fortune in being treated by Freud—and traveled abroad to boot—were not likely to criticize the benefits they may have received.

Despite the disappointments in what Freud had appeared

to promise, the more time has passed the greater his intellectual stature has seemed to grow. In Britain, for example, which has a history of skepticism about Freud's teachings, psychoanalytic studies centers are now being established at a number of the newer universities. And Argentina, the most European of South American countries, has been a central training center for analysts all over Latin America. Margaret Thatcher, currently a heroine in Buenos Aires for having so humiliated the military over the Falklands—or Malvinas—is also responsible for the success of psychoanalysis in Britain's newer centers of higher learning; she cut off money to Oxford and Cambridge in favor of these fresh institutions.

Freud was a great spellbinder, and his system of thought has permanently influenced how we think about human nature. Helping people to change may be a more intractable issue than Freud had hoped, and identifying with him may be one of the hidden sources of the effect he had. Even if certain of Freud's claims now seem discredited, his writings continue to exert an impact that is unrivaled by any of the alternative thinkers who have presented themselves. The frequency with which Freud has been attacked and criticized is testimony to the continuing vitality and relevance of what he proposed. Only the most credulous of naive believers could expect that after all these years what Freud had argued could be taken as literally true. And yet his worldview has had enough validity so that in spite of the passage of time, key aspects of what he had to say still strike home. He remains a contemporary presence because what he had to contribute went beyond the confines of the culture of his own era.

Although any thinker has to bear responsibility for the uses to which his ideas are put, Freud has sometimes been unfairly blamed for events that were well beyond his control. For example, it is often rightly pointed out the extent to which Freud shared in many cultural prejudices of his own time, and in particular his view of women was necessarily an aspect of the civilization of which he was a part. Jokl's critique of Freud skipped over the issue of the social atmosphere in which Freud had grown up. Yet as one reflects on Freud's contact with the patients who are interviewed here, I think it is impossible to adopt a simplistic version of how he treated women.

Psychoanalysis and feminism, two of the most important currents in the last hundred years of thought, have a complicated interlocking relationship. Freud's profession proved enormously open to female talent. As early as 1910 some of Freud's Viennese followers, men who were at least a generation younger than he, wanted to exclude women from the Vienna Psychoanalytic Society. Even though Freud took a clear stand against such a policy of keeping the membership of the group exclusively male, regarding it as "gross inconsistency" were women to be left out "on principle," the vote to support Freud's position was only eight in favor with three opposed (Nunberg and Federn 1967). In the milieu Freud was working in he was hardly a reactionary. Over the course of Freud's lifetime—and especially when he was an old man—women came to occupy leading positions, both as theoreticians and practitioners, within the psychoanalytic movement. Freud's general points about the differences between the psychologies of men and women are elaborate ones, not to be reduced to some stereotypes about how Freud supposedly held back the emancipation of women (Deutsch 1991, Roazen 1985). (No one I saw emphasized Freud's having ever made much of the now notorious concept of penis envy.) The examples of how well he got on with some of his female patients, especially those who were exceptionally talented, should help put to rest the myth that Freud ranks among those hostile in the context of his times to the legitimate rights of women.

Here sometimes Freud's own writings can be misleading, and the model of how he conducted himself warrants more attention if we are to understand him historically. But paradoxically Freud's continuing stature has seemed to mean that particular words he published, often taken out of appropriate context, get unfairly singled out. For example, one of Freud's former female patients, Joan Riviere (1934), objected in print to some of Freud's most recent theoretical writings on the nature of femininity; she said then that it was "not a credible view of women," and that "Freud himself has not always looked on women thus" (p. 336). With all that Freud succeeded in doing, it has been easy to miss the center of gravity of what he accomplished. But even though Freud's convictions about women should be no more wholly defensible than anything else he argued and his approach to femininity ought to be as subject to critical scrutiny as all his other ideas, the examples of his clinical practices, at least as I was able to reconstruct them, do not support the proposition that he was a misogynist.

Now that Freud's various correspondences are steadily appearing in print, and these volumes of his letters will continue to be published over the next generation, it is going to be increasingly common to find Freud on many occasions saying apparently contradictory things. There will be little dispute, though, about how great a literary stylist he was, and it will be intriguing to read what he might have written about these ten patients. But it is precisely those capacities of Freud as a writer that are apt to obscure how devoted he was to his practice as a psychoanalyst. Despite how hardworking he was as a clinician, and the importance he attached to good practical results, it is all too easy for people nowadays to think of Freud as a closet philosopher thinking up his ideas independently of concrete, practical pressures.

At times, especially late in his life, Freud could choose to emphasize the significance of psychoanalysis as a purely theoretical contribution. The older Freud grew, the more detached he could become from human conflicts. Still when one thinks of the extent to which he was suffering from cancer of the jaw, and yet how concerned he continued to be with the therapeutic effects of his form of treatment, what may stand out most is how, in spite of all his personal suffering, he continued to take as much interest as he did in the problems people brought to him. Mark Brunswick was abundantly critical of many aspects of Freud's approach to him, but he never doubted Freud's concern about Mark as a patient.

It can hardly be suggested, though, that Freud was a gentle humanitarian, and he was surely no sentimentalist. He was a relentless critic of religion, even if with certain patients Freud (1918) could acknowledge how useful religious teachings could be. Freud was outspokenly an opponent of the pieties of Christian ethics. Pfister believed that in spite of everything Freud may have supposed, psychoanalysis stood in Pfister's view for a variation on the Christian version of love. Pfister dissented from many of Freud's opinions, and thought that Freud's outlook on art, philosophy, and psychotherapy shared certain defects, but Pfister (1993) still maintained that within Freud's psychoanalysis was a viewpoint thoroughly consistent with Christian morality. Although Pfister was restating many of the central points that Jung had earlier tried to establish, Freud could tolerate Pfister's views and allowed them to be published in one of his journals. Others subsequently in the history of psychoanalysis would try to find a basis within Freud's thinking for buttressing traditional religious thought (Roazen 1976).

Freud possessed an exceptional hardness within him that was an essential constituent of the strength he had in fulfilling what he saw as his special mission. Freud succeeded historically in part because of his exceptional talents as a fighter. Early reviewers accused Freud of fitting data to theory. From our own point of view today it does sound prescient, to me at any rate, for such a reviewer to have objected that Freud "seeks sexual causes and sexual nexus always and everywhere." I wish that more analysts had taken to heart the early warning that "anyone who can give his questions a suggestive twist, whether done consciously or unconsciously, can obtain from susceptible patients any answer which fits into his system" (Roazen 1990c, p. 199). That principle is still applicable today, even to the latest and most up-to-date seeming non-Freudian therapeutic recommendations.

The success of the Freudian revolution in the history of ideas makes every critical insight into his work that much more valuable. In my opinion some of the earliest reviewers of Freud's work were right on the mark in seeing flaws in his approach. Within about ten years of *The Interpretation of Dreams* Freud had already achieved the basic power that enabled him to triumph later on. It is no wonder that he was appalled by reviews that were less than wholly enthusiastic; he early understood the kind of control he would ultimately be able to exert, and therefore disdained those who were in any way halfhearted in their admiration. By and large the Central European response to Freud's work seems to have been sophisticated. Contemporary critics of his, especially among his former students who were knowledgeable enough to be insightful "dissidents," were often right in pointing out various flaws in Freud's approach. At the end of Jung's friendly contact with Freud he provocatively asked whether "perhaps" Freud really hated neurotics, and in Ferenczi's own period of acute disillusionment with Freud he quoted Freud as having referred to his patients as worthless "rabble" (McGuire 1974, Roazen 1990d). It is more important, I think, to evaluate the significance of these disquieting aspects to Freud's thinking than to obsess about issues connected with Strachey's translations of Freud, which too often end up like counting angels dancing on the head of a pin.

Freud made few pretenses about being an indiscriminate lover of mankind. He insisted that traditional moral teachings were a cheat, and he designed psychoanalytic treatment for the exceptional few; Eva Rosenfeld was telling in her discussion of his ideal of psychoanalysis. Freud admitted being angry about how mankind as a whole failed to live up to the most elementary standards of decency that he thought should be reasonably expected of people. Phony spiritualism was no sort of reliable help, and just misled the unwary about what could be expected in life. When all is said and done, however, Freud's complicated sort of irony can be easy to misunderstand. In 1924, for example, when his picture appeared on the cover of *Time* (October 27), he was quoted as having said of himself that he was "the only rogue in a company of immaculate rascals."

Inevitably Freud tended to universalize insights that were in fact personal. All of psychoanalytic theory can be seen as Freud's autobiography writ large. But Freud took great offense at efforts by others to show him how he tended to project his own conflicts into the minds of his patients. As early as 1901, Fliess had warned that "the reader of thoughts merely reads his own thoughts into other people" (Masson 1985, p. 447); if that is how Fliess understood Freud's psychoanalytic efforts to understand the minds of others, then Freud concluded that Fliess's accusation had rendered all Freud's "efforts valueless." Their friendship could never survive such a criticism from Fliess.

And yet when one reads through Freud's letters to Fliess, one has to agree with Eva Rosenfeld about how similar he sounds to the later Freud. A remarkable strain of consistency runs through all Freud's thinking, and there never was a time, at least when anyone I encountered knew him, when Freud was not working from a well-thought-out system of ideas. It is not as if, when these ten people were seeing him, Freud was in his early years, or fumbling around in the dark. He was 46 years old by 1902, when he first started assembling a following in Vienna; it was only a year or two later when he first saw Hirst. Someone of Freud's age then, within old-world culture, would not have been used to being easily challenged. Still, when Freud was able to be on good terms with patients, and I hope these ten examples give some notion of him at his best, he could relax and be relatively at ease. With certain people he could even question some of his own apparently most cherished concepts. But strict limits always existed beyond which it would not be allowable for possible skeptics to go. Some of his poorest therapeutic results, as for example with David Brunswick, wound up paradoxically earning him one of his most fervent followers.

The complexities of Freud's interaction with these ten people should, I think, indicate how insufficient it is to cite Freud's most abstract writings as evidence of his most valuable or characteristic modes of thinking. The published clinical descriptions that Freud did offer, as in his five famous case histories, are only a small fraction of Freud's actual practices and convictions. Oral history, such as I accumulated, has its own inadequacies, and I have no doubt that if these people were still alive to be questioned, different information about their contact with Freud might surface. But even though there have to be inevitable limitations to the kind of material that I collected, I am convinced that it is worthwhile to preserve it for the sake of showing something of Freud's unique scope.

An unfortunate set of preconceptions exists about not only how Freud acted as a therapist, but also the proper role of a psychotherapist. Concerning pupils Freud disagreed with, he could be intransigent. In 1931 he wrote in disapproval of Ferenczi's supposedly having started to kiss his patients, and allowed them allegedly to kiss him:

> Now when you decide to give a full account of your technique and its results you will have to choose between two ways: either you relate this or you conceal it. The latter, as you may well think, is dishonorable. What one

does in one's technique one has to defend openly. Besides, both ways come together. Even if you don't say so yourself it will soon get known, just as I knew it before you told me. [Jones 1957, pp. 163–164]

Ferenczi's response remains unpublished.

One of Freud's principal reproaches against Ferenczi is directly relevant to the stories that these ten patients had to report. For if it is true that "what one does in one's technique one has to defend openly," then our conception of Freud as a psychoanalyst has to be considerably expanded beyond the stereotype fostered by so many textbook accounts of how he went about things. Yet the taboos have been such that it has taken a longer time than one might expect for Freud's own techniques to become known.

I have not tried to gloss over or hide some of the most disconcerting aspects of Freud's failures as a practitioner. It can be no accident that even after all these years since Ruth Brunswick's death, for example, so little about her has appeared in the literature and that what has been published has been so biased. The tragedy of Ruth's life can of course not be blamed on Freud; the fact that she was overwhelmed by her own troubles says something about the inevitability of human pain and suffering, which Freud's own skeptical philosophic approach never tried to minimize. Yet the failure to explore the details connected with Ruth's life, or the perhaps more sensational disaster associated with Horace Frink's debacle, can only perpetuate a dangerous set of myths about how psychoanalysis can be counted upon to rescue humanity from some of its most conflicted sorts of problems.

Intellectuals are apt to be some of the most credulous propagators of illusions concerning the early days of psychoanalysis. Critically to examine the historical origins of a discipline like psychoanalysis is to run the risk of being accused of being a debunker; all organizations live by means of a shared mythology, which is why genuine historical research has never been welcomed in any authoritarian setting. Yet the true model of what Freud was actually like, as best we can reconstruct it, makes for a far more interesting and instructive figure than any of the various idealizations of him.

No matter how positive some people's experiences with Freud could be, he was no miracle worker. The successes he had were often attributable to factors that he either was unaware of or chose to downplay. By today's standards he was too puritanical, and the moral positions he espoused are by no means as exempt from critical examination as he liked to think. Out of a misplaced loyalty to him an industry of orthodox defenders of Freud has arisen, even though such expressions of false piety should long since have been unnecessary in shielding him from historical scrutiny.

In Great Britain, for example, the impact of Kleinian thinking has been welcomed not just within the clinical community but among some of the most sophisticated British philosophers. When I was told in the mid-1960s by a leading apostle of Klein's that all analyses should, as a matter of principle, last for ten years, I meekly asked what could justify that sort of intrusion on someone's life. I got a one-word response: "Research." I was as appalled then as now; if patients are going to be treated as guinea pigs, they have a right to be told beforehand.

When I related that story about psychoanalytic pretentiousness in the early 1990s in France, I heard a parallel example from a French child analyst. A friend of hers, an English mother, had taken her young child, who unaccountably was not yet talking, to the same disciple of Klein's. The parent was told that she should bring the child for a year, and the psychoanalyst would then tell her what she "thought." The mother had another child, and getting to the daily analytic sessions from the other side of London meant not only a disruption in her family life but a challenge to her maternal responsibilities. The analyst once again had a one-word answer: "Move." Freud had soberly proposed by means of analysis to transform neurotic misery into everyday unhappiness, but a messianic streak in him has been picked up by others.

One sometimes thinks that all Freud's cautiousness can get swamped in the idealism that he bequeathed to his professional descendants. In France today the enthusiasm for Freud, even though the psychoanalytic wave arrived in that country later than elsewhere, has meant that some of the most educated of the world's intelligentsia are at the same time unaware about defects in the Freudian approach that should have been long since securely established. There is a history of debate about both the advantages and the limitations to the use of the analytic couch, for example, and the experience of the last hundred years has much to teach about where therapists are characteristically most apt to go wrong.

In America the medical community has been so disappointed in the early exaggerated claims in behalf of the therapeutic efficacy of psychoanalysis that the pendulum has radically swung back to a strictly somatic approach. If Freud could ever have made extravagant claims for what psychoanalysis could accomplish, which would be implicit in patients staying in treatment with him for years, nowadays psychopharmacological advocates feel free to prescribe medication on the basis of only the briefest of contact with suffering clientele. General practitioners may understand that psychotherapy, combined with appropriate modern medication, makes the most clinical sense, but it is difficult to find therapists who are conversant with the latest chemical developments as well as the history of the whole discipline.

Whatever the natural tendency of any profession like psychiatry or psychotherapy to advance its own claims, in

America some of its most distinguished writers have been among Freud's most ardent propagandists. For example Lionel Trilling, the eminent literary critic at Columbia University, falsely wrote in 1957 of both Rank and Ferenczi in the Sunday *New York Times Book Review*: "Both men fell prey to extreme mental illness and they died insane" (Lieberman 1985, p. 400). Trilling later co-edited a one-volume version of Jones's biography without acknowledging how tendentious Jones consistently had been. And even as late as 1972 Trilling could write: "The Freudian clinical theory is by no means to be written off as irrelevant to schizophrenia, but its characteristic therapeutic procedure is not decisively efficacious in the treatment of this pathology" (pp. 167–168). Trilling's prose is so pretentious that it may be hard to find him "comic," as Nabokov reacted to the the Freud–Bullitt study of Wilson.

It would be laughable, if Trilling as a source were not such an influential and representative one, to find someone that late in the day writing of Freud's approach that it was not "decisively efficacious" in treating schizophrenia, when anyone halfway savvy should have known long before then that psychoanalysis required all kinds of adaptations to be in any way suitably used in such cases. It does not make Trilling any the less misleading for him to have added: "As for the Freudian ethos, what I have called its patrician posture of simultaneous acceptance of and detachment from life in civilization makes it patently—and bitterly—inappropriate to the situation of the psychotic person" (p. 168).

But Trilling seems to have had no realistic understanding of what Freud himself had thought. There is considerable literature on the distinction between neurosis and psychosis, which despite Jung's insistence Freud only belatedly drew, and abundant evidence has existed about why and how Freud was reluctant to accept some of the essential limitations of his own form of treatment. His own experience with psychiatric cases like psychotics was limited, even if he was willing to sanction what others might experiment with in trying to reach such patients by changing his own preferred techniques. Therefore no grounds were there at all for any bitterness about accepting the inappropriateness of Freud's ethos to "the situation of the psychotic person."

Unfortunately Trilling's kind of naïveté is no isolated phenomenon. One can find Janet Malcolm's recent reliance on psychoanalytic reasoning not only promoting a subtle form of orthodoxy, but also reflecting a widespread credulity among the intelligentsia. Malcolm does not seem to have any idea what sort of dinosaur position she has been defending, either in terms of how long treatment should last or how analysts ought to behave. It is in keeping with her orientation that Malcolm (1984) has sought to do her best to glamorize Eissler (cf. Roazen 1990a), who has so prominently stood as a guardian on behalf of the most reactionary forces within psychoanalysis. Anyone, including me, who has ever challenged the status quo has evoked the kind of polemical wrath from Eissler and Malcolm, which among impartial observers is likely to discredit the whole enterprise of psychoanalytic thinking.

It is in the context of the unfortunate dogmatism that has marred this field that I have tried to present these ten examples of real people, as opposed to the attention that has been lavished on the handful of written cases Freud himself offered. Whatever Freud may have sometimes made it sound like, practical results did matter to him. And however dubious he may have rightly been about the possibilities of moral progress, nothing can be gained by citing isolated Freudian texts, as is done in so much of the professional literature today. Freud's words can be used to justify almost any contemporary practice, with the result that what he was like in his own time is less likely to survive. As

Finley Peter Dunne's Mr. Dooley said, "The further ye get fr'm any period the better ye can write about it. Ye are not subject to interruptions by people that were there" (O'Brien 1992, p. iii).

It is real people I have tried to talk about, and not just because individuals are more important than concepts. I believe that ideas like these arise in a human context, and are an expression of the hopes and fears of imperfect but struggling actors. The history of psychoanalysis is full of interesting but forgotten figures—not just those about whom there are scandals—who for one reason or another have remained unknown. Irma Putnam may have been smart as a whip, but she has not up to now made any impact in the literature.

I have presented the story of Freud's patients from their points of view. While doubtless this perspective has built-in biases of its own, at least it avoids the kind of stereotypes about psychoanalysis that have proved so curiously attractive to some intellectuals. Marxism had at one time a similar sort of attraction as a surrogate religion. Although it may be impossible ever to achieve the ideal of recovering history as it actually happened, and the most we can hope for are different perspectives on how Freud behaved, these ten people demonstrate sides to Freud that neither Nabokov or Trilling were able to appreciate.

Science in the context of psychotherapy merely means that one generation is able to learn from an earlier era's mistakes. Freud can be allowed his flaws, without denigrating his place in history. Nor should he be idealized, so that reading about his flaws becomes unduly shocking. I suspect he would have been disappointed if he ever failed to disturb the complacent peace of the everyday world.

All the past quarrels in the history of psychoanalysis have produced a regrettable degree of defensiveness. If one mentions the fate of Ruth Brunswick or writes about some of the suicides on the part of the early analysts, then the implication is that one is accusing Freud of having been personally responsible for other people's troubles. It should not be necessary to whitewash the past, obliterating human tragedy from the story of psychoanalysis, in order to be entitled to be listened to. In this field there are abundant false continuities, and for parochial reasons certain thinkers are known in certain places rather than other theorists. Transferences that have arisen in the context of training are another common source of distortion.

Freud's stature within intellectual history is secure, even if his technical recommendations not surprisingly are in thorough need of revising; right from the start people were credulously looking for manuals of how to proceed, and Freud only rarely offered the kind of guidelines that have been naively craved. Plenty of thinkers have respectfully tried, over the last hundred years, to offer alternatives to how Freud went about his work. To give them a decent hearing one does not have to be deemed subversive of Freud himself. He knew that to the extent that a better world is ever possible, it can only come from critical examination.

The old Vienna of which Freud was a representative is no more, but his civilization represents one of the high points of human thought. We can only benefit from becoming more familiar with what he and his culture were like. At his best Freud invoked the concept of the unconscious as a way of setting limits to what we can know about ourselves or others. It would be in his own most genuinely humble spirit if we were to acknowledge that even now, when the literature about him has grown so vast, there is little about him we can securely know. Some such acceptance of our own inevitable shortcomings makes a valuable corrective to the arrogance and self-righteousness that has marred the field of psychotherapy.

Freud, as we have seen, had his own set of moralisms, which stands out in part simply because of the passage of time. It is hard ever to establish the question of influence, but it would appear that Freud took a leading role in criticizing traditional family life. Although he could work with family members of his patients, and even treat members of the same family simultaneously, one of the core appeals of Freud's approach was his indictment of the upbringing that his patients had had. As a therapist, however, Freud was often acting as a parental substitute. Freud could be giving with one hand while taking away with the other; he offered the ideal of autonomy and self-determination at the same time as he was laying down certain rules for the procedure of psychoanalysis. In terms of traditional philosophy, he shared Jean-Jacques Rousseau's conviction that because of the way in which we can become enslaved to our own passions, it makes sense to force people to be free.

The world as we know it is apt to be far more anomic than the context in which Freud was functioning. Instead of the large extended families that were once taken for granted, we increasingly have lonely and isolated people who turn to therapists for support and meaningfulness. Traditions reinforce and sustain as well as interfere and Freud knew this implicitly, although he only rarely paused to spell it out.

Freud once made some enduringly valuable comments about what he had in mind for people in the course of a discussion on suicide. He was addressing the role of secondary schools in the education of the young, and he observed that they "should achieve more than not driving its pupils to suicide." Such institutions should give students "a desire to live and should offer them support and backing at a time of life at which the conditions of their development compel them to relax their ties with their parental home and their family." Here Freud (1910) went on the attack:

It seems to me indisputable that schools fail in this, and in many respects fall short of their duty of providing a substitute for the family and of arousing interest in life in the world outside. This is not a suitable occasion for a criticism of secondary schools in their present shape; but perhaps I may emphasize a single point. [pp. 231–232]

And this is the part of Freud's remarks that seem to me most significant: "The school must never forget," he believed, "that it has to deal with immature individuals who cannot be denied a right to linger at certain stages of development and even at certain disagreeable ones." For Freud thought that "the school must not take on itself the inexorable character of life; it must not seek to be more than a *game* of life" (pp. 231–232). Freud was defending a point of view that may sound unprogressive, even reactionary, but I think his words are worth pondering precisely because they are so unlikely to seem popular now. Schools, he thought, should be unlike life if they were to fulfill the task of promoting genuine maturity. And the same went, I think, for the treatment situation he devised.

I have presented my accounts of the contact I had with these ten patients of Freud's for the sake of making us more tolerant of human variety. Some of the situations that I have described may seem bizarre or inappropriate: Hirst's bragging about his youthful sexual prowess; the Brunswick family complexities; Edith Jackson's involvement with Freud's eldest son; the Levys and their problems raising a child; the suicide of the Putnam daughter; Jokl's financial proposals; Eva Rosenfeld's talking behind Anna Freud's back; the Strachey marriage; or Freud's having analyzed his daughter Anna.

There was much about these people I could not find out. Each of these vignettes only scratches the surface of what might have happened. And yet I think perhaps I found out not too little but too much. I wonder whether it is proper for the world to know all these intimate details. Freud devised a form of treatment that transgressed human privacy in an unprecedented way.

I have put these tales together for what I hope is an emancipatory purpose. Stereotypes of psychological "normality" and what psychotherapy can ever hope to achieve are necessarily more impoverished than they ought to be. Human beings are so interesting precisely because they cannot be captured by prefabricated formulas. Freud may have been playing with fire as the creator of psychoanalysis, and not everyone unambiguously thrived thanks to contact with him. But our world has inherited Freud's impact, and we should make the best of what we have by being as tolerant as we can about the different choices people must make.

Above all, the focus must shift away from the words Freud wrote, which are ritualistically cited in the literature, to what he did in practice. There should be a reciprocal relationship between Freud's life and his writings, so that we can eventually turn to Freud's texts with an enhanced understanding. But all this effort at exploring the historiography of psychoanalysis should be for the objective of enhancing our humaneness. I never proceeded with any conviction about the superiority of the present over the past. History has the most to teach when it takes us outside of ourselves. To be truly loyal to Freud's spirit involves, I believe, our willingness to follow his example by going beyond him.

A stern taskmaster might be tempted to dismiss all the ten human beings I have chosen to write about as "spoiled," people without qualities, to invoke Robert Musil's term, left-overs from a time which has quickly passed them by. Perhaps psychoanalysis is neither an illness nor a cure—it grabs the imagination and pushes it forward or leaves behind those who use it not to learn but to get by. Such a possibility also does not diminish Freud who was driven on and on. The inevitable limitations of these people—and I lean toward tolerance, not moralism—should teach us something about the shortcomings of the human condition. Ideas like Freud's either retain a presence which stimulates or they become minor games which kill them for sure. Personally I am keeping my fingers crossed about Freud and psychoanalysis.

References

Albrecht, A. (1973). Professor Sigmund Freud. In *Freud As We Knew Him*, ed. H. Ruitenbeek, pp. 23–25. Detroit, MI: Wayne State University Press.

Alexander, F. (1940). Recollections of Berggasse 19. *Psychoanalytic Quarterly* 9(2):202.

Appignanesi, L., and Forrester, J. (1992). *Freud's Women*. New York: Basic Books.

Bernfeld, S. (1962). On psychoanalytic training. *Psychoanalytic Quarterly* 31(4):463.

Bertin, C. (1982). *Marie Bonaparte: A Life*. New York: Harcourt Brace Jovanovich.

Bilinsky, J. (1969). Jung and Freud. *Andover Newton Quarterly* 10(2).

Blanton, S. (1971). *Diary of My Analysis with Sigmund Freud*. New York: Hawthorn.

Bonomi, C. (1994). Why have we ignored Freud the "paediatrician"? In *100 Years of Psychoanalysis*, ed. A. Haynal and E. Falzeder, London: Karnac.

Brabant, E., Falzeder, E., and Gampieri-Deutsch, P., eds. (1993). *The Correspondence of Sigmund Freud and Sandor Ferenczi, Vol. I, 1908–14*, trans. P. T. Hoffer, intro. by A. Haynal. Cambridge, MA: Harvard University Press.

Brown, T. M. (1987). Alan Gregg and the Rockefeller Foundation's support of Franz Alexander's psychosomatic medicine. *Bulletin of the History of Medicine* 5(61):155–182.

Cocks, G., ed. (1994). *The Curve of Life: Correspondence of Heinz Kohut 1923–1981*. Chicago: University of Chicago Press.

Crews, F. (1993). The unknown Freud. *New York Review of Books*, November 18, pp. 55–66. (Also see later exchanges, February 3, 1994, pp. 34–43; April 21, 1994, pp. 66–68; August 11, 1994, pp. 54–56.)

Darnton, R. (1968). *Mesmerism and the End of the Enlightenment in France*. Cambridge, MA: Harvard University Press.

Deutsch, H. (1965). Psychoanalytic therapy in the light of follow-up. In *Neuroses and Character Types: Clinical Psychoanalytic Studies*, pp. 339–352. New York: International Universities Press.

———— (1991). *Psychoanalysis of the Sexual Functions of Women*, ed. P. Roazen, trans. E. Mosbacher. London: Karnac.

———— (1992). Occult processes occurring during psychoanalysis. In *The Therapeutic Process, the Self, and Female Psychology: Collected Psychoanalytic Papers*, ed. P. Roazen, pp. 223–238. New Brunswick, NJ: Transaction.

Diaz de Chumaceiro, C. L. (1990). A brief comment on Freud's attendance at opera performances: 1880–90. *American*

Journal of Psychoanalysis 50(3):285–288.

Douglas, C. (1993). *Translate This Darkness: The Life of Christiana Morgan*. New York: Simon and Schuster.

Dufresne, T. (in press). An interview with Joseph Wortis. *Psychoanalytic Review*.

Edmunds, L. (1988). His master's choice. *Johns Hopkins Magazine,* April, pp. 40–49.

Ellman, S. J. (1991). *Freud's Technique Papers: A Contemporary Perspective*. Northvale, NJ: Jason Aronson.

Erikson, E. H. (1963). *Childhood and Society*, 2nd ed. New York: Norton.

Falzeder, E. (1994). The threads of psychoanalytic filiations or psychoanalysis taking effect. In *100 Years of Psychoanalysis: Contributions to the History of Psychoanalysis*, ed. A. Haynal and E. Falzeder. Special issues of the *Cahiers Psychiatriques Genevois*. London: Karnac.

Freeman, E. (1971). *Insights: Conversations with Theodor Reik*. Englewood Cliffs, NJ: Prentice-Hall.

Freud, A. (1965). *Normality and Pathology in Childhood: Assessments of Development*. New York: International Universities Press.

_____ (1978). In memoriam Edith Jackson. *Journal of the American Academy of Child Psychiatry* 17:731.

Freud, E. L., ed. (1970). *The Letters of Sigmund Freud and Arnold Zweig*, trans. Prof. and Mrs. W. D. Robson-Scott. London: Hogarth.

Freud, M. (1957). *Glory Reflected*. London: Angus and Robertson.

Freud, S. (1895). Studies on hysteria. *Standard Edition* 2.

_____ (1901). Autobiographical note. *Standard Edition* 3.

_____ (1905). Jokes and their relation to the unconscious. *Standard Edition* 8.

_____ (1909). Notes upon a case of obsessional neurosis. *Standard Edition* 10.

—— (1910). Contributions to a discussion on suicide. *Standard Edition* 11:231–232.

—— (1912). Recommendations to physicians practising psychoanalysis. *Standard Edition* 12.

—— (1916/1917). Introductory lectures on psychoanalysis. *Standard Edition* 16.

—— (1918). From the history of an infantile neurosis. *Standard Edition* 17:17–122.

—— (1920). Dr. Anton von Freund. *Standard Edition* 18:267–268.

—— (1921). Psychoanalysis and telepathy. *Standard Edition* 18:177–193.

—— (1925) An autobiographical study. *Standard Edition* 17.

—— (1926). Psychoanalysis. *Standard Edition* 20.

—— (1931). Female sexuality. *Standard Edition* 21.

—— (1937). Analysis terminable and interminable. *Standard Edition* 23.

—— (1938). Splitting of the ego in the process of defence. *Standard Edition* 23:275–278.

—— (1963). *Psychoanalysis and Faith: Dialogues with the Reverend Oskar Pfister,* ed. H. Meng and E. Freud, trans. E. Mosbacher. New York: Basic Books.

Friedman, L. J. (1990). *Menninger; The Family and the Clinic.* New York: Knopf.

Gardiner, M. (1983). *Code Name "Mary".* New Haven: Yale University Press.

Gay, P. (1987). *A Godless Jew: Freud, Atheism, and the Making of Psychoanalysis.* New Haven: Yale University Press.

—— (1988). *Freud: A Life for Our Time.* New York: Norton.

Gilman, S. L. (1993). *Freud, Race, and Gender.* Princeton, NJ: Princeton University Press.

Glover, E. (1955). *The Technique of Psychoanalysis.* New York: International Universities Press.

Grubrich-Simitis, I. (1993). *Zurück zu Freuds Texten*. Frankfurt: Fischer.

Heller, P., ed. (1992). *Anna Freud's Letters to Eva Rosenfeld*. New York: International Universities Press.

Hendrick, I., ed. (1961). *The Birth of an Institute*. Freeport, ME: Bond Wheelwright.

Higgins, M., and Raphael, C. M., eds. (1967). *Reich Speaks of Freud*. New York: Noonday.

Hinshelwood, R. D. (1995). Psychoanalysis in Britain: points of cultural access, 1893–1918. *International Journal of Psycho-Analysis* 76 (1):135–152.

Holroyd, M. (1971). *Lytton Strachey: A Biography*. London: Penguin.

Jones, E. (1955). *The Life and Work of Sigmund Freud,* vol. 2. New York: Basic Books.

———— (1956). *Sigmund Freud: Life and Work*, vol. 1, 2nd ed. London: Hogarth.

———— (1957). *The Life and Work of Sigmund Freud*, vol. 3. New York: Basic Books.

Kardiner, A. (1957). Freud: The man I knew. In *Freud and the Twentieth Century*, ed. B. Nelson, pp. 48–49. New York: Meridian.

Kleinman, A. (1988). *Rethinking Psychiatry: From Cultural Category to Personal Experience*. New York: Free Press.

Knapp, B., and Chipman, M. (1964). *That Was Yvette: The Biography of the Great Diseuse*. New York: Holt, Rinehart & Winston.

Levy, K. (1949). The eternal dilettante. In *Searchlights on Delinquency*, ed. K. R. Eissler, pp. 65–76. New York: International Universities Press.

———— (1960). Simultaneous analysis of a mother and her adolescent daughter. *Psychoanalytic Study of the Child* 15:378–391.

Lévy-Freund, K. (1990). Dernieres vacances des Freud avant le fin du monde. *Le Coq-Heron* 17:39–44.

Lieberman, E. J. (1985). *Acts of Will: The Life and Work of Otto Rank*. New York: Free Press. Amherst, MA: University of Massachusetts Press, 1993.

MacLean, G., and Rappen, U. (1991). *Hermine Hug-Hellmuth: Her Life and Work*. New York: Routledge.

Mahony, P. J. (1986). *Freud and the Rat Man*. New Haven: Yale University Press.

Malcolm, J. (1981). *Psychoanalysis: The Impossible Profession*. New York: Knopf.

———— (1984). *In the Freud Archives*. New York: Knopf.

———— (1992). *The Purloined Clinic: Selected Writings*. New York: Knopf.

Masson, J. M. (1984). *The Assault on Truth: Freud's Suppression of the Seduction Theory*. New York: Farrar, Straus, & Giroux.

Masson, J. M., ed. and trans. (1985). *The Complete Letters of Sigmund Freud to Wilhelm Fliess*. Cambridge, MA: Harvard University Press.

McGuire, W., ed. (1974). *The Freud/Jung Letters*, trans. R. Mannheim, and R. F. C. Hull. Princeton, NJ: Princeton University Press.

Meghnagi, D., ed. (1993). *Freud and Judaism*. London: Karnac.

Meisel, P., and Kendrick, W., eds. (1985). *Bloomsbury/Freud: The Letters of James and Alix Strachey*. New York: Basic Books.

Menaker, E. (1989). *Appointment in Vienna*. New York: St. Martin's Press.

Micale, M. S., ed. (1993). *Beyond the Unconscious: Essays of Henri F. Ellenberger in the History of Psychiatry*. Princeton, NJ: Princeton University Press.

Molnar, M., ed. (1992). *The Diary of Sigmund Freud*. New York: Scribner's.

Monk, R. (1990). *Ludwig Wittgenstein: The Duty of Genius*.

New York: Free Press.

Nunberg, H. (1942). In memoriam: Ruth Mack Brunswick. *Psychoanalytic Quarterly* 15(2):142.

Nunberg, H., and Federn, E., eds. (1967). *Minutes of the Vienna Psychoanalytic Society,* vol. 2, trans. M. Nunberg. New York: International Universities Press.

O'Brien, C. C. (1992). *The Great Melody: A Thematic Biography of Edmund Burke.* Chicago: University of Chicago Press.

Paris, B. J. (1994). *Karen Horney: A Psychoanalyst's Search for Self-Understanding.* New Haven: Yale University Press.

Paskauskas, R. A. (1985). *Ernest Jones: A Critical Study of his Scientific Development.* Ph.D. Dissertation, Institute for the History and Philosophy of Science and Technology, University of Toronto.

Paskauskas, R. A., ed. (1993). *The Complete Correspondence of Sigmund Freud and Ernest Jones.* Cambridge, MA: Harvard University Press.

Pawel, E. (1989). *The Labyrinth of Exile: A Life of Theodor Herzl.* New York: Farrar, Straus, & Giroux.

Pfister, O. (1993). The illusion of a future: a friendly disagreement with Prof. Sigmund Freud, ed. and introductory note by P. Roazen. *International Journal of Psycho-Analysis* 74(3):557–579.

Puner, H. W. (1947). *Sigmund Freud: His Life and Mind,* New York: Howell, Soskin. (Second edition with a new introduction by P. Roazen, 1992. New Brunswick, NJ: Transaction.)

Riviere, J. (1934). Review of *New Introductory Lectures. International Journal of Psycho-Analysis* 15:336.

Roazen, P. (1968). *Freud: Political and Social Thought.* New York: Knopf. (Second edition and new preface. 1986. New York: Da Capo, pp. 300–322.)

_____ (1969). *Brother Animal: The Story of Freud and Tausk.* New York: Knopf. (Second edition with new introduction.

New Brunswick, NJ: Transaction, 1990.)

―――― (1975). *Freud and His Followers*. New York: Knopf. (Reprinted New York: Da Capo, 1992.)

―――― (1976). *Erik H. Erikson: The Power and Limits of a Vision*. New York: Free Press.

―――― (1985). Epilogue. *Helene Deutsch: A Psychoanalyst's Life*, 2nd ed. with new introduction. New York: Anchor Books.

―――― (1989). Book review of Brownell and Billings' *So Close to Greatness: Biography of Williams C. Bullitt*. *American Scholar*, Winter, pp. 135–140.

―――― (1990a). *Encountering Freud: The Politics and Histories of Psychoanalysis*. New Brunswick, NJ: Transaction.

―――― (1990b). Tola Rank. *Journal of the American Academy of Psychoanalysis* 18(2):247–259.

―――― (1990c). Book review of *Freud Without Hindsight*. *Journal of the History of the Behavioral Sciences* 26:197–202.

―――― (1990d). Book review of *The Clinical Diary of Sandor Ferenczi*, ed. J. Dupont. *American Journal of Psychoanalysis* 50:367–371.

―――― (1991a). Nietzsche and Freud: two voices from the underground. *Psychohistory Review*, Spring, pp. 327–349.

―――― (1991b). Freud in France. *Virginia Quarterly Review*, Autumn, pp. 780–784.

―――― (1991c). Book review of Burlingham, *The Last Tiffany: A Biography of Dorothy T. Burlingham*. *Psychoanalytic Books*, January, pp. 32–40.

―――― (1991d). Freud and Lytton Strachey: an uncanny parallel. *Psychologist-Psychoanalyst*, Summer, pp. 43–44.

―――― (1992a). Book review of *The Freud–Klein Controversies 1941–45*. *Psychoanalytic Books*, Fall, pp. 391–398.

―――― (1992b). The rise and fall of Bruno Bettelheim. *Psychohistory Review*, Spring, pp. 221–250.

―――― (1993a). *Meeting Freud's Family*. Amherst, MA: University of Massachusetts Press.

_____ (1993b). Book review of *The Complete Correspondence of Sigmund Freud and Ernest Jones. Psychoanalytic Books*, Fall, pp. 478–488.

_____ (1993c). Review of *Anna Freud's Letters to Eva Rosenfeld. Bulletin of the History of Medicine* 67:739–740.

_____ (1994a). Book review of Magda Whitrow's *Julius Wagner-Jauregg. History of Psychiatry*, March, pp. 148–150.

_____ (1994b). Book review of *The Correspondence of Freud and Ferenczi. American Scholar*, Spring, pp. 315–318.

_____ (1995). Erich Fromm's Courage. In *A Prophetic Analyst: Erich Fromm's Contributions to Psychoanalysis*, ed. M. Cortina and M. Maccoby. Northvale, NJ: Jason Aronson.

_____ (in press-a). Book review of *Translating Freud. The Forum*, American Academy of Psychoanalysis.

_____ (in press-b). *Canada's King: An Essay in Political Psychology*, chapter 2.

Rosenfeld, E. M. (1951). The Pan-headed Moses—a parallel. *International Journal of Psycho-Analysis* 32:83–93.

Rosenzweig, S. (1992). *Freud, Jung, and Hall the King-Maker: The Expedition to America, 1909*. St. Louis: Rana House.

Silberman, S. L. (1990). Pioneering in family-centered maternity and infant care: Edith B. Jackson and the Yale rooming-in research project. *Bulletin of the History of Medicine* 64:262–287.

_____ (1994). The curious pattern of a distinguished medical career: a psychoanalytic portrait of Edith B. Jackson. *Biography* 17(3):223.

Sterba, R. F. (1982). *Reminiscences of a Viennese Psychoanalyst*. Detroit, MI: Wayne State University Press.

Strachey, J. (1934). The nature of the therapeutic action of psychoanalysis. *International Journal of Psycho-Analysis* 15(2–3):147.

Tausk, V. (1991). *Sexuality, War and Schizophrenia: Collected*

Psychoanalytic Papers, ed. P. Roazen. New Brunswick, NJ: Transaction.

Thomas, D. M. (1981). *The White Hotel.* New York: Viking.

Thompson, M. G. (1994). *The Truth about Freud's Technique: The Encounter with the Real.* New York: New York University Press.

Timms, E. (1986). *Karl Kraus: Apocalyptic Satirist: Culture and Catastrophe in Habsburg Vienna.* New Haven: Yale University Press.

Trilling, L. (1972). *Sincerity and Authenticity.* Cambridge, MA: Harvard University Press.

Warner, S. (1994). Freud's analysis of Horace Frink, M.D.: A previously unexplained therapeutic disaster. *Journal of the American Academy of Psychoanalysis* 22(1):137–152.

Wessel, M. A. (1978). Edith B. Jackson. *Journal of Pediatrics,* July, pp. 165–166.

Wilson, E. (1987). Did Strachey invent Freud? *International Review of Psycho-Analysis* 14:299–315.

Winslow, E. G. (1986). Keynes and Freud: Psychoanalysis and Keynes's account of the "animal spirits" of capitalism. *Social Research* 53:549–578.

––––– (1990). Bloomsbury, Freud, and the vulgar passions. *Social Research* 57(4):785–819.

Wortis, J. (1954). *Fragments of an Analysis with Freud.* New York: Simon and Schuster.

Young-Bruehl, E. (1988). *Anna Freud: A Biography.* New York: Summit.

Index

Abraham, K., 67, 164, 219, 241, 242–243, 247
Abstinence, 218
Acton, Lord, 144
Adler, A., xiv, xvi, xx, 35, 96, 120, 127, 128, 147, 182, 185, 200, 221, 243
Aggression
  Brunswick, Mark, 73
  Brunswick, Ruth, 80
Aichhorn, A., 105, 155–156, 163

Alcohol abuse, Brunswick, Mark, 78–79
Alexander, F., 51, 52, 131, 175, 260, 261
America
  Freud and, 12–14, 44–46, 83, 106, 109, 135, 186–187
  psychoanalysis and, 271–272
Andreas-Salomé, L., 107, 131, 217

Anger, Freud, 109
Anschluss, 116
Anthropology, 62
Anti-Semitism, 14–15, 25–26,
    108, 249. *See also*
    Religion
Anxiety, libido and, 74
Appignanesi, L., 40, 144,
    196, 204, 205, 218
Art, 70
Austria
  civil war in, 85
  World War II, 116
Austro-Hungarian Empire
  Anti-Semitism, 14
  society in, 8, 15

Bak, R., 73
Balint, A., 161
Balint, M., 146, 155, 161
Benedek, T., 199
Bernays, Minna (Freud's
    sister-in-law), 207–209,
    218, 221
Bernfeld, S., 28, 107, 116,
    117, 119
Bertin, C., 72
Bettelheim, B., 124, 239
Bibring, E., 105, 163
Bibring, G., 105
Bilinsky, J., 208n1
Biological psychiatry, xvi, 37,
    271–272

Blank screen, 104
Blanton, S., 91, 107, 108
Bleuler, E., 125–126, 128
Bleuler, M., 128
Blos, P., 199
Blumenthal, 84
Blumgart, H., 38, 44, 59, 66,
    76
Blumgart, L., 38, 66, 68
Bonaparte, Marie, 64, 65, 80,
    82, 87, 99, 101, 105,
    107, 162, 174, 191, 198,
    203, 222, 224, 235, 236
Bonaparte, Napoleon, 15
Bonomi, C., 113
Borderline disorder, Freud
    and, 120
Brabant, E., 43, 46, 144,
    158
Brandes, G., 10
Breuer, J., 17–18, 137, 246
Brill, A. A., 68, 69, 132, 239
Brown, T. M., 96
Brunswick, D., 31–60, 62,
    63, 69, 73, 74, 80, 102,
    115, 132, 174, 175, 184,
    190, 196, 268
Brunswick, M., 38, 40, 42,
    44, 46, 50, 56, 61–88,
    89, 94, 97, 103, 110,
    134–135, 136, 155, 184,
    189, 192, 193, 206,
    218–219, 223, 252, 265

Brunswick, R. M., 38, 39, 40,
    42, 44, 48–49, 50, 53,
    55–57, 59, 64, 65, 66,
    67, 68–69, 71, 74, 75,
    76, 77–88, 95, 98, 103,
    105, 122–123, 137,
    138,183, 184, 196, 198,
    202, 203, 218–219, 222,
    224, 252, 269, 274
Brunswick, T., 81, 97
Bullitt, W. C., 65, 83, 84, 87,
    93, 108, 207, 246, 260,
    272
Burlingham, D., 93, 97, 101,
    107, 131, 159, 199, 210,
    213, 222, 229
Busch, W., 136

Campbell, M., 172
Cassirer, S., 101
Castration anxiety, Jokl and,
    127
Charcot, J.-M., 240
Child analysis, 188–189,
    270–271
Chipman, M., 210
Clift, Montgomery, 90
Cocaine, Freud and, 4–8, 9,
    51, 57
Cocks, G., 144
Co-dependency, 78–79
Coldness, of Freud, 21,
    29–30

Communism, 187
Condom, 26
Confidentiality, 258
Conrad, J., 254
Coriat, I. H., 171
Countertransference
    Brunswick, David, 43,
        50–51
    Brunswick, Ruth, 57, 69
    Freud and, 135
    Frink and, 68
Creativity, women and, 127
Crews, F., xii
Culture, women and, xxi
Cushing, H., 171

Darnton, R., 260
da Vinci, Leonardo, 199
Death, 129, 139–140, 252
Depression, 228
Deri, F., 47, 52
Deutsch, F., 105, 138, 176
Deutsch, H., 29, 43, 80, 92,
    97, 105, 111, 121,
    122–123, 138, 175–176,
    184, 192, 222, 236, 263
*Diagnostic and Statistical
    Manual*, 37
Dias de Chumaceiro, C. L., 70
Dollfuss, E., 85–86
Dooley, L., 104
Doolittle, H., 112
Dora case (Freud), xix

Dostoyevski, F., 156, 157, 191, 251, 254
Douglas, C., 172
Drug dependency, Brunswick, Ruth, 55–56, 78–79, 82–83, 137
Dubovitz, M., 153
Duff, G., 228
Dunne, F. P., 274

Eckstein, E., 4, 10, 11–12, 16, 23, 183
Eckstein, F., 4
Eckstein, G., 4
Eder, D., 228
Edmunds, L., 68
Ego psychology, 103
Eissler, K., 6, 27, 28, 31, 32, 34, 37, 38, 67, 69, 90, 92, 93, 105, 108, 125, 163–164, 207, 242, 273
Eissler, R., 113
Eitingon, M., 214
Elizabeth I (q. of England), 232–233
Erikson, E. H., 138–139, 199
Ethics, sexual abuse, 258–259
Euthanasia, 230
External conditions, psychoanalysis and, 42

Falzeder, E., 77, 237, 259
Federn, E., 263

Federn, P., 17, 18, 19, 67, 103, 121, 122, 128, 134, 161, 163, 176, 251
Federn, W., 85
Feminism, 263–264
Fenichel, O., 47, 52, 118, 121, 235
Ferenczi, G., 107
Ferenczi, S., 76, 86, 132, 135–136, 144, 145, 146–149, 158, 161, 174, 243, 246–247, 269, 272
Fetishism, 77
Fichtl, P., 159–160
Fliess, R., 85, 223, 235–236, 267
Fliess, W., 11, 210, 211
Forrester, J., 40, 144, 196, 204, 205, 218
Forster, E. M., 245
Forsyth, D., 228
Free association
    Brunswick, David and, 47
    Brunswick, Mark, 63
    Brunswick, Ruth and, 59
    politics and, 102
Freeman, E., 158n1
Fremont-Smith, F., 175
French Revolution, 15
Freud, Alexander, 210
Freud, Anna, 3, 5, 6, 7, 8, 17, 31, 37, 44, 47, 58, 68, 71, 73, 74–75, 80, 84, 85, 87, 89–90, 97, 99,

107, 109, 112, 113, 124,
129, 130, 131, 138, 139,
143, 150–151, 152, 154,
155, 156, 160, 164–165,
167, 179, 188, 193,
196–197, 199, 200, 201,
205, 207, 210–211, 213,
217, 219, 224, 227, 229,
230, 235, 236, 237, 248,
277
Freud, Ernst, xiv, 65, 131,
144, 160, 199, 209
Freud, H., 107
Freud, Jacob, 210
Freud, Martha, 16, 17, 95, 130,
141, 151–152, 159, 209
Freud, Martin, 67, 81, 85–86,
93, 94, 97, 100, 109,
110, 130, 131, 153, 209
Freud, Oliver, 52, 130, 209
Freud, Sigmund, xii, xxi,
xxiii, 29, 35, 42, 47, 55,
63, 65, 77, 153, 154,
157, 240, 244, 254, 258,
276–277
Freud, Sophie, 153
Freud Archives, 67–68, 69
Friedlander, K., 229
Friedman, L. J., 118
Frink, H. W., 68, 69
Fromm, E., 123, 180

Gardiner, M., 85
Gay, P., 116, 146

Germany, 84
Gershwin, G., 186
Gift giving, 106–107,
121–122, 157–158
Gilman, S. L., 8
Glover, E., 36, 120, 170, 220,
228
Goebbels, Joseph, 203
Gorer, G., 234
Grant, D., 237
Greer, G., 122
Gregg, A., 96
Grinker, R., 108
Groddeck, G., 244
Grubrich-Simitis, I., 77
Guilbert, Y., 100, 157,
209–210, 221

Handshakes, 36, 101
Hartmann, H., 80, 113, 128,
129, 138, 161
Hauptmann, G., 157
Heimann, P., 227, 229
Heller, P., 201, 203, 211,
218, 229
Hendrick, I., 171, 173, 183
Herman, W., 170
Herzl, T., 10
Higgins, M., 53, 118
Hinshelwood, R. D., 233
Hirst, A., 1–30, 31, 36, 37,
39, 40, 44, 46, 51, 63,
83, 131, 183, 209, 220,
224

Hirst, M., 17
Hitchcock, A., 21
Hitler, A., 134, 203
Hitschmann, E., 58, 105, 116, 131, 251
Hoffer, W., 159
Hollitscher, M., 17, 70, 210
Holroyd, M., 232
Holt, E. B., 39
Homosexuality, 72, 129, 234, 245
Horney, K., 122, 123
Hug-Hellmuth, H. von, 123

Id, 58, 70
Identification, Hirst, 19
Impartiality, psychoanalysis and, 31–32, 47, 63
Impersonality. See Blank screen; Coldness
Impotence, Hirst, 20, 31
Inferiority concept, 185
Infidelity, 76–77
Intelligence, as resistance, 48
Intolerance, Freud, 109

Jackson, E., 89–113, 115, 119, 129, 133, 137, 158, 159, 168, 169, 173, 174, 177, 181, 191, 242
Jackson, G., 93
Jackson, H. H., 92, 93
Jefferson, T., 14
Jekels, L., 154, 161

Jensen, W., 139
Jokl, R., 115–141, 143, 159, 160, 212, 223
Jones, E., 2–3, 4, 8, 28, 49, 56, 69–70, 75, 76, 88, 91, 94, 99–100, 116, 132, 146, 148, 149, 164, 200, 212, 218, 228, 234, 241, 243, 245, 246, 247, 251, 255, 269, 272
Jones, K., 107
Jung, C. G., xiv, xvi, xx, 13, 26, 35, 96, 119, 125, 128, 137, 147, 170, 172, 173, 174, 178, 179, 182, 184–185, 200, 206, 221, 243, 244, 246, 259, 272

Kann, Loe, 57, 76, 78n2, 218
Kappers, A., 170
Kardiner, A., 45, 68, 128, 173–174, 186
Kendrick, W., 64, 234, 238, 249n2
Kennedy, Jacqueline, 37
Keynes, J. M., 245
Kirs, M., 99
Klein, M., 81, 146, 164, 188, 203, 205, 216, 219, 220, 225–227, 228, 241, 247–248, 270
Kleinman, A., 260–261
Knapp, B., 210
Kohut, H., 34, 144

Koller, C., 4, 5, 6, 7, 9, 14, 51
Königstein, L., 5
Kovacs, W., 160, 161, 162
Kraus, K., 258
Kris, E., 75, 80–81, 87, 128, 161, 235, 236
Kris, M., 69, 70, 75, 81, 97, 101, 113
Kubie, L. S., 170, 173

Lacan, J., 129, 205, 241
Lambda, P., 156
Lampl, H., 242
Lampl-de Groot, J., 107
Lassalle, F., 10
Lay analysis, 33, 44, 103
Leopold and Loeb case, 93
Lerhman, P., 68
Levy, K., 143–165, 167, 176, 182, 186, 196, 197, 217, 229, 238, 251, 254
Levy, L., 145–146, 149, 150, 153, 155
Lévy-Freund, K., 161
Lewin, B., 192
Libido theory, 72, 73–74, 173. See also Sexuality
Lieberman, E. J., 272
Literature, Freud and, 25
Little Hans case (Freud), xix-xx, 62, 130, 139
Loewenstein, R., 129
Looney, J. T., 254

Love, sexuality and, 27
Low, B., 228
Loy, Myrna, 85

Mack, J., 38, 85
Mahler, G., 253
Mahony, P. J., xii
Malcolm, J., 32, 147, 273
Mann, H., 25
Marxism, 250
Masson, J. M., 11, 267
Masturbation, 26, 72, 73, 74, 110
McGuire, W., 266
McLean, G., 123
Meghnagi, D., 14
Meisel, P., 64, 234, 238, 249n2
Menaker, E., 78
Menninger, K., 85
Menuhin, Y., 158
Mesmer, F. A., 260
Meyer, A., 169
Meyer, C. F., 156, 254
Meyers, F., 233
Micale, M. S., 198, 261
Millett, K., 122
Mind/body relationship
  Freud and, xv–xvi
  Putnam and, 185–186
Molnar, M., 65, 78, 145
Money, 249–250
Monk, R., 18, 157, 250

Monroe, Marilyn, 37
Moralism, 70, 72, 74,
    206–207, 224–225, 265,
    275–276
Morgan, C., 172
Mother–infant relationship,
    59, 216
Mozart, W. A., 100, 136, 175
Murray, H. A., 208n1
Music, 69–70, 100, 136,
    174–175, 216, 252–253
Musil, R., 278

Nabokov, V., 260, 272, 274
National character, 161–162
Neurology, psychiatry and,
    132
Neurosis
  Freud and, 120, 180
  trauma and, 21, 23
Nietzsche, F., 71, 214
Note taking, Freud and, xii
Nunberg, H., 78, 105, 119,
    263

Oberndorf, C. P., 48
O'Brien, C. C., 274
Obsessive-compulsive
    disorder, Freud and, 120
Oedipus complex, Jokl and,
    127
Opera, 70, 100, 174–175
Osler, W., xx

Paine, T., 14
Paris, B. J., 123
Parsons, T., 93
Paskauskas, R. A., 78n2, 138,
    148, 255
Pawel, E., 10
Payne, S., 229
Penis envy, 127, 263
Pfister, O., xiii, 198, 214, 265
Pharmacology, xvi-xviii, 37,
    271
Politics
  free association and, 102
  Freud and, xv, 24, 135,
    250
  Jones and, 3
  World War II, 134–135
Popper, K., 206
Pötzl, O., 126, 199
Prohibition, 93
Psychiatry, neurology and,
    132
Psychoanalysis
  curative quality, 32
  external conditions and, 42
  impartiality and, 31–32,
    47, 63
  medicine and, 33
Psychoanalytic training
  Freud on, 119
  Kleinians, 120
Psychopharmacology. See
    Pharmacology
Public libraries, 14

Public toilet, 13–14
Puner, H. W., 212
Putnam, I., 99, 101, 104,
        107, 167–193, 195, 196,
        210, 214, 215, 228
Putnam, J. J., 96, 168, 171
Putnam, M., 107, 169
Putnam, T., 168, 170

Rado, S., 86, 146, 205
Ramsey, F., 250
Rank, O., 71, 88, 96, 119,
        120, 124, 128, 147, 182,
        185, 219, 243, 246, 272
Raphael, C. M., 53, 118
Rappen, U., 123
Rat Man case (Freud), xx
Reich, W., 53, 74, 118, 121
Reik, T., 67, 122, 124,
        157n1, 250, 254
Religion, xiii, 16, 108, 116,
        168, 198, 212, 221, 249,
        265. See also
        Anti-Semitism
Resistance
    Brunswick, David, 48
    Brunswick, Mark, 62, 73
    Jokl and, 118
Rickman, J., 227, 228
Rie, O., 97, 163
Riviere, J., 100, 229, 264
Roazen, P., xxiii, 3, 4, 7, 9,
        13, 17, 32, 33, 35, 43,
        52, 57, 60, 65, 68, 71,
        80, 83, 89, 94, 111, 116,
        117, 119, 120, 122, 123,
        124, 129, 139, 147, 152,
        163, 168, 169, 178, 197,
        201, 209, 217, 232, 241,
        252, 260, 263, 265, 266,
        273
Roheim, G., 162–163
Roman Catholic Church,
        Austro-Hungarian
        Empire, 14–15, 16
Roosevelt, F. D., 38, 135
Rosenfeld, E., 107, 195–230,
        231, 239, 267, 277
Rosenfeld, H., 227
Rosenzweig, S., 13
Ross, H., 111
Rousseau, J.-J., xxiii, 276
Russell, B., 250
Russia, World War I, 15

Sacco and Vanzetti trial, 93
Sachs, H., 51, 121–122,
        189–190, 192, 251
Sadger, I., 121, 161, 251–252
Sadism, 251
Schiller, F. von, 254
Schiller, M., 209
Schizophrenia, 272
Schlesinger, T., 8
Schreber case (Freud), xx
Schur, M., 80, 84, 85
Science, 261, 274
Scopes trial, 93

Searle, N., 228–229
Self psychology, 34
Sexual abuse, 258–259
Sexuality. *See also* Libido
    theory
  Freud and, 26–27
  Hirst, 20
  prohibition against, 109,
    110
  United States and, 12, 14
Shakespeare, W., 254
Shamdasani, S., 243
Shapre, E., 228–229
Short-term analysis, 34, 43
Silberer, H., 117, 121, 130,
    137, 223, 224
Silberman, S. L., 90, 92, 98,
    104, 113
Silence, Freud and, 73
Simmel, E., 47, 51, 52, 150,
    199, 220
Socialism, Freud and, 135,
    250
Stekel, W., 120, 126, 138, 246
Stephen, A., 234
Stephen, K., 234
Sterba, R., 105, 123
Strachey, A., 231–255
Strachey, J., 100, 231–255
Strachey, L., 232, 234
Suicide, 229
  Freud, 230
  Hirst and, 9
  Silberer, 116, 121, 130

Tausk, 121
Surgical analogy, Freud and,
    29, 42
Swales, P., 244n1
Syphilis, 23

Tausk, V., 117–118,
    119–120, 138, 150, 223,
    224, 225
Thatcher, M., 262
Thomas, D. M., 111
Timms, E., 258
Tolerance, Freud and, 23–24
Transference
  Freud and, 217
  Hirst, 19
Transference love,
    Brunswick, Ruth, 69
Trauma, 21, 23, 84
Trilling, L., 272–273, 274

Unconscious, 58
United States. *See* America
Unwin, S., 251

Van der Hoop, J. H., 170
Versailles Treaty, 246
Vienna, Austria
  civil war in, 85
  Freud and, 25–26
  population of, 8
  World War I, 83–84
Vienna Psychoanalytic
    Society, 115–141

Virgil, 10
von Freund, A., 149–150, 153, 182, 214
von Freund, T., 229, 259

Waelder, J., 105, 183
Waelder, R., 104–105, 138, 183
Wagner, R., 70
Wagner-Jauregg, J., 7, 126
Warner, S., 68
Weiss, E., 213, 240
Wessel, M. A., 98
Wild analysis, 75
Wilson, E., 240, 260
Wilson, W., 83, 207, 245, 260, 272
Winslow, E. G., 245
Wittgenstein, L., 157

Wolf Man case (Freud), xx, 39, 48–49, 62, 69
Women, Freud and, xxi, 122, 127, 129–130, 136–137, 141, 159, 227, 263–264
Woolf, L., 245, 250
Woolf, V., 234, 245, 249, 250
World War I, 15–16, 83–84, 126
World War II, 52, 64, 65, 80, 113, 116, 134–135, 236, 246
Wortis, J., 109, 190

Young-Bruehl, E., 83, 145, 151

Zilboorg, G., 186
Zweig, S., 8